JEAN FOUQUET AND HIS TIME
BY PAUL WESCHER

TRANSLATED BY EVELINE WINKWORTH

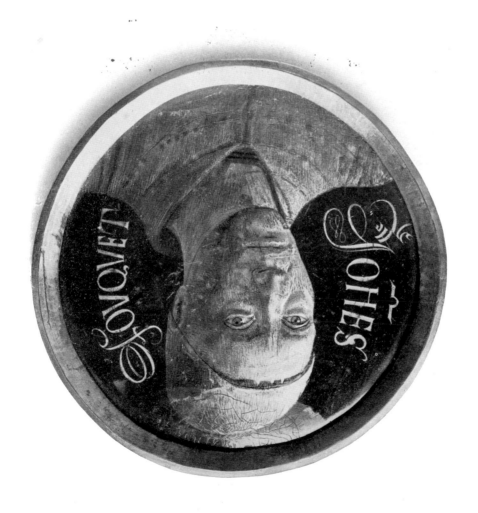

JEAN FOUQUET

AND HIS TIME

*

BY PAUL WESCHER

*

MCMXLVII
REYNAL & HITCHCOCK
NEW YORK

Published 1947 by Reynal & Hitchcock
Originally published in Switzerland
by Holbein Publishing Company, Basle

TABLE OF CONTENTS

France at the Time of Fouquet   7

Fouquet's Art   15

The Tradition of Fouquet's Life   23

Fouquet's Work

    The Miniatures   36

    The Panel Paintings   48

The Master of King René of Anjou   55

Jean Colombe and Jean Bourdichon   72

Bibliography   91

Plates

Notes to the Illustrations   97

List of Illustrations   105

Index of Names   109

FRANCE AT THE TIME OF FOUQUET

From the depths of her defeat, when the moral and material life of France was at its lowest ebb at the end of the Hundred Years' War with England, the French genius arose again in two important artists: Jean Fouquet and François Villon, Painter and Poet, the first two great realists in the history of French art, and the founders of French pictorial and literary style. The Miracle of Jeanne d'Arc, a military and political miracle of national reawakening, was here repeated in the intellectual sphere.

When Fouquet and François Villon were born, within the space of a decade—Fouquet was born about 1420 at Tours, Villon about 1430 at Paris—the once powerful realm of France had dwindled to half its size, torn by party strife, its capital besieged by enemies; and with the decline of trade, commerce and agriculture, poverty and insecurity were universal.

At Fouquet's death in about 1480 (the end of Villon's life, like the greater part of his adventurous and sordid career, is lost in obscurity) France had recovered and had again become great, strong and prosperous, thanks to the inexhaustible fertility of her soil and the vigour of her people; thanks, too, to the progressiveness, the power of organization, the statesmanship and realism of her two kings, Charles VII and Louis XI, and their counsellors and officials.

The new realistic outlook which was so typical a feature, not only of the government but of the whole life of France, was the result of the Hundred Years' War, in which the feudal and romantic Middle Ages came to a violent if timely end. The war itself, an outcome of the conflict of the feudal powers of the Middle Ages, had in effect resulted in a transformation of power; for, while the feudal lords were liquidated, a new centralized state, a new conception of absolute monarchy triumphed. France experienced at this time the greatest rebirth of her history, a true *Renaissance* in every sphere of her life.

This Renaissance had little in common with the Italian Renaissance. It was a purely national affair. The cosmopolitan ideal of Humanism, which in Italy inspired and united every form of life, was lacking. In the French universities no Greek or classical Latin was taught, only mediaeval dog-Latin, which, abhorred by the Humanists, was still, even at the University of Paris, held to be the key to knowledge. It is true that during the war, new universities were founded at Toulouse, Caen, Bordeaux, Angers and Poitiers, but even at

these seats of learning there was no critical translation of classical texts, no knowledge of antiquity, and, as a consequence, no strict historical or philosophical discipline of thought. Not until after the fall of Constantinople (1453) were some Greek scholars received at the University of Paris. Guillaume Fichet was the first librarian of the Sorbonne to treat humanistic studies from a standpoint other than that of the Stoics and ancient moral philosophers, till then regarded as the link between pagan and Christian views of life. In 1470, he encouraged the production of the first printed French book, the *Lettres* of the Humanist Gasparino da Bergamo. Owing to persecution, he left Paris, however, after only a brief period of activity (1464–1472) and went to Rome, never to return. After 1472, Robert Gaguin, the General of the Trinitarians, and leader of the *"Fichetistes,"* or followers of Fichet, as the enlightened, humanistically inspired school of learning was called among the schoolmen, taught in Paris; from 1476 to 1478 Filippo Beroaldo lectured there. In the course of these years, the first translation of Petrarch's *Trionfi* saw the light, in a manuscript illuminated by Maître François.[1] Yet the Florentine Humanist, Pico della Mirandola, like Johannes Reuchlin before him, came to Paris in 1485, with the acknowledged object of studying scholastic learning and the old authors. Scholasticism, with its theocratic system, its distorted learning composed of dogmatism, dialectics and religious observance, of heathen and mediaeval Christian elements of culture, continued, therefore, before and after the end of the century to be taught with unabated vigour. In the artistic sphere, it corresponded perfectly with the flamboyant Gothic style which at that time dominated French architecture.

In spite of the persistence of the mediaeval spirit, it is permissible to speak of an artistic Renaissance in France, as the great French scholar, Count Louis de Laborde, was the first to do, being followed in this by E. Müntz; it is apparent not only in the work of Fouquet, but also in the work of Michel Colombe, the leading sculptor of his time. Apart from stylistic forms, borrowed from Italy, about which we shall have more to say later on, it was first and foremost the new, all-embracing aesthetic concept which we call realism, with its sense of solidity and spaciousness, the new way of expressing individual and natural forms, which linked their art to the spirit of the age.

The fundamental difference between French and Italian art remained and continued to prevail until the pillaging of Italy by Charles VIII and Francis I, at the end of the century. Fouquet's art was formed by no particular cultural

---

1) Munich, Bayrische Staatsbibliothek, Cod. Gall. 16.

8

ideal or aesthetic theory. It drew its inspiration from the French spiritual life, at once rational and mystical, which survived the Middle Ages. Its positive aspect, its deep feeling for life, for order, for construction, developed in reaction to the prodigious disturbance and chaos which had overtaken France, and was simply part of the awakened vitality of the French nation, everywhere perceptible.

In order to gain a better understanding of the state of the arts in France at this time, a short retrospective view of contemporary events is necessary; for French painting at the time of Fouquet reflected in the clearest way the national discord and the conflict between old and new tendencies. Since the siege of Paris by the English, various regional centres—Dijon, Moulins, Blois, Bourges, Angers and Aix—had taken the place of the ancient capital, formerly the heart and cultural centre of France. The importance of these seats of the Dukes of Burgundy, Bourbon, Orléans, Berry, Anjou and Provence increased as these princes won independence for their realms. At Tours and Bourges, the residences of the exiled King, new centres of art grew and flourished. Provincial France came into her own, as she was to do again later, in the 17th century, and brought to light many-sided talents, which, as in Italy and Germany, took their colour from local conditions. Avignon, still a Papal enclave, was not only a haven of peace during war, but gave rise at this time to an independent school of art which, strongly influenced by Italian masters, in particular the Sienese, differed essentially from that of the royal dominions.

The defeat at Agincourt (1415) was largely due to internal division arising under the mad King Charles VI, to the struggle for power among the Royal Princes, and in particular to the deadly enmity between the Houses of Orléans and Burgundy. The old realm of the French Kings had ceased to be a united kingdom and was divided into various vassal states, of which the most powerful, the Dukedom of Burgundy, strengthened, after the murder of Duke Jean sans Peur, by the forces of the Netherlands, had cut itself completely free and was openly allied with the English. By the Treaty of Troyes, the sequel to Agincourt, the English King was declared Lord of France in his own right, and the nineteen-year-old Dauphin Charles, on hearing of his father's death in 1422 at Mehun-sur-Yèvre, had lost his claim to the throne. The English Regent, the Duke of Bedford, made his triumphal entry into Paris; his power was based not only on the resources of England, but also on the captured revenues of the rich provinces of Normandy, Picardy, Champagne and the Ile-de-France. The Dauphin had few resources at his command. His most

powerful supporters, Dukes Charles of Orléans and John of Bourbon, the Count of Angoulême and others, were prisoners of the English; the Duke of Anjou and of Provence was taken prisoner at the battle of Bulgnéville (1431) by the Duke of Burgundy; the Dukedom of Brittany remained neutral. The devastated and anarchical state obtaining in the provinces which remained loyal to the crown is described by Alain Chartier with the words: "*En France, les pays champêtres sont tournés à l'état de la mer, où chacun a tant de seigneuries comme il a de force.*" No substantial subsidies for waging war were to be derived from them.

In this truly desperate state of affairs, the Dauphin led an isolated existence in retirement in his castles of Mehun, Saumur or Chinon, which seem to have been alike palace, fortress and chapel, and at Poitiers or at Bourges. Mistrustful and melancholy, of a pious disposition, filled with doubts, even as to his own birth (doubts justified by the immoral conduct of his mother, Isabella of Bavaria), he was shy, uncertain, weak, dependent on those surrounding him. During the first fifteen years after his father's death, he completely abandoned the government to his counsellors and favourites, who shamelessly enriched themselves, intrigued and made war upon each other, invading each other's territory. In vain Alain Chartier, in his *Quadrilogue invectif*, held before his eyes the example of the rise and fall of Nineveh, Babylon, Troy, Athens and Rome, the greatness of France, her riches, the industry and intelligence of his subjects, the number of men capable of defending him, also the troubles and disasters brought about by defeat. In vain he depicted, as did Jean Juvénal des Ursins in his *Epistres au Roy* (1433 and 1440), the lamentable state of the land and the peasants, the need for relief and for action. "*Quare abdormis, domine?*"—"Why do you sleep, Lord?"—so Jean Juvénal ended his first letter. Charles did not listen to these counsellors; war was hateful to him, and he still hoped to dislodge the English by means of diplomacy. In 1428, he gave his side up for lost, and even the Miracle of Jeanne d'Arc and the *Sacre* at Reims could not for long arouse him from his apathy and indolence. Inactive, he remained an onlooker at the trial and martyrdom of the *Pucelle*; dumbly he acquiesced in the retirement of his disastrous favourite, La Tremoille, and submitted to the Connétable de Richemont and to Charles d'Anjou; inactive, he witnessed the growth of feudal anarchy. Without his aid, the English were gradually pushed back by a series of bold single actions, and even in the negotiations preceding the Peace of Arras, which were chiefly conducted by his counsellors, by the Pope and by the Duke of Savoy, he was ready to yield the third and best part of his kingdom.

Illustration I   *Fouquet: St.Margaret*

The worst time of all for France began after the signing of the Peace of Arras, so eagerly awaited by the people. But if it ended the enmity with Burgundy, it also set free a large number of soldiers who had hitherto been employed in the conduct of the war, and who now, unpaid, were left to roam the countryside, and to make a living by plundering, robbing, murdering, and devastating the whole country. For nine years, until the Armistice of Tours (1444), these *Ecorcheurs* were the terror of the whole population; they held up traffic on the roads, paralysed trade and caused infinite insecurity and misery.

In the midst of these grievous times, however, the government unexpectedly began to take practical steps towards the work of reconstruction. This used to be ascribed on the one hand to the altered bearing of the King, under the influence of his new counsellors, and on the other, to his mistress Agnes Sorel. Charles VII, who seemed old at thirty, at forty was suddenly young and energetic. Soon after his return to Paris, the working out of the first financial decrees

11

was begun, which, passed in 1439, governed the raising of taxes and insured their collections by the appointment of royal tax-gatherers *(Elus)* in every province. At the same time, the right of the aristocracy to levy their own armed forces was prohibited, and the consequent *Praguerie* was defeated without trouble. These decrees were followed in subsequent years by others designed to consolidate the royal prerogative; lawlessness and insecurity gradually ceased, and finally a standing army of fifteen companies of artillery and a militia of 16,000 crossbowmen was set up. In order to end the problem of the *Ecorcheurs*, they were sent in 1444 under the leadership of the Dauphin to the support of King René d'Anjou and of the Emperor Frederick III against the people of Lorraine and the Swiss and fought the battle of St. Jakob on the Birs.

In England the Wars of the Roses, which brought about conditions similar to those which had prevailed earlier in France, facilitated the withdrawal of troops from the still-occupied provinces. After the death of the Duke of Bedford in 1435, the warlike spirit of the English had abated; the young King Henry VI himself wished for peace, and although the campaigns in Normandy, Guyenne and Brittany dragged on, throughout the rest of France the King's standard waved peacefully. Charles VII had gained through his enforced exile what Paris alone would never have given him in times of peace—he had won back the wide French provinces, with the allegiance of the whole people of France, with their patriotism, their faith and their unshaken vitality. He had united France under the Crown, and was gradually subduing the feudal lords, great and small. He increased the number of provincial parliaments, despite opposition from Paris, and thus created an instrument with which to enforce his will against the opposition of the aristocracy and at the same time to maintain the support of the common people, who, as the born opponents of feudalism, were to play an increasingly prominent part from now onwards as the propertied citizens of the towns. Under his successor, Louis XI, the *"roi bourgeois,"* these changes were made quite openly, but they had their origin in the time of Charles VII and the Hundred Years' War.

Even in the worst days of the war, the *"bonnes villes"* had repeatedly and willingly contributed the necessary subsidies to the King, while the feudal aristocracy, as a result of the destruction of their lands, were unable, and sometimes also unwilling, to render material help; and the citizens of besieged towns—such as Rouen and Orléans—remained loyal to the King and opposed the English domination. The King had not forgotten this support and rewarded it with

Illustration II   *Colombe: Jacques Cœur*

far-reaching privileges. He had recognized the value of civil magistrates, experienced in administration, and he therefore chose his secretaries, counsellors and
ministers of finance—Guillaume Cousinot, Jean Bourée, Etienne Chevalier,
Laurens Gyrard, Guillaume Gaufier—with a preference for this section of the
community. It was thus inevitable that the influence of the middle classes should
penetrate social and cultural life. With their commercial instinct and realistic
attitude towards money, property and individual achievement, the rich citizens
became of increasing importance; their personal ability and initiative, which
under the rigid feudal system had remained latent, received new impetus. As
again in the 18th century, they acquired sovereign rights, land investments,

13

incomes from such sources as land tenure, ground rents and fines, as well as official and remunerative positions in the administration. *"Chacun ne vault désormais que par l'argent ou l'esprit qu'il possède,"* reported a contemporary chronicle. This was indeed a change from the idealistic romanticism of the feudal age. *"En ceste même saison,"* reports Chastellain of the year 1462, *"fut dit que le roy fit ennoblir par cryée tous ceux qui voudroient marchander en son Royaume et leur accorda privilège de noble homme et pareillement estat."*

The example of Jacques Cœur, who from an obscure master of a mint rose to be the first really great merchant in France, controlling not only trade with the Levant but also industry, mining, salt taxes, the mint and other financial concerns, and of whom it was said: *"il gagnoit chacun an tout seul plus que ne faisoient ensemble tous les autres marchands du Royaume,"* was an encouragement to all. He lent the king 40,000 *écus* for the ransom of Normandy, and his name became proverbial in his life-time as "rich as Jacques Cœur." We find to-day examples of the cultural importance of these acquired riches in Cœur's magnificent palace at Bourges, in the chapel and the great stained glass windows of the Cathedral. His sudden fall from power, his trial and condemnation for which the court nobles were chiefly responsible, denote the opposition of powers, parties and ideologies characteristic of the age.

For, though the influence of the feudal system had been discredited, it must not be forgotten that, as an institution, it had retained its significance and that, as far as court circles were concerned, this had rather increased in importance. The old aristocracy was still the arbiter of taste and fashion, the King himself was in favour of retaining the existing hierarchy, and court poetry and court painting were, at least in theory, in harmony with aristocratic ideals. On the other hand, it was inevitable that the more progressive section of the aristocracy, especially the landed gentry, the *"gens de petits états,"* should conform to the new conditions, ideas and outlook. It also followed that their political views were more realistic and frequently coincided with those of the middle classes, and that, deprived of their independence, their contribution to the life of the nation should follow a new direction. After the death of Charles VII, the *"Ligue du bien public"* allowed the conflict between the old and the new political ideals, between the old and the new order of things, to flare up once more. It interrupted the progress of affairs no more, however, than the conservative paintings of the old masters could arrest the development of new conceptions of art and the sturdy reality of life itself.

14

FOUQUET'S ART

That Fouquet's appearance on the scene coincided with the liberation of his country and the great changes taking place in France at that time, is no accident, either historically or from the point of view of the art historian. Fouquet made good the setbacks of those disastrous years from 1420 to 1445 during which he grew to maturity; setbacks which did not exist for those born under luckier stars and in other lands, in Italy, the Netherlands or Germany. At the end of a long period during which all values were annihilated, the people of France were ready for a fresh start, for new ideas and a new outlook, an eagerly awaited change from the constant dwelling on the transience of earthly things and the meaninglessness of existence, which filled with despair the departing Middle Ages and which speaks so clearly to us from the spineless forms, the weak lines and the tender, faded colours of its paintings.

That the old order of things was passing had long been apparent to writers, especially to the older and more introspective ones, such as Chartier and Deschamps: *"Il n'y a plus de noblesse, ni de foi, ni loyaulté, ni modération, ni honneur."* *"Que vault le monde? Hélas, il ne vault rien!"* so runs the end of Chartier's ballade *"Quant union n'est plus en sainte église."* Antoine de La Sale, the Dauphin's companion during his exile in Burgundy, went so far as to ridicule knightly ideals, very much with the approbation of his lord, in his *Petit Jehan de Saintré*. The old hierarchical order of the world, in which only the upper classes counted and in which this life was only considered as a preparation for the life hereafter, had collapsed. Life was fundamentally worth living, even in the face of misfortune, poverty, and misery, for all was human. Villon mocks Alain Chartier's lament:

> *Il n'est dangier que de Villain*
> *N'orgueil que de povre enrichy*
> *Ne seur (sûr) chemin que le plain*
> *Ne secours de vray amy ...*

with:

> *Il n'est soing que quant on a fain*
> *Ne service que d'ennemy*
> *Ne maschier qu'ung botel de foing*
> *Ne fort guet que d'homme endormy ...*

and he composed his superbly defiant and sarcastic poem:

Fy de bonté, fy de fiance
fy d'honneur, fy de leaulté
fy de force, fy de sapience ...
fors que de ceulx qui ont argent.

The development of individuality, the reaction against the social attitude of the Middle Ages, were the dominating motives; the desire to see the world with new eyes is nowhere more clearly expressed than by Villon in his famous ballade, the refrain of which runs: "*Je connois tout fors que moi même.*" Nothing is in fact more remarkable than this preoccupation with self which runs through French literature of the 15th century—the perpetual consciousness of the contrast between the individual and the rest of the world. Only out of this consciousness was a new objective representation, such as was rendered in their respective ways by Villon and by Fouquet, made possible. For an artist who observed the world from this angle could no longer content himself with the old decentralized style. He needed a more scientific construction, in which the knowledge of perspective provided him with a better understanding of the nature of things, and he needed, too, anatomical knowledge of the form of man himself.

This world of sharply defined contrasts, the dawn of a new cultural epoch in France, is reflected in the works of Villon, in the *Petit Jehan de Saintré*, in the *Cent nouvelles nouvelles* of Antoine de La Sale and in the *Farce de Maître Pathelin* among others; it was a stimulus to spiritual life, and endowed the open-minded with a deeper insight than would have been theirs in times of peace. Fouquet's awareness of reality was so intense because he lived in a time of unrest and strife, of contrasted brilliance and misery, and of violent change. Sturdy and independent, with a penetrating gaze in the honest expression of the frontispiece eyes, as he is shown in his self-portrait, he did not indulge in pessimistic reflections or join in the lament for the transience of earthly glory, but, aided by a fertile imagination, mastered reality with the native instinct of the French for essential facts.

Fouquet's art was courtly art; not only was it intended for courtly patrons and persons of high rank but it served to epitomize the spirit of the court. It surveyed the world from a height, from the point of view of the mighty, just as François Villon, the penniless vagabond, saw it from the depths of his poverty. Fouquet's world was a solemn, ceremonious world, a world of state proceed-

16

Illustration III   *Fouquet: Etienne Chevalier and his Patron St.Stephen*

ings, like that of Froissart's *Chronicle*. Almost all the gaiety of earthly life, as we find it in the Limburg brothers, is absent from his pictures. The world of Fouquet is one of battles, intrigue and treason, devotion and sacrifice. The scenes of the Redemption and Passion of Christ, which in those days accompanied mankind from the cradle to the grave, bore the same ceremonial features, the same devotional forms, which accompanied the meeting of queens, the birth, marriage and death of princes. The Heavenly Redemption of mankind, as it was set forth in the Death and Ascension of Christ, the Coronation of the Virgin, the Holy Trinity, the Miracle of Pentecost, is made by Fouquet more brilliant and hieratic, is intended more for kings than for ordinary mortals, and thoroughly conformed to the way of thinking of the pious Charles VII and his followers. Louis XI, in other ways cool-headed and calculating, was quite convinced that the saints always interceded for him. He believed in their miracles, sought to win their favour through pilgrimages and large sums of money spent in pious benefactions and hoped, through their intercession, to achieve eternal sanctity just as on earth he had increased his power through successful political alliances and appropriate presents. Fouquet was no mystic, like the ecstatic master of the Rohan prayerbook. He had seen Rome and the Pope, he had experienced in his own lifetime the ending of the schism, he recognized the unshakeable power and brilliance of the Catholic Church and its teaching. The Passion of Christ and the Lives of the Saints were for him, as for all painters of that time, stories of humanity, universal, contemporary. In the Adoration of the Chantilly miniatures, he gave to the kneeling King Melchior the features of Charles VII, just as Rogier van der Weyden in his Columba Altar gave to the same king the features of Charles the Bold. St. Stephen, in the Altar of Melun, ill. v is painted from a living model, as faithful in portraiture as Chevalier himself, kneeling beside him as a donor, or as the Madonna with the features of Agnes Sorel, as real as all the saintly figures in the Pietà of Nouans.

Like Jan van Eyck, Dirk Bouts and Hugo van der Goes, like Pisanello, Fra Angelico, Piero della Francesca, like Conrad Witz, Stephan Lochner and all his famous predecessors and contemporaries, exponents of the new style of painting, Fouquet, with the precision of a miniaturist in his care for detail, portrays the world with truthful clarity.

We must consider now the other, the unofficial side of his art, provincial, perhaps, but independent and vital. All painters of middle-class origin derived their individuality from keeping closely in touch with everyday life, their facility

and unerring sense of quality from the traditions developed by generations of craftsmen. They were craftsmen in feeling as well as in practice, like all the other craftsmen in the narrow streets of the towns in which they lived. The standard of their work was kept at a high level by the control of the guilds. These mediaeval craftsmen were masters of their profession; their work ranged from purely decorative activities, from the painting of sculpture, litters and state-carriages, coats of arms and banners, to the sublimest creations of imaginative art. The refined sense of a right application of the decorative arts to the varying needs of all ranks of society was a characteristic of mediaeval life in general.

If, therefore, Fouquet depicted the hierarchy of a courtly world, his means of expression were derived from middle-class surroundings and the realistic outlook of his own class of society. His style was, in a certain sense, abstract and idealized, to suit the spirit of courtly patronage. But it was based, as with van Eyck, more on a detailed approach than on a generalized and independent conception of the bourgeoisie, a conception at this period only possible for the German and Italian masters, whose social background was different. But in spite of that, his style was expressive in the strongest degree of the mentality of the French nation as a whole, that same rustic, provincial middle class, from which the great realists of the 17th century arose.

How much Fouquet combined French mentality with French feeling for style, how much of his work, like that of all painters of genius, was prophetic of the future, modern in its appeal, was apparent at the great exhibitions of French art in London in 1933 and in Paris in 1937. Fouquet's Antwerp Madonna with the features of Agnes Sorel is the prototype of such paintings as François Clouet's *Maîtresse au bain*, or the *Gabrielle d'Estrées au bain* and *Sabina Poppaea* of the time of Henri IV, of Pierre Mignard's *Marie Mancini* and Nattier's *Mademoiselle de Clermont*, as well as Fragonard's *Mademoiselle Colombe* and finally David's *Madame Récamier* and Ingres' *Belle Zélie*.[2] The rational, realistic and at the same time idealistic outlines of the art which united him and his followers, Jean Colombe and Jean Bourdichon, to the court painters of Francis I, to Jean Clouet, Godefroy de Batave, Corneille de Lyon and others, formed an almost unbroken sequence till the end of the *Ancien Régime* and even till the Classical Revival. When at the beginning of the 18th century, the aesthetic philosopher de Piles, as spokesman of the academic world, with a strong bias

plate 38

2) Richmond (Surrey), Sir Herbert Cook coll. – Dijon, Musée des Beaux-Arts and Chantilly, Musée Condé. – Geneva, Musée d'Art et d'Histoire. – Berlin, Kaiser-Friedrich-Museum. – Chantilly, Musée Condé. – Paris, Gabriel Cognacq coll. – Paris, Musée du Louvre. – Rouen, Musée des Beaux-Arts.

20

towards classicism, contended that art forms should be abstracted from the forms of everyday life, *réalité vulgaire*, while at the same time imitating these forms, not only was his theory upheld by the art of the 17th and 16th centuries, but he could point to the very beginnings of modern French painting, to Fouquet himself, who introduced the tradition and gave life to the ideal of abstract thought and realistic appearance in French painting.

The uncompromising art of Fouquet, based on entirely new conceptions, must have made an extraordinary impression on his contemporaries. His quick success at court, the direct, lively imitation of his fellow artists, bear witness to the distance which divides him from all painters of his own and former times. While, however, the fame and the masterpieces of the Netherlandish painters, of van Eyck, Rogier, Dirk Bouts, Memling, van der Goes, outlived their day, for three hundred years the name of Fouquet was forgotten. In the 16th century, a few art historians knew his name from hearsay, but the historical tradition of an early school of French painting was already broken when innumerable monuments were destroyed by the iconoclasm of the Huguenots. When the Abbé Gaignières began again to examine and to have copies made of what remained, the artists and the dates of the works of art were mostly unknown; among them, Fouquet's portrait of Charles VII which, until 1757, hung in the Sainte-Chapelle ill. VIII at Bourges. On the other hand, Gaignières enables us to recognize from his copy that the companion-portrait of Marie d'Anjou, the wife of Charles VII, which is lost to us to-day, was also from the hand of Fouquet.

The so-called Diptych of Melun was seen by Denis Godefroy in the middle of ill. V, Plate 38 the 17th century in the church of that place and described as an anonymous work in his *Histoire de Charles VII;* in 1775 it was removed and, with so many church possessions, sold for a song during the Revolution. Through an extraordinary chance, the panel portrait of Chevalier with the greater part of his miniatures came into the hands of the Frankfort patrician Georg Brentano, the step-brother of the Romantic poet, Clemens Brentano. He had acquired the miniatures in 1816, on his return journey from Italy, from the Basle art dealer Peter Birmann, who in his turn had bought them in Paris during the Revolution.

With Victor Hugo's *Notre-Dame de Paris* a romantic light was thrown upon the whole of the late-Gothic Middle Ages. Champollion-Figeac excavated from the depths of the Bibliothèque Nationale and published in 1826 the Tournament Book of good King René, while a novel entitled *La Fille de Foucquet* by Crespy-le-Prince appeared in 1834. The time was ripe for scientific research.

21

Two manuscript entries by François Robertet, the secretary of Duke Pierre de Bourbon, in two volumes of the Bibliothèque Nationale, the *Antiquités Judaïques*[3] and the *Très riches Heures*[4] of the old Duke of Berry, led in due course to the recognition of Master Paul of Limburg, Fouquet and Jean Colombe. This François Robertet, who came of a family prominent in the magistrature, was, like his brother Jacques, interested in literature, an antiquarian, and a thoroughly cultured personality. The two brothers transcribed the works of Henri Baude, collected the poems of Chastellain, Villon, Molinet, and played an important role in the intellectual life of France at the end of the 15th century. Their father, Jean Robertet, as the first secretary of the Order of St. Michael, had known Fouquet personally, for Fouquet had executed the title-page miniature for the Statutes of the Order as well as other works for the Order. Robertet therefore spoke with the best authority when he remarked, at the end of the second volume of Josephus' *Antiquités Judaïques*, that the first three miniatures were by the Miniature Painter of the Duke of Berry, the others by Jehan Fouquet, "*natif de Tours.*" Of no less importance was the note in the *Très riches Heures*, by which he bequeathes to us the names of Paul of Limburg and Jean Colombe. In Italy, Fouquet's fame found valuable documentary evidence in the architectural treatise of Antonio Filarete, who, in 1461, recommended to the Duke Francesco Sforza the best masters of his time for a model cultural state. A much-travelled Florentine, Francesco Florio, who, in 1476–77, paid a long visit to Tours, wrote of Fouquet that he surpassed not only contemporary but also all old masters; and the poet and archaeologist Jean Lemaire, who at the beginning of the 16th century was in the employment of Anne de Bretagne and Margaret of Austria, the *Statthalterin* of the Netherlands, mentions him in two of his writings next to Jan van Eyck and Rogier van der Weyden.

With the help of these and other documents brought to light since about 1830, French scholars, and in particular Count P. Durrieu, have gradually pieced together, with the discovery of archives, dates and works, the main outlines of Fouquet's life and career which, even if there are still many gaps in our knowledge of the artist, may be sketched in the following way.

3) Paris, Bibliothèque Nationale, Ms. fr. 247 and Nouv. Acq. fr. 21013.

4) Chantilly, Musée Condé.

THE TRADITION OF FOUQUET'S LIFE

Jean Fouquet was born at Tours about 1420 and, if a document discovered by Yves de Raulin is to be trusted, was the illegitimate child of a priest and an unmarried woman. In a papal brief of the year 1449, by which his birth was legitimized, at his own proposal, he is mentioned as a cleric of the Diocese of Tours, which meant that, probably with the help of his father, he had studied and had taken holy orders. The position of cleric, held also by Villon and Henri Baude, carried the privilege of being subject not to the jurisdiction of the state but to that of the church, and brought with it the possibility of appointment to all secular and ecclesiastical offices not excepting the highest honours under the Crown. The clerics at that time were recruited from a large section of educated middle-class youth, the progressive, often rather restless and discontented elements of society. They represented the first germs of a new order of society in which rank and birth counted for less than personal gifts and ability. Many of the secretaries and counsellors, of the *Elus de finance*, etc., who under Charles VII and still more under Louis XI played such important roles, were drawn from the ranks of these middle-class clerics.

It is not known at which university Fouquet studied or where he learnt his craft, but it may be assumed that it was in Paris about the year 1440. The famous tradition of illuminated books, in spite of the occupation, and in spite of the fact that many artists at that time had migrated to the South, was still carried on in several workshops, and the English Regent himself, the Duke of Bedford, a patron of the arts, like his brother-in-law, Duke Philip the Good of Burgundy, gave them every encouragement by commissioning them to work for him. Among others, "the Master of the Duke of Bedford," who has been identified, perhaps wrongly, with Haincelin, or Hans of Hagenau, the most famous master of the time, illuminated some of the most beautiful prayerbooks for him. Perhaps younger painters were trained in his workshop, such as the prolific Maître François or Bénigne Guyot and Jacques de Besançon, and possibly also Fouquet. A manuscript, the *Mer des Histoires*,[5] executed in 1443 for Jean Juvénal des Ursins and several other illuminated manuscripts in Brussels, Geneva and the Bibliothèque Nationale at Paris, serve well to illustrate the rather antiquated style of the school over which the old Haincelin of Hagenau presided.

5) Paris, Bibliothèque Nationale, Ms. lat. 4915.

The view that the hand of Fouquet is to be seen here has been superseded; even his early work must have looked quite different. It is, however, tempting to believe that Fouquet received his first instruction and mastered his art in that Parisian circle, and that he derived his first artistic impressions from the versatile, gay and mighty city. Again and again the famous ancient monuments and buildings characteristic of the city appear in his later miniatures, such as the Palais-Royal, the big and little Châtelet, Notre-Dame, the Sainte-Chapelle, the Temple, the Bastille, the gates of Saint-Martin and Saint-Denis. It is not difficult, therefore, to imagine the young Fouquet in the spirit of a Romantic revivalist, and to see him looking at the Dance of Death on the walls of the Hôpital des Innocents, before which mendicant friars preach to the crowd in the street on the transience of earthly glory. It is scarcely to be disputed that, in Paris or elsewhere during these years, he saw also works of the great realistic painters of the Netherlands, Jan van Eyck, Campin, Petrus Christus and Rogier van der Weyden.

The journey to Italy which Fouquet, like Dürer, undertook when already a master, was to mark an important stage in his career. He was in Rome after 1445 and before February 1447, that is to say before the death of Pope Eugene IV, whose portrait he had the opportunity of painting. Filarete, whom we have mentioned before, and with whom he was in close personal relationship, for he calls him only by his Christian name, Giachetto francioso—mentions in his architectural treatise: "*Il quale fè a Roma papa Eugenio e du'altri de'suoi appresso di lui; che veramente parevano vivi proprio. I quali dipinse in sù uno panno collocato nella sacristia della Minerva*," and he adds: "*Io dico così perchè a mio tempo li dipinse.*" This portrait of the Pope with two of his "nephews" hung, in Filarete's time, in the sacristy of S. Maria sopra Minerva and, like most of the paintings on canvas of that time, has not been preserved. The marked Italian style of the shield-bearing *putti* in several of his miniatures are evidence of the fact that Fouquet must have been acquainted with the monumental tombs for the Cardinal of Portugal and Pope Martin V in Rome, designed by Filarete.

In order to paint the Pope's portrait, it was necessary to have introductions and recommendations from the highest quarters. It is permissible to assume that Fouquet was sent on a special delegation by the French court for that very purpose; for at this time negotiations, between Charles VII and the Papal See, about the rescinding of the Pragmatic Sanction of 1438 and over the ending of the Schism were in progress. Twice in the summer of 1446 and after the death

24

of Eugene IV, in July 1448, high French dignitaries, Jean Juvénal des Ursins, Archbishop of Reims, Thomas de Courcelles, Chancellor of the University of Paris, Jean d'Estampes, Bishop of Carcassonne, and Jacques Cœur, who was held in great favour by the Pope, arrived in Rome with a large and splendid retinue, to continue the negotiations, which in 1449 resulted in the abdication of the Anti-Pope Felix V, Duke Amadée of Savoy. Jacques Cœur took this opportunity to commission Filippo Lippi to paint the altar-piece of the Annunciation with his coat of arms, now in the Munich Pinakothek.

Had Fouquet's visit been restricted to Rome, what could he have seen there of contemporary Italian painting, or better still, what did he see? There is no doubt that, like other foreign artists who travelled to Italy, he was eager to see as much as possible. E. Müntz's *Les Arts à la cour des Papes* and J. Pératé's *Les Papes et les Arts* give exhaustive information on this subject. Numerous works by Masaccio and Masolino, the actual founders of the new Italian school, painted under Pope Martin V between 1424 and 1428, were then in existence. In S. Clemente in the chapel of Cardinal Branda, their frescoes of the Passion and of the Life of St. Catherine as well as Masaccio's Crucifixion, were pointed out to the admiring visitor. In S. Maria Maggiore, the Colonnas had commissioned Masolino to paint the two altar-pieces of the Ascension and the Miracle of the Snow for their Tabernacle, which hang to-day in the Naples Museum. In S. Giovanni in Laterano the frescoes which Gentile da Fabriano and Pisanello had painted there between 1430 and 1432 were to be seen.

Of even greater interest for Fouquet than these older masters were the paintings which the venerable Fra Angelico was carrying out at that time in S. Maria Sopra Minerva (High Altar) and in the so-called Chapel of the Sacraments in the Vatican. These Vatican frescoes representing the Passion of Christ were destroyed under Pope Paul II. The slightly later cycle of frescoes of St. Stephen and St. Laurence in the Chapel of St. Nicholas, which may have been begun at Fouquet's time, gives us a good idea of the impressions which Fouquet received from Fra Angelico's art and which obviously created a lasting influence. He took from him not only certain architectural details and some peculiarities of the grouping of figures for his Chantilly miniatures, but also certain poses and gestures which are typical of Fra Angelico. For example, figures placed in the foreground with their backs to the spectator, or half turned away, striding towards the vanishing point, and thereby accentuating the perspective. This similarity of movement is striking when one compares Fra Angelico's panel

paintings, such as the Scenes from the legends of Cosmo and Damian[6] or of Nicholas of Bari,[7] with the miniatures of the Martyrdom of St. Peter, the Execution of St. John or the Pentecost at Chantilly. In sacred and miraculous subjects, Fra

plate 24 Angelico's influence is especially apparent. The pictures of the Holy Trinity, seen through what can only be described as a veritable tunnel of radiant angels, who with rows of Apostles and Fathers of the Church form the concave walls, and the rainbow-coloured tiers of angels flanking the Coronation of the Virgin are unthinkable without Fra Angelico's Last Judgement and Coronation of

plate 4 the Virgin.[8] The scenery of the Visitation, a white wall in the background behind which dark cypresses are silhouetted against a pale sky, recalls a motif which is frequently used by Fra Angelico and his pupils.

It is not known whether Fouquet also knew any of the works of the great Umbrian Master Piero della Francesca, the harsh strength of whose style must have appealed to him even more than the art of the pious Frate. The superficial formal connection between Fouquet's Antwerp Madonna and the Urbino Madonna of Piero della Francesca[9] is no sufficient proof. Opinions about Piero della Francesca's work in Rome at this time are contradictory. Vasari remarks that Piero painted for Nicholas V in 1453–54, that is after Fouquet's time, "*due storie nelle camere di sopra*" in the Vatican. On the other hand, in these frescoes, painted in what was later known as the "*Stanza del'Eliodoro*," the Master painted the portraits of several well-known personalities of the first half of the century, among them that of Charles VII of France. Clément and Prutz have assumed that he went to France himself, but he could just as well have seen and used a portrait of the King by Fouquet. Before the destruction of the frescoes to make room for those by Raphael, Raphael had the portraits copied and bequeathed them to Giulio Romano, who gave them to Paolo Giovio, the friend of Vasari.

In Rome Fouquet learnt through the treatise *Della Pittura* (1435) of Leon Battista Alberti, the *Commentarii* of Ghiberti (1447) and perhaps also through Piero della Francesca, who had already planned his *Treatise on Perspective*, the new laws for composing a picture which revealed to the artist the possibilities of completely realistic representation. Instead of the former antiquated juxtaposition, the arbitrary superimposing of actions, planes and figures, each

6) München, Ältere Pinakothek. – Dublin, National Gallery. – Paris, Musée du Louvre. – Florence, Galleria dell'Accademia.

7) Rome, Pinacoteca Vaticana. – Perugia, S. Domenico and Galleria Civica.

8) Berlin, Kaiser-Friedrich-Museum. – Florence, Galleria dell'Academia. – Florence, Uffizi.

9) Urbino, Palazzo Ducale.

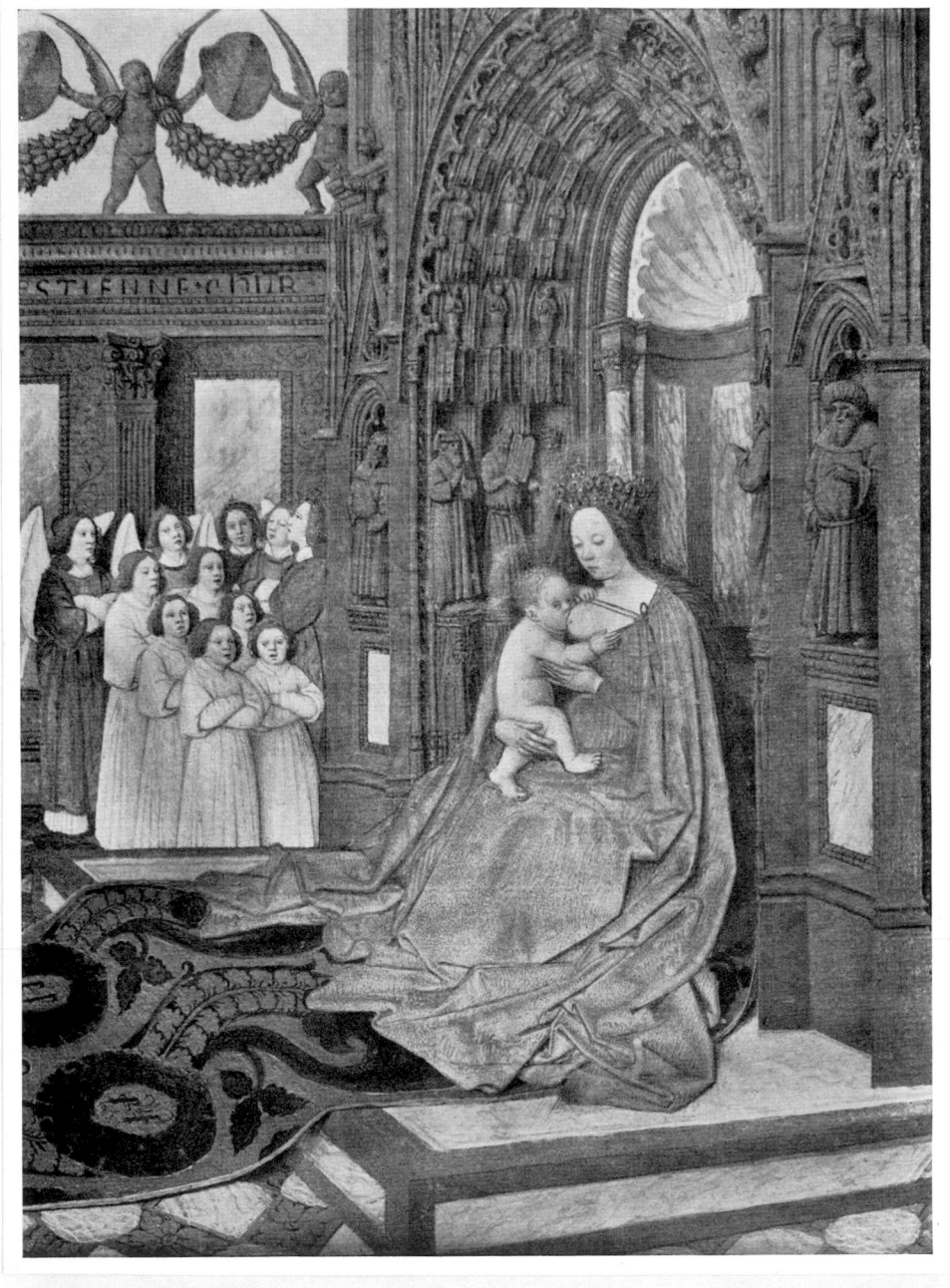

Illustration IV   *Fouquet: The Madonna*

subject had its firmly constructed place in the composition, its distance in space and depth was exactly determined, and the vanishing lines of perspective gave a firm construction to the whole. Proportion, and the proportion of the human body in particular, was a preoccupation with Italian artists. Horses seen in perspective, to be rendered later with such perfect mastery by Fouquet, were, after the famous battle pictures painted by Paolo Uccello for Cosimo de'Medici, the subject of eager study in Italy and are to be met with especially in numerous miniatures and *cassoni* pictures after Petrarch's *Trionfi*.

As for Renaissance architecture, only a few typical examples of which were to be seen in Rome at that time, Fouquet was too much under the influence of the Gothic tradition to absorb more than a few decorative details, wall-ornaments, columns, etc., borrowed from pictures and bas-reliefs rather than from actual buildings. The Roman reminiscences which appear in his pictures are chiefly those of mediaeval and antique buildings, such as the Castello di S. Angelo, the Forum, the interior of the old Basilica of St. Peter, Trajan's Column and the Triumphal Arch of Marcus Aurelius. When Fouquet left the Italian metropolis in 1447 or 1448, after a prolonged stay, he took away with him not only the new theories of Italian art, its new rhythm and lively images, but the very breath of a new life; he had discerned the many-sided intellectuality, the new value of the individual which gave Italian art its universal character.

Immediately after his return to Tours, he opened his own workshop, married and took over his father's house in the Rue des Pucelles. Soon afterwards the first commission from the court must have reached him, for Agnes Sorel, who probably posed for the Madonna of the Melun Diptych, died on February 9, 1450. Etienne Chevalier, who commissioned the picture for his native town, acted with Jacques Cœur as her executor.

Fouquet's work in Tours constituted only a part of the widespread artistic and architectural activity which, interrupted during the war, was now developing in most French towns, especially in Touraine. After 1430, the building of the Cathedral of Tours was continued under the patronage of the Archbishops Philippe de Cœtquis and Jean Bernard; the great sacristy was erected; the work on the façade was continued and the Archbishop's Palace adjoining the Cathedral was completely restored. The Duke of Bourbon gave one of the great Cathedral windows, Jean Gilbert, goldsmith to Charles VII, a chapel dedicated to St. Eligius. The church of St. Clement was newly constructed as well as the Gate of St. Martin, which was decorated by the painter Mathelin Poyet with

coats of arms and two winged stags, the King's heraldic emblem. The palaces of Count Dunois and the rich Mayor Jean Briçonnet, at whose expense the church of St. Clement was also constructed, as well as the palace of Jacques Cœur at Bourges, were superb examples of the new style of secular architecture.

The famous Basilica of St. Martin, in which Jean Gerson (Jean Charlier de Gerson, the well-known scholar and divine, chancellor of the University of Paris from 1363 to 1429) dedicated a series of tapestries for the choir, became, especially under Louis XI, the royal chapel, and a monument of great repute. In its newly erected *Chapelle Royale* hung a portrait of Charles VII and above the numerous precious golden reliquaries, to which Charles had added the magnificent *Chasse de Saint Martin*, enclosed by Louis in a silver grill worth 72,845 *livres*, twenty heavy silver lamps burnt day and night. Fouquet himself executed a series of paintings, presumably frescoes, for the Church of Notre-Dame-la-Riche, to which the Italian Florio referred when he declared him to be "the most excellent master."

The ten years between 1450 and 1460, the first decade of peaceful reconstruction and at the same time the last of Charles VII's reign, witnessed in quick ill. V, plate 38 succession the production of Fouquet's happiest creations: besides the Melun ill. I, III, IV, plates 1–27 pictures, there were also the book of hours of Etienne Chevalier, the portraits ill. VIII, plate 40 of the King and his Chancellor, Guillaume Juvénal des Ursins, the Munich ill. VI, VII, plates 28–30 *Boccaccio*, the *Grandes Chroniques de France*, several more painted prayerbooks plates 41, 42 and probably also the great altar-piece of the Pietà of Nouans.

At the death of King Charles VII, on July 22, 1461, Fouquet was in Paris, and Pierre de Hannes, the sculptor, who, together with Colin d'Amiens and Jacques de Litemont, had taken his death-mask and cast the *effigy*, speedily travelled there so that Fouquet could paint it "*comme au vif*." This leather effigy, clothed in the robes of the dead king, served, according to the old custom, for the funeral celebrations and the translation of the body to Saint-Denis.

In the autumn of 1461, Fouquet was busy with two assistants making decorations and plans for the triumphal entry of the new king, Louis XI, among them settings for Mystery Plays or *tableaux vivants* of a similar character. As the King let it be known to the City Council "*qu'il n'y prenoit nul plaisir*," the festivities were cancelled and Fouquet was remunerated with 100 *sols*.

The next record referring to Fouquet's activity is dated 1463 and is contained in the will of that date of Jean Bernard, Archbishop of Tours, which was drafted three years before his death, by his secretary François Thouars, who later acted

Illustration V

Fouquet: Etienne Chevalier and his Patron St.Stephen

as host to the Italian Florio. In it he bequeathed an altar-piece of the Ascension of the Virgin, to be executed by Fouquet, to the Church at Candes, the summer palace of the Archbishops of Tours, for the price of 70 *écus*, the artist taking in part exchange from the bishop a picture of the Madonna worth 25 *livres* already paid for. As the Huguenots destroyed the Church of Candes in 1562, no doubt this work also fell a victim to the iconoclasts.

In 1469, Louis XI finally took up his residence at Tours and founded the Order of St. Michael, following the example of Duke Philip the Good of Burgundy, who had founded the Order of the Golden Fleece. On this occasion Fouquet was commissioned to paint the title miniature of the Statutes of the Order[10] and Jean Robertet, secretary of the Order, paid him also 55 *livres* in December 1470 "*pour la façon de certains tableaux que le dit seigneur (Louis XI) lui a chargez faire pour servir aux chevaliers de l'ordre de Saint-Michel.*" It is uncertain whether they consisted of coats of arms only, or were pictorial representations of St. Michael slaying the dragon, as depicted in the background of the title miniature. It is clear from this that Fouquet kept the privileged position he had gained under Charles VII under the less art-loving Louis XI. As the King, in 1474, planned to erect a monumental tomb for himself, he ordered designs from Fouquet and the sculptor Michel Colombe. The highest proof of royal favour was bestowed on the master in the following year, in which he obtained at last the official title of the "*peintre du roy,*" took up permanent employment in the royal household, was freed of taxes and various compulsory duties, and obtained other privileges which went with the appointment.

At the beginning of his career, most of his works had been commissioned by members of the ennobled officials; now, at the height of his fame, he was patronized especially by the higher aristocracy. Thus in 1472 he was called to Blois to illuminate a prayerbook for Marie de Clève, widow of Charles d'Orléans, and he was employed in the same way by Charles de Guyenne, the King's brother, and Pierre de Bourbon, his brother-in-law. If the document of the Fillon collection is to be trusted, Philippe de Comines, the new favourite of the King, commissioned him to paint two prayerbooks for which he only paid 39 *écus* instead of the agreed 62 and in 1477 the painter had to sue in the Paris law courts to recover the balance.

In the Louvre is preserved a life-sized and very realistic portrait in sculpture from the tomb of Comines, one of the most interesting personalities at the

10) Statuts de l'ordre de S. Michel, Paris, Bibliothèque Nationale, Ms. fr. 19819.

French Court. Although a Fleming, born at Ypres, he had left the service of Charles the Bold in 1472 to seek employment with Louis XI, whom he served so well as a diplomat of truly Macchiavellian ingenuity, that he was loaded with honours, and acquired both property and riches. His *Memoirs*, written later, give a vivid impression of the age of Louis XI, and in their psychological insight surpass all the historical works of the 15th century. He had in his possession an early masterpiece by Jan van Eyck, The Maries at the Sepulchre,[11] which is of especial interest in connection with our subject. He had probably taken this picture with him to France, and Fouquet may therefore have had the opportunity of seeing with his own eyes this work of his great predecessor. Of his two prayerbooks, only one is now to be found in the Bibliothèque Nationale; the second one, published by Leo Baer, cannot be attributed to Fouquet, but was executed by Jean Colombe and his workshop, whose style was partly based on Fouquet's Chevalier prayerbook.[12]

Certainly the most generous and most art-loving among these later patrons of Fouquet was Jacques d'Armagnac, Duke of Nemours, the grandson and worthy successor of Duke Jean de Berry, the famous bibliophile, of whose manuscripts he had inherited a certain portion, besides being himself a passionate collector of books and works of art of all kinds. When the Duke was arrested by royal command in 1476 and soon afterwards executed in Paris because he was found guilty of continuous conspiracy since the times of the "*Ligue du bien* plates 31–35 *public*," the two volumes of the Josephus, mentioned above, were found in his library in the Castle of Carlat and confiscated. Although Jacques d'Armagnac employed several well-known miniaturists of his own, as Jan ten Eycken, Evrard d'Espingues and Guillaume Alexandre, he considered Fouquet alone worthy to finish this work which the brothers Limburg had begun.

In the same year 1476, in which the Duke of Nemours fell victim to the intrigues of Louis XI, the King of Portugal came to visit the French King at Tours, and Fouquet was commissioned to prepare a design for the painted canopy to be used at the triumphal entry. It is possible that on that occasion he came into contact with Nuno Gonzalves, the court painter of the Portuguese King, whose art is related to his own in many respects.

A final work of miniature painting, begun by him, but never finished, is

11) Richmond (Surrey), Sir Herbert Cook coll.
12) Ms. lat. 1417. – In: The Burlington Magazine, XXV, 1914, p. 40 (then by Joseph Baer & Co., Frankfort-on-the-Main, from the Huth Library).

preserved in an *Histoire Romaine* by Livy,[13] translated by Pierre Bersuire. It was commissioned after 1477 by Guillaume d'Harcourt, Comte de Tancarville, the brother-in-law of the famous Dunois; two of the miniatures, an Assembly in the Roman Forum and the Rape of the Sabines, were entirely carried out by Fouquet. A third was conceived and largely painted by him, but with additions plate 36 by another hand, at the instigation of a later owner of the manuscript, François de Rochechouart, Chancellor of Louis XI and Governor of Genoa.

The reason why Fouquet did not complete these miniatures is clear from an entry in the records of the Collegiate Church of St. Martin, his parish church at Tours. Under the date of 8 November 1481 are mentioned *"la veufve et héritiers de feu Jehan Foucquet, peintre"*; Fouquet was therefore dead before that date. A few years later, after the death of Louis XI (1483), the royal residence at Tours was given up, and under the Regent Anne de Beaujeu and during the reign of Charles VIII, Paris once more became the seat of the Court, with Moulins or Blois as alternatives. The centralization of France began again with Paris as its focus. Tours relapsed into its former provincial status; only the Tourangean school of painting remained as the proof of its former importance.

13) Paris, Bibliothèque Nationale, Ms. fr. 20071.

FOUQUET'S WORK

The Miniatures

ill. I, III, IV The illustrations in Etienne Chevalier's book of hours undoubtedly take prece-
plates 1–27 dence over all other known miniatures by Fouquet. They are the crowning
achievement of all his artistic endeavour, his *"Grand testament,"* as it were. In
its original condition, this prayerbook must have been of incredible splendour;
with the *Très riches Heures* of the Duke of Berry and the prayerbook by Jan van
Eyck at Milan, it was certainly the most beautiful manuscript of the 15th century painted in Northern Europe. The miniatures, some of them cut down and
framed in a most barbarous fashion, are each a small masterpiece. Although they
were conceived as parts of an entity and composed to blend with the written
text, they are each in themselves perfect and command our highest admiration.
As it is impossible to form a complete impression of the original book, the
order in which the miniatures were arranged can only be guessed by applying
the general liturgical rules to the opening lines of text where they have still
survived under the pictures.

The calendar pictures of the activities appropriate to each month, which
would have been most instructive as a study of everyday life and its background,
are missing. Three of the pictures of the Evangelists are replaced by the Epi-
plate 1 phany, the Ascension of Christ and the Birth of St. John the Baptist; St. Luke
the Evangelist is missing but the composition of this picture seems to have been
the same as those preserved in other prayerbooks by Fouquet and Jean Colombe. Of the two pictures appropriate to the devotions of the Virgin, the
Mater Dolorosa for the prayer *"O intemerata"* is missing. When illustrating the
plates 2, 5 Hours of the Virgin, Fouquet varied the general practice by putting a second
plates 6 Annunciation in the place of the Tidings to the Shepherds and the Death of the
plate 7 Virgin and Funeral of the Virgin instead of the Adoration of the Magi, the
plates 10–13 Purification or the Circumcision. The Hours of the Cross are rendered in seven
stages in the usual way and, with the exception of one, *Terce*, which would probably have been represented by the *Ecce Homo*, all are preserved, as are also
plate 14 the three Hours and Vespers of the Holy Ghost, consisting of Pentecost—
plates 16, 15 twice, like the Annunciation—the Spring of the Apostles and the Ascension
of the Holy Ghost. For the service dedicated to the Virgin, Fouquet chose as
plate 17 his most important illustration the Marriage of the Virgin; for the seven peni-

tentiary psalms, David in Prayer, on the battlefield with two corpses in the — plate 20
foreground, the realistic painting of which immediately reminds one of Carpaccio's painting of the Entombment.[14] The Vespers for the Dead show, as
always, a funeral procession and the Vigil of the Dead, a representation of — plate 18
Job and his three friends. Of the subsequent Fifteen Joys of the Virgin — plate 19
every one of the pictures is missing. To the *Stabat Mater Dolorosa* belongs the — plate 21
Lament of the Virgin, the background of which shows Notre-Dame and the
Mont Sainte-Geneviève at Paris. The Seven Prayers of Intercession are decorated with the picture of St. Bernard of Clairvaux among his Friars. Of the — plate 23
prayers to individual saints, introduced by a picture of the Holy Trinity— — plate 24
these prayers are of great variety according to the place of origin and the personal use of the owner of such prayerbooks—seventeen miniatures in all have — plates 22–27
survived: twelve dedicated to male saints and five to female saints, among
them, of course, St. Stephen, the patron saint of Chevalier, St. Martin, the — ill. III, plate 25
patron saint of Tours, St. Margaret and St. Michael as the favourite saints of the — ill. I
French King. Henry Martin assumed that at least thirteen of the miniatures of
this prayerbook are lost; two of the miniatures, the Vespers of the Holy Ghost — plate 14
and St. Veranus, have been recently discovered. The original number would have — plate 22
been about sixty.

Etienne Chevalier, for whom this magnificent work, as well as the altar-piece
of Melun was painted, was one of those middle-class court officials who, through — ill. V, plate 38
their ability and loyalty, had gained great influence and prestige as well as great
wealth. He was a native of Melun, the son of a secretary of the King's, and
became when still a youth *Conseiller* and *Maître des Comptes*, later *Contrôleur de
la recette*, and finally rose to be *Contrôleur Général des Finances*. In that capacity
he was for many years a member of the select circle of the *Grand Conseil Privé*
which presided over the fate of the country. The majority of the *Grandes
Ordonnances*, or financial decrees, were drafted and signed by him. In 1445 he
was sent to England, with Guillaume Cousinot and Jean Juvénal, to negotiate
the peace treaty, and, as he enjoyed the King's full confidence, was nominated
Trésorier in 1452. When Louis XI ascended the throne in 1461, he was, like
most counsellors of Charles VII, temporarily relieved of his office. However he
was soon reinstated and, in 1463, the King sent him to Lille, to discuss the re-
purchase of the towns on the Somme. His portrait appears twice in the miniatures of the prayerbook: on the first two-page illustration he is seen praying — ill. III, IV

14) Berlin, Kaiser-Friedrich-Museum, Nr. 23 A.

37

before the Madonna and also in the Entombment. In both cases he so clearly resembles his portrait in the Berlin altar-piece, even in age, that only a short time can have elapsed between the painting of these two works. Throughout the prayerbook, not only are his initials but also his full name and title, "Maistre Estienne Chevalier" repeatedly displayed; a sign that the owner felt a justifiable pride in the ownership of this precious volume.

Several of the miniatures, in a new and striking fashion, are divided into an upper and a lower scene, the upper containing the main subject and the lower a subsidiary scene with figures engaged in some everyday activity, or wild men such as often appear in the marginal decorations of illuminations of the period, or angels holding placards. The origin of this divided scene is made fairly clear to us by the picture of the Martyrdom of St. Apollonia. The background is a faithful representation of the stage of a Mystery Play, with its various compartments, ranged side by side, in which different scenes were enacted at the same time. Sometimes these compartments which were also used for *tableaux vivants* such as formed part of triumphal processions, were composed of two or even three platforms, raised one above the other, often hung with placards and Fouquet obviously employed this arrangement in the composition of his pictures. The influence of the Mystery Plays, that is to say, the Passion Plays of that time, on the Chevalier miniatures is probable also for another reason, as E. Mâle was the first to indicate. At that time the longest and most important Mystery Play of the 15th century was well known. Written by Arnoul de Gréban, *Maitre ès arts* and organist of Notre-Dame de Paris, before December 1, 1452, its subject was that of the redemption of mankind and the liberation of Adam and his successors through Jesus Christ. It contained 34,500 lines, and took four days to perform. The first day, that of the Redemption, began with Adam and Eve awaiting the return of the Messiah, and led, with innumerable parallels and symbolical interludes, to the scene of Jesus among the Wise Men; the second day represented the Life of Christ from his Baptism up to the Betrayal by Judas; the third day of the performance, Good Friday, brought the representation of the Passion; the fourth, Easter Day, the Resurrection and reappearance of Christ and the Ascension, and it ended with a *Moralité*, as an epilogue, in which God the Father, the Archangel Michael and the Virtues, personified as Wisdom, Justice, Truth and Charity, appeared with singing angels. Choirs of angels, such as are to be seen in the pictures of the Madonna, the Birth of Christ and the Coronation of the Virgin, played an im-

portant part in Gréban's play; he himself conducted the choir-boys of Notre-Dame. The realistic secondary characters and subsidiary scenes, which enlivened the play and established greater contact with the audience, were also represented by Fouquet in two miniatures of the Passion: the carpenters who fashion the plate 10 cross and the smithy in which the nails for the crucifixion are forged. The real plate 11 importance of the Mystery Plays, as far as art was concerned, lay, however, not so much in their stage-settings as in their large casts and dramatic action, and also in their topical spirit and method of instruction.

In all Fouquet's representations two traits are conspicuous: his pleasure in dramatic action and his joy in everyday life. They are like variations on a great theme: God in France, the ever-present Christ and the saints seen under a French sky, standing resolutely on French soil. Man holds the centre of the stage on which this mystery is enacted, with the leaders of Christianity, Jesus, Mary, the apostles and martyrs, all equally human, to aid him by their example. In representing these human beings in their most perfect form, the artist worked in the best service of religion, according to the wise precepts of the church of those days. In following the example of Italian art, the art of those days doubtless underwent a kind of profanation, while at the same time teaching a spiritual comprehension of humanity on a higher plane. Coming as they did after the ascetic and ecstatic figures which the mediaeval artist loved to paint (those thin lifeless figures depicted by the Maître François and most other French and Flemish miniature painters), Fouquet's pictures of saints in the form of contemporary human beings of flesh and blood, with their feet firmly planted on a ground which is no *terra incognita* but some recognizable place, must indeed have seemed an innovation. Fouquet comprehended the anatomy, movement and functions of the human body as well as he understood those of the horse, that emblem of the age of chivalry, and all natural objects. He was a tireless observer of movement and of life. Had his sketchbooks been preserved, we should doubtless find them filled with studies from Nature of every kind, like those of Pisanello or Leonardo. In comparison with many old masters whose creations were purely fantastic, Fouquet, with his fanatical objectivity, may appear prosaic. His poetry lies less in vivid expressionism than in the harmonious relationship of colour, light, space and the plasticity of objects—in the revelation of a new life. It lies above all in a lofty, monumental style which connects it with the best traditions of French sculpture, with the anonymous mediaeval sculptors of the great French cathedrals as well as with Claus Sluter.

That Fouquet himself regarded the illuminations for the Chevalier prayer-book as his most important artistic creation is evident from the fact that he and his pupils copied a number of them in smaller and simplified versions for other prayerbooks. The Kiss of Judas and the Crucifixion are to be met with again in a prayerbook at The Hague and in the prayerbook of Charles de Guyenne; St. John on the Island of Patmos, the Visitation, the Marriage and Death of the Virgin, the Crucifixion, the Lamentation and the Job in the so-called Prayer-book of Diane de Croy and in a manuscript at Paris; the Annunciation, Birth of Christ, Visitation, Lamentation, Pentecost, the Madonna and the Funeral Procession in the prayerbooks illuminated for Pierre de Bourbon and for an unknown patron whose initials read AR.[15] The probable identity of those minia-tures missing from the prayerbook of Chevalier, such as the St. Luke the Evange-list, the Tidings to the Shepherds, the Presentation in the Temple, the Flight into Egypt and the Baptism, has been determined in this way. Only compara-tively few fresh compositions are to be found in these small prayerbooks. There was an established rule for the sequence of pictures in books of hours, and it was only natural in a busy workshop, such as Fouquet's undoubtedly was, that the best compositions and figures should be used repeatedly. This was the accepted practice of the painters of that time, and is no disparagement of Fou-quet's inventive ingenuity which we see so convincingly demonstrated in his profane and historical works, such as the Munich *Boccaccio*, the *Antiquités* of Josephus and the *Grandes Chroniques de France*.

Boccaccio's work, entitled in the translation by Laurent de Premierfait *Des Cas des nobles hommes et femmes malheureux*, had become a favourite at that time with the world of fashion. Duke Charles of Orléans had it with him during his captivity in England and in reading it pondered over the transience of earthly glory. It was like an ever-present mirror, a *"miroir des princes,"* as was also the symbol of the wheel of Fortune, so frequent a feature in pictorial re-presentations of that time, and which Fouquet used twice in the larger illustra-tions of this book.[16] The long series of *Cas* is illustrated with nine large minia-tures, introducing the nine parts of the book, and eighty small ones, at the be-ginning of each chapter; the latter are miniatures in the strictest sense of the word, that is to say pictures on a very small scale indeed. The frontispiece, the

15) The Hague, Koninglijke Bibliotheek, Ms. 74 G 28. – Paris, Bibliothèque Mazarine, Ms. 473. – Sheffield, Ruskin Museum. – Paris, Bibliothèque Nationale, Ms. Nat. lat. 13305. – Copenhagen, Kongelige Bibliotek, GKS 1610. – London, formerly Chester Beatty coll.

16) Munich, Staatsbibliothek, Cod. Gall. 369.

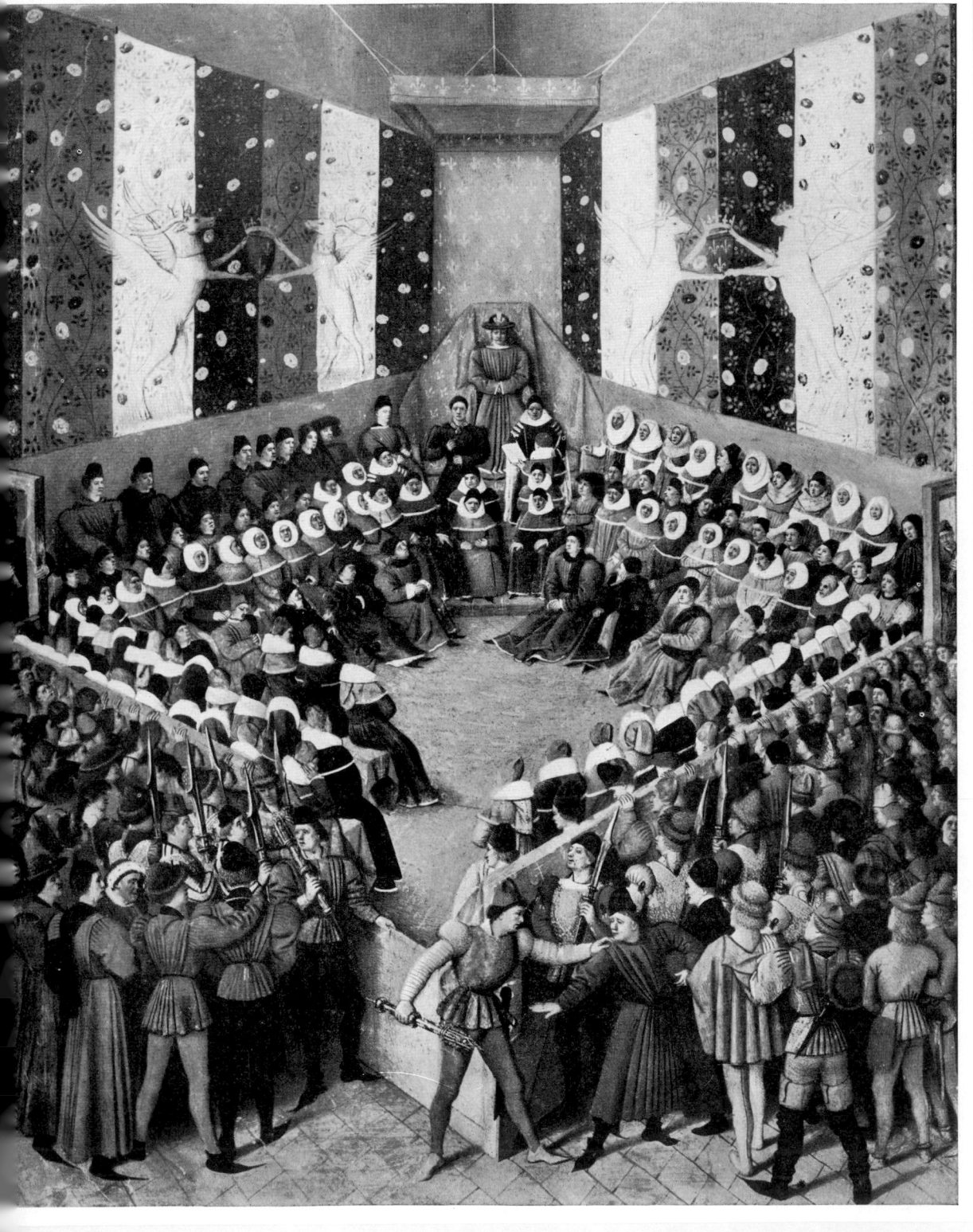

Illustration VI   Fouquet: The Trial at Vendôme in 1458

largest and most magnificent of the pictures, represents the trial of the Duke of ill. VI
Alençon at Vendôme and was apparently ordered by the patron of the manuscript. The picture has nothing to do with the contents of the book; the
event, however, had not long before greatly stirred the people of France and
inspired the artist to illustrate yet another striking and topical example of the
downfall of a mighty man, in keeping with the tenor of the book.

The motto *"Sur l'y n'a regard,"* which appears in several places in the Munich
manuscript, was at first connected with Etienne Chevalier because, according to
Godefroy, his house in the Rue de la Verrerie at Paris bore a similar inscription.
With the help of the initials L. G., which frequently appear in the manuscript,
the partly deleted calligrapher's note at the end of the book and the anagrammat-
ical inscription contained in the motto, Count Durrieu discovered the name of
Laurens Gyrard, the real owner of the book. Since 1453 Laurens Gyrard had
been *Contrôleur de la recette* in the Treasury and successor to Chevalier. Like
Chevalier, the middle-class magistrate Gyrard stood in high favour with the
King, who nominated him, among others, executor of the will of André de
Villequier, his first favourite. For the second time, therefore, we see Fouquet
occupied with a work of great magnificence for an ennobled official—a proof
of the growing influence of that class in the political as well as in the cultural
sphere. Unlike the Chevalier prayerbook, the exact date of this work is known,
for the copyist, Pierre Faure, Curé of Aubergenville near Paris, has left a note
at the end of the book to the effect that he finished this work on November 24,
1458. According to the custom of the time, the painting of the miniatures was
carried out partly at the same time as the work of the copyist and partly afterwards.

In the same year Fouquet had received the commission of yet another important work of miniature painting and this time from the King himself, whose
portrait he must have already painted. The *Grandes Chroniques des Rois de* ill. VII, plates 28–30
France[17] set the standard for official writing of history. As early as the last
decades of the 13th century, it became the custom for one or more of the monks
of Saint-Denis to record the most remarkable events of their time, and so one of
the best known of them, Guillaume de Nangis, wrote the history of France up
to the death of Philippe Auguste. This work was continued regularly, so that
the chronicler of the day was able to take advantage not only of his own personal information but also of the memoirs of other contemporaries. In this way,

17) Paris, Bibliothèque Nationale, Ms. fr. 6465.

as time went on, a historical corpus came into existence, such as is to be found nowhere else.

To illustrate this important work, newly edited in 1458 by the King's secretary Noël Frébois, a miniature painter had to be officially commissioned. The work demanded singular gifts, especially adapted to the circumstances: a dignified style and a vivid imagination. Fouquet conceived the mediaeval subjects of the history of France in the spirit of his own time, although there were older pictures in the richly illustrated *Grandes Chroniques* which he could have used as models. These subjects consisted, as they had in the past, mostly of triumphal processions, meetings of monarchs, banquets, coronations, state funerals and battle scenes. To follow the strict rules of etiquette, as Aliénor de Poitiers described them in full detail in the *Honneurs de la Cour*, and to depict them correctly, was all the more obligatory, as the book was ordered for the King himself. Most of the pictures have therefore a measured and ceremonial style which contrasts with the freedom of the earlier miniatures. The old kings, such as Dagobert and Childerich, are endowed by Fouquet with the features of Charles VII, just as he represents several of the old emperors with the personal appearance of the Emperor Sigismund of Austria. Similarly the *temps barbares* of the early Middle Ages are not shown in the style and costume of their period but in that of Fouquet's own day. The deeper historical understanding, which had already awakened in Italy, was still alien to the French. In this difficult task Fouquet proved himself once more a great master of his craft; one who had the power to create a vivid impression of these comparatively uninspiring historical events and to endow them with greatness, through his skilful grouping of the figures in their beautifully coloured robes, with backgrounds showing realistic views of Paris and its neighbourhood, of Tours, Orléans, Reims and Montpensier; through effects of light and shade of sublimely picturesque sensibility and, above all, through his unique power of expression.

plates 31–35 In the two volumes of the *Antiquités Judaïques* by Flavius Josephus,[18] the only manuscript of which Fouquet's authorship (thanks to François Robertet's note) is certain, we meet him again as an illustrator of historical events but under different conditions and in quite a different style. Here his imagination is no longer forced to conform to certain conditions and to court etiquette. He was free to choose his own subjects, and the large pictures of this manuscript, almost too crowded and bursting with life, are, next to the Chevalier minia-

18) Paris, Bibliothèque Nationale, Ms. fr. 247 and Nouv. Acq. fr. 21013.

44

feuſſent gardez iuſques alautre audience
Cr fine lem.e luire des cronicse des Rois de ſnce

Cr commence le iii.e luire qui fait mencion
des fais & hiſtoires le Roy Gontran qui eſtou

Illustration VII   *Fouquet: Gontran and Childebert*

tures, his most representative and extensive work and most typical of his later
style. It was commissioned before 1476, but certainly not before 1470, by
Jacques d'Armagnac, Duke of Nemours, who had inherited the two volumes
from his grandfather, Jean de Berry, and who wished to see the illustrations
completed. The books were at that time adorned with three miniatures from
the Limburg workshop and spaces for the additional illustrations had been
left blank. Paul of Limburg's work was considered in its day, that is at the
time of Fouquet's birth, a model of modern art and nowhere else can Fouquet's
incredible progress be better assessed than here, when one compares the three
pictures of the older master with his. No greater gulf could divide them. The
first volume of Josephus contains eleven large miniatures from Fouquet's hand,
the second, which is incomplete, ten pictures; not all, however, entirely by him

plate 31

45

and partly in an antiquated style. As already in the Munich *Boccaccio*, the smaller prayerbooks and also in parts of the *Grandes Chroniques* Fouquet seems, towards the end, to have delegated some of the work to his assistants.

This history by Josephus, known since the latter part of the Middle Ages, and, like the Bible, widely circulated, is in its main theme a history of continual battles and conquests, of heroic deeds and atrocities. The illustrations reveal Fouquet as a painter of battle scenes. He groups his crowds with all the skill and subtlety of an experienced theatrical producer and each scene seems to be taken directly from the war-like life of his own time. For Fouquet has transferred the history of the Jews to France, to the valley of the Loire, the banks of the Seine and to his own day. Only a few fantastic mountain ranges and invented forms of Oriental architecture hint that the action is taking place in a distant plate 34 land in times long past. Jerusalem with its Temple, is Tours with its Cathedral in the course of construction, here crowned with an Oriental cupola instead of its spires. In only a few of the Chevalier miniatures has Fouquet given so much plate 33 space to the wide landscapes, or depicted with so much detail as here the meandering rivers and low hills of his native region, the simple, friendly charm of its towns and villages. It seems as if he had wanted once more to bring together all that had moved him in his youth—the contrast between the never-ending, futile war and the eternal peace of nature. Judea and the Jewish War, with its repeated destruction, is for him a symbol of contemporary France. In these pictures, just as in those times, the fate of the individual is of no importance. Everything is seen as from a distance from which the crowd alone is distinguishable. Two parties only emerge, joined in a hand-to-hand struggle, one of which is condemned to suffer the cruel fate of the vanquished. The first picture—the Punishment of Korah, Dathan and Abiron—may have been traced by the older master of Limburg, for it differs from Fouquet's own style in the lack of unity of composition and in the representation of the horses. The design, too, which shows Salmanzar leading the ten Tribes of Egypt into captivity, based partly on that of a coin of Heraclius owned by the Duke of Berry, may be traced back to the older painter. Where Fouquet aimed at a more Oriental setting, as in the view of the Inner Shrine of the Temple, or the pictures of Pompey's and Herod's Entry into Jerusalem, a bizarre mixture of Gothic and Renaissance styles of architecture appears, with reminiscences of the twisted columns of the old Basilica of St. Peter, which he had seen in Rome, and of San Giovanni in Laterano. The exaggerated use of gold gives to most of the

46

pictures a pompous and ritualistic appearance which emphasizes their legendary and biblical character.

Closely related to the Josephus miniatures, as far as subject, composition and style are concerned, are five pictures and illuminated pages, which have been preserved, cut out and detached from yet another larger manuscript, the *Histoire ancienne jusqu'à Jules César et des faits des Romains*. Two of these pages refer directly to the history of Caesar, who as one of the "*Neuf Preux*," heroes of Antiquity, had long been popular. They are: Caesar about to cross the Rubicon plate 37 and Pompey escaping after his Defeat at Pharsalia; the three others are: Samson slaying the Lion and the Destruction of the Temple, the Coronation of Alexander the Great and the Battle of Cannae.[19] Their date must be roughly contemporary with the Josephus illustrations and the three representations of Roman history form in subject and in style a link between this and Fouquet's last known work, an unfinished Livy.[20] plate 36

The growing interest in these old Roman histories clearly shows that the historical spirit of the Renaissance, with its interest in the ancient world, had at length penetrated into France, too late, however, to have a fruitful influence on art. For these illustrations of Fouquet are not conceived in a style that is any more antique or classical, than are his early works or the Josephus. These last three paintings, which form an artistic unity, show a marked change of style when compared with the *Grandes Chroniques*, the *Boccaccio* and the Chevalier miniatures, but not in the sense of progressive development. The freshness and realism of the Chevalier miniatures have given way to an almost mechanical precision and their monumental strength is replaced by the outward trappings of greatness. The prospect is wider, the effect richer and more magnificent, the artist's technical mastery is as accomplished as ever, but the burning conviction of the earlier works is absent. His long years of association with and dependence on the Court have transformed him into a court painter. Fouquet had become in a sense more of a miniature painter than he had been when he painted the more panel-like Chevalier illustrations; on the other hand, this change to a more illustrative and narrative style occurred at a time when the woodcut, with its simplified linear technique, was setting new standards for the art of book decoration.

19) London, Henry Yates Thompson coll. – Amsterdam, Rijksprentenkabinet, Nr. 1943. – Paris, Musée du Louvre.

20) "Histoire Romaine." Paris, Bibliothèque Nationale, Ms. fr. 20071/72.

Fouquet was not only a miniature painter but also a painter of panel pictures. In a sense his importance in this field is the greater since in it he broke more new ground and laid completely new foundations for the art of painting. Whether he considered himself a better painter of panels than of miniatures seems unimportant compared to the essential fact that, as a painter of illuminated books, he could appeal to only a very small number of privileged persons, whereas through his altar-pieces he could address a wide public. After Bellechose and Malouel, that is since the time of Charles VI, the art of panel-painting in France, if not extinct, seems to have declined and degenerated through the effects of war. The only known example, the votive-picture of the Ursins from their chapel in Notre-Dame,[21] is a mediocre work. Even if we allow for the loss of several monuments, the total lack of important works cannot be ascribed solely to a broken tradition but corresponds without doubt to the historical facts. Patrons and funds for the maintenance, not to mention the decoration of the churches, were lacking and the absence of schools and practical experience was responsible for the scarcity of competent artists.

In Italy, Fouquet saw an abundance of paintings, and here and there perhaps the work of a Netherlandish artist. His portrait of Pope Eugene proves, however, that he had evolved his technique of panel-painting before his Italian journey, and that, like van Eyck, independently he had found ways and means to enhance the character of panel-painting. His first known work, the so-called ill. V, plate 38 Diptych of Melun,[22] reaches a very high level of creative power and is a remarkable revelation of his fully developed talents. The plastic strength of the modelling, the accomplished simplification and the big sweep of outline, the clearcut brilliance and the delicacy of the colour harmonies, and finally the commanding portraiture are all in evidence. The Antwerp Madonna, in view of its monumental strength and almost life size, can be compared only with the Madonnas of Piero della Francesca. The poetic conception of the Angels of Day and Night, with their brilliant, effective colour, has scarcely ever been so impressively represented. The resemblance of the Madonna to the funeral effigy of Agnes Sorel at Loches suggests that the altar may have been dedicated in her honour. We have already mentioned that Chevalier, in his peculiar quality as *Trésorier*, was probably much associated with her, and was destined to be an executor of her

21) Paris, Musée du Louvre.
22) Berlin, Deutsches Museum. – Antwerp, Musée Royal des Beaux-Arts.

48

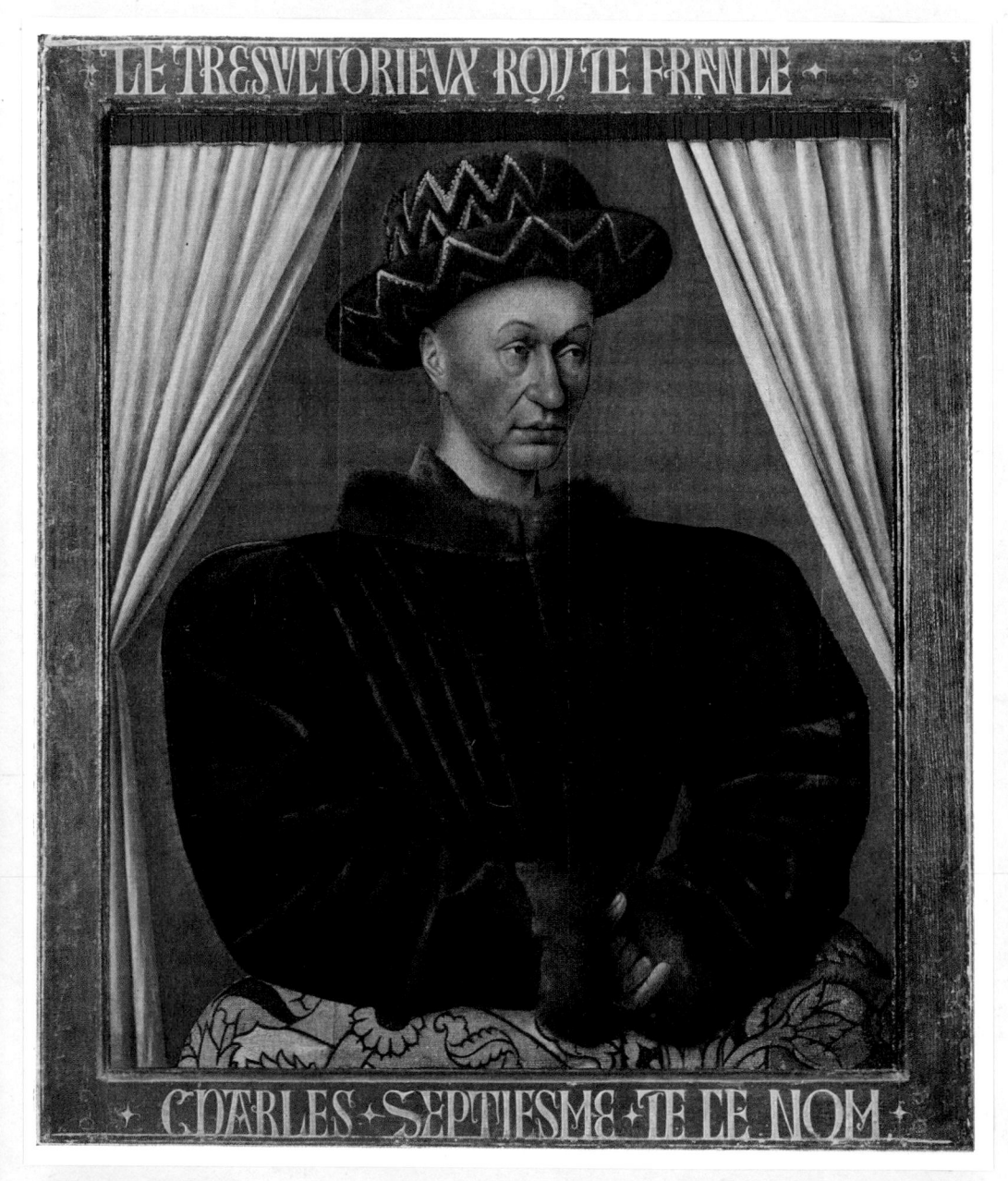

Illustration VIII   *Fouquet: Portrait of Charles VII*

49

will. Chevalier's wife, Catherine Budé, however, died soon after, in 1452, after having received at the New Year as a present from the King a dress valued at 50 *écus*, and this has given rise to the belief that this altar was erected to her memory. Finally there is a third possibility to be considered, that it was a joint gift from both husbands and destined for Chevalier's birthplace. In this case, in spite of Godefroy's testimony that the pictures were no longer in their original place, but that he had seen them hanging in the choir, one beside the other, it must have been originally a triptych. The composition of the two panels, the relationship of which we feel to be incomplete, actually points to such an arrangement. A right wing, showing Catherine Budé with her patron saint, St. Catherine, facing to the left, would complete the whole composition and give it the harmonious form of a semicircle.

In the portrait of the donor, Etienne Chevalier, as well as in the portrait of   ill. V
Charles VII and of his chancellor Guillaume Juvénal des Ursins, Fouquet proves   ill. VIII, plates 39, 40
himself to be a profound psychologist, unsurpassed by any of the great portrait painters of the 15th century, the century rightly celebrated for the discovery of the human countenance.[23] If we compare them with the only two important portraits of an earlier date, the portrait in profile of Louis II d'Anjou (about 1417), and the portrait of Pierre de Luxembourg (about 1430/40),[24] the greater clarity and precision of the outward characteristics of the sitter, as well as the psychological insight and the grasp of the whole personality, are very remarkable. As one can see in the portrait of Charles VII, whose personality is best known to us, Fouquet depicts not only one side of the sitter but all the different sides of his character, his whole complex nature. An unsurpassed master of theatrical production, he enhances these invisible characteristics with an appropriate setting, the surroundings in which he places his figures: the unfathomable monarch who keeps shyly to himself is placed between the half-drawn curtains of his box in church, his hands clasped on a velvet cushion, near, yet inaccessible, separated from mankind by his majesty; the ostentatious chancellor, on the other hand, is posed before a Renaissance background, richly decorated with gilded ornaments in the style of the "*ouvraige de Lombardie*," the pilasters of which bear in the most conspicuous place his coat of arms, adopted from the Roman family Orsini. In spite of their individual likeness, the difference of pictorial treatment between these two por-

23) Berlin, Deutsches Museum. — Paris, Musée du Louvre. — Berlin, Staatliches Kupferstichkabinett. — Paris, Musée du Louvre.
24) Paris, Bibliothèque Nationale. — Avignon, Musée Calvet.

traits and the Chevalier portrait is enormous. Here everything is seen in a strong light with plastic shadows, there the harmonies of the colours are flatter, as if plunged into the semidarkness of a room. The date of the King's portrait is disputed, as some even suppose it to have been painted before Fouquet's journey to Italy. But it can be dated only after the Treaty of Arras (1444) or more probably after 1450. It was only after the victory of Formigny (1450) which, with the conquest of the Guyenne, more or less put an end to the war, that he was able rightfully to assume the title *"très victorieux,"* which forms part of the inscription on the frame; his age also is about the same as in the miniature of the Adoration in the Chevalier prayerbook, whereas in the portrait in the *Grandes Chroniques* he is more portly in stature. The portrait of the chancellor may have been painted shortly before or after that of the King. Either it may have caused the King to have his portrait painted by the same artist, or, which is more likely, it may have been commissioned in imitation of the King.

frontispiece   The self-portrait of Fouquet,[25] painted in grisaille on an enamelled medallion, presents us with a new and twofold problem: it is the first known self-portrait of a French master and it is the first product of its kind as far as the technique of the enamelling is concerned, a technique which soon afterwards rose to great importance through its use by the School of Limoges. It can reasonably be assumed that Fouquet had learnt this technique in Rome from Filarete, who made just such an enamelled medallion for Piero de'Medici, to be inserted into a bronze copy of the statue of Marcus Aurelius. It is an attractive theory that this self-portrait, together with another medallion of the same size at the Berlin Kunstgewerbe-Museum representing Pentecost, may have once formed part of the original frame of the so-called Melun Diptych. But as Charles Sterling has shown, this is not mentioned in the text of Godefroy.

plates 41, 42   The only life-size altar-piece, the Pietà of Nouans, appears at first sight, by comparison with the Melun panels, a work of cold solemnity, and we can only assess its artistic significance when we recall what its importance was in its own time and make allowance for its being incomplete, cut and reduced, and its background plate 21 painted over. The same idea which Fouquet carried out in the two Lamentations of the Chevalier prayerbook is used here on a greater scale, with great pictorial force and impressive realism, reminiscent of the monumental sculpture of the Holy Sepulchre. Among all the surviving works by painters from central France, there is not one which represents the essence of the new art, its inner

25) Paris, Musée du Louvre.

52

significance as well as its outward greatness, as perfectly as this one. Only in the outlying parts of the kingdom, in the domain of René of Anjou, have comparable examples survived, in the altars of Enguerrand Charenton and Nicolas Froment at Villeneuve-les-Avignon and in the Altar of the Annunciation at Aix. In this respect Fouquet's Nouans Pietà, the first achievement of French painting on a large scale and the most poignant expression of the French artistic revival, is of equal value with Jan van Eyck's Ghent altar or Rogier's Descent from the Cross at Louvain, with the panels of Conrad Witz, or the frescoes of Masaccio. It can here be demonstrated once more that Fouquet's creative power is above all essentially optical, that his inner vision is dependent on reality. The nun-like figures of the three Maries are conceived in the same naturalistic spirit as Louis Le Nain's pictures of peasants two centuries later. The well-thought-out balance of the composition of this Pietà is simple, clear and true to nature. A scene of mourning conjures up before the eyes of the pious church-goer the whole significance of our Lord's painful death; it is rather a scene of the living than of the dead. That the priestly donor, who commissioned the picture, is to be identified with Jean Bernard, the famous bishop of Tours, is improbable because the patron saint behind him, who lays his hand on his shoulder, is St. James of Compostella and the donor's Christian name must therefore have been Jacques and not Jean.

While all these pictures form a coherent group, characteristic of Fouquet's style between 1450 and 1460, a further portrait (should it be from his hand) must belong to a later period of his life. It is a small roundel, a picture of a young noble- plate 43 man with a turban like those worn till about 1470;[26] it was shown under Fouquet's name for the first time in 1927, in the exhibition of Primitive French Painting at F. Kleinberger's in New York, and has not been mentioned hitherto in any of the literature about Fouquet. Certainly the artistic intensity of the technique and the individual expression are suggestive of Fouquet, but it seems to be related most closely to the miniatures of the last decade of his life, beginning with the title miniature, adorned with numerous portraits, of the Statute of the Order of St. Michael, in which the typical and unique quality of the earlier works is lost in a greater variety of form. After all, only a fragment of the corpus of his work is known and it would be an unfair depreciation of the many-sided talents of a great master to limit him to a certain type. Fouquet, like most pioneer artists of the 15th century, was in full command of his powers of expres-

26) New York, Arthur Sachs coll.

sion from the beginning of his career and appears to us as a complete personality. He changed, as far as we can see, more as a miniature painter and this change was obviously effected through the influence of the court and the nobility who claimed his services increasingly. In the present state of our knowledge of his development, more than this may not be said.

THE MASTER OF KING RENÉ OF ANJOU

In epochs which have been little explored and are poor in surviving monuments, the archaeologist always tends to concentrate his interest on works of historical significance and on those of outstanding artists. This applies to 15th century France and for this reason Fouquet commands our attention. But experience shows that progress on a large scale in any given subject is never restricted to one principal figure; others are always involved. Thus, although the revival of French painting was initiated by Fouquet, he was not the only exponent of it. Other contemporary painters were also held in great repute—among them Colin d'Amiens, and Mathelin or Maturin Poyet, both, like Fouquet, appointed court painters in 1475, Coppin Delf, the Painter of King René of Anjou, and Piètre André, Court Painter to Marie de Clève, who decorated the chapel of the Castle of Plessis. We have as yet no authentic record of their work. On the other hand, miniatures and panel-paintings of Fouquet's time have been preserved which are still anonymous although of the highest artistic quality.

Since the great exhibition of Primitive French Painting in Paris in 1904, where all the primitives then known were assembled, two unusually expressive portraits have been ascribed to Fouquet. Only very recently these two, together with a third newly discovered portrait of a woman, were recognized as the work of a different painter. They are the portrait of the Old Man with a Wine Glass and plate 44 the Portrait of a Young Man[27] with the date 1456. Compared with Fouquet's ill. IX portraits, the sitters of the so-called "Master of 1456" seem tougher, more monumental in their broad, matter-of-fact calm, more angular, of heavier build and more plastic in aspect. They are extremely expressive figures of a singular vitality, which is only a little modified by the slight tiredness of their expression. All they have in common with the Portuguese Court Painter Nuno Gonzalves is their masterly grasp of form; their technique is much more refined. The luminous hues, the strong and contrasted colouring and the facial type, on the other hand, point rather to the South than to the North and remind one of the master who next to Fouquet is known as the second great realist in the history of French painting—the so-called "Master of King René of Anjou."

This anonymous artist shared all the qualities which distinguish Fouquet: the same fresh approach to his subject, the same sure eye for essentials and the same

27) Paris, Louvre. – At present Vaduz, Galerie Liechtenstein.

masterly execution. The difference lies in the personality and in the intellectual and physical environment of the two masters. The Master of King René was a Southerner, or at least an artist living and acclimatized in the South, like Enguerrand Charenton of Laon, and thus shows more sensibility and vivacity of expression and colour, more imagination, and an almost pagan-archaic outlook, influenced by the Romanesque and antique monuments of Provence. While Fouquet reflects the narrower, Christian, late-mediaeval life of Central France and of the French Kingdom, the Master of King René depicts the civilization of the realm of Anjou, which was only slightly connected with the former.

The intellectual life of the Court of King René at Angers and Aix was, in spite of family ties with the French reigning house, very different from the life at Tours and, on account of the history of the House of Anjou, was more cosmopolitan in outlook. The old hope of regaining the throne of distant Naples, where the Duke of Anjou had reigned in the 13th and 14th centuries and which was to revert to René through the legacy of Joanna II, the last Neapolitan queen, nourished many adventurous plans and gave politics and artistic endeavour a strong impetus towards the South and the Italian peninsula. The only Italian artists who can be traced in France at that time, Francesco Laurana and Piero da Milano, had been summoned there by King René. Both had collaborated as sculptors and architects in the triumphal arch of the Castel Nuovo in Naples which King Alphonso of Aragon had erected as the first Renaissance monument to commemorate his entry into that city. After the death of King Alphonso I, they were summoned by King René, and Francesco Laurana remained in France, with short interruptions, till his death. He lived first at Marseilles, and later at Bar-le-Duc, making numerous medallions, not only of King René and his entourage but also of Louis XI. Amongst other activities he executed in 1471 the tomb of Charles d'Anjou, and in 1478 a relief of the Crucifixion for the Celestine monks in Avignon. King René was also well versed in Italian literature. In his first chamberlain, Louis de Beauvau, the translator of Boccaccio's *Philostrates* and (after Filelfo) Dion Chrisostomo's *History of Troy*, and also in his seneschal, Giovanni Cossa, he had two ill. X first-class Italian scholars. In the Venetian nobleman, Jacopo Antonio Marcello, he had a Humanist who was devoted to him and who sent him among other things a beautifully illuminated manuscript[28] of Guarino's translation of Strabo.

King René's life was both fortunate and unfortunate—fortunate because it passed in a world of beautiful illusions and ideals; unfortunate in all its ventures

28) Albi (Dep. Tarn), Bibliothèque.

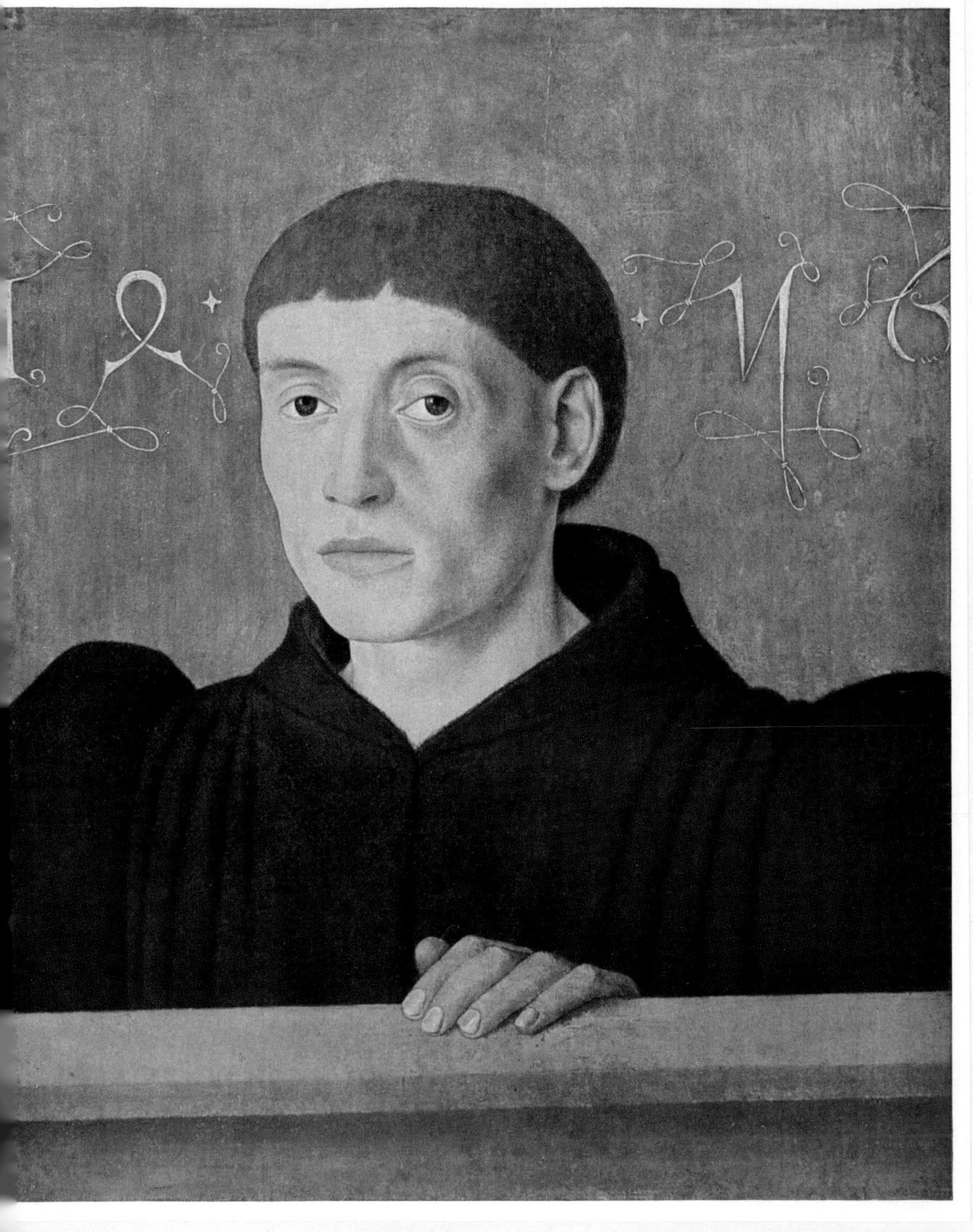

Master of 1456: Portrait of a Young Man

and disappointed hopes. In more than one respect, he resembled his cousin, Duke Charles of Orléans. Like Charles, who, in his long years of captivity in England had found consolation in the realm of fancy and of poetry, René became a poet and aesthete while a prisoner of the Duke of Burgundy at Dijon from 1431 to 1437. There, in captivity, he learnt that though he had till then been only reigning Duke of Anjou, Provence and Lorraine he had inherited the Kingdom of Naples and the two Sicilies. He was now able to add the romantic mediaeval title of King of Jerusalem to his other numerous honours, and had his prayer-book of 1436 adorned with pictures of that city with the Church of the Holy Sepulchre and the Mosque of Omar. Actually, René only reigned over Naples for four short years, years of continuous struggle. After he had obtained his liberty by paying an enormous ransom, he set out for Naples with an army, only to be driven thence by his rival, King Alphonso of Aragon, as early as 1442. But for many more years, he still clung to the hope of recovering his distant kingdom, seeking partisans in Italy, borrowing large sums of money from the Florentine bankers Pazzi and Medici, and undertaking a second abortive expedition to Italy in 1453. He kept the title until his death.

King René had as many residences as there were different French territories under his rule. He could live at Angers, in the fantastic old Castle of Saumur, depicted by Paul of Limburg, or in the Castle of Gardanne, at Bar-le-Duc, at Aix or at Tarascon. On account of their geographical position, close contacts with Dijon and Burgundy on the one hand, and with the Papal enclave of Avignon on the other were inevitable. Marseilles, already at that time a flourishing Mediterranean port, was within his sphere of influence; and on several occasions he went to war for Genoa but failed to maintain his hold over it. Many accounts of the adventurous and fantastic traits in his character have come down to us. In Angers, where he made his *Entrée* in 1454 and where he lived longest (till 1469), he kept a zoo which was widely famed for its *bêtes des Indes*. One of his favourite occupations was collecting maps of the world, oriental arms, curios and oddities from strange countries. At one moment he was occupied with worldly affairs, at another he sought relief from them. One day when out hunting near Angers he met an old hermit, and after talking with him was so impressed by his virtue and wisdom that he ordered a cell and chapel to be built for the old man, and next to it a summer house for himself, decorated with allegorical paintings. He often went to this *Ermitage de Reculée* to converse with his artists and scholars. About 1450–1452 he commissioned the sculptor Jacques Moreau to execute his tomb

after his own designs in the Church of St. Maurice at Angers, and above the tomb a fresco painting by Coppin Delf, representing himself as the *Roi mort*— a corpse eaten by worms, the head resting on one emaciated hand holding a tottering crown. The same *Roi mort* appears in two of his prayerbooks,[29] one of which, preserved in the British Museum, is illuminated by an outstanding miniature painter, a worthy predecessor of the Master of René. Until the Revolution, there was a painting of a similar subject in the Celestine Monastery at Avignon, traditionally ascribed to King René himself. It showed the corpse of a woman with a headdress and the legend

"une fois sur toute femme belle
mais par la mort je suis devenu telle."

Yet another painting in the Castle of Angers showed Death piercing a lover with an arrow, as in a *Miroir des Morts* painted by a certain Arnaud Tavernery in 1479. All these pictures point to the fact that René, like his cousin Charles of Orléans, was dominated by the thought of mortality and the impermanence of earthly glory, so typical of the dying age of Chivalry.

King René, like Philip the Good and Charles of Orléans, still cherished the old chivalrous ideals. He founded the Order of the Knights of St. Maurice in 1448 and had many young noblemen of his court brought up according to its precepts. In 1445, a famous tournament was held at Nancy on the occasion of his daughter's wedding to the King of England. In 1446 he commissioned a large commemorative painting of the tournament held at Saumur in honour of Charles VII, for which his chancellor, Gui de Laval, paid the artists 100 *écus*. He himself wrote at that time a book on tournaments,[30] which he had illustrated by his best miniature painter, our Master of King René. The most remarkable tournament was one held in 1455, when he had fallen in love with Jeanne de Laval, who became his second wife. A wooden castle *De la joyeuse garde* was erected near Saumur and there a festival was held which lasted forty days. A *"Pas d'armes de la bergère"* was one of the features in which the King and all the participants dressed as shepherds and shepherdesses in costumes of grey, gold and silver. It was then that he wrote a pastoral poem, influenced by Virgil's Bucolics, entitled *Regnault et Jeanneton*, the first example of a genre which was to re-appear in the pastoral plays at the Petit Trianon in the days of Marie-Antoinette.

29) Paris, Bibliothèque Nationale, Ms. lat. 1156 A. – London, British Museum, Ms. Egerton 1070.
30) Paris, Bibliothèque Nationale, Ms. fr. 2695.

60

Illustration X   *Giorgio Schiavone: Jacopo Antonio Marcello*

From all these poetic traits and from his keen interest in every artistic activity arose, as early as the 15th century, the legend that King René had tried his hand not only at poetry but also at painting. Jean Robertet mentions the "*Paînctures du feu roy de Cecille*," and the Italian Summonte writes in 1524: "*Etiam de mano soa pinse bene, et a questo studio fu sommamente edito, pero secundo la disciplina di Fiandra.*" Whether this legend was merely based on some amateurish efforts or not, seems immaterial. King René surely had a share in the illustrations of his works in as much as he gave his painter instructions about the subjects of his pictures.

His best known work, the romance *Cuer d'amours espris*,[31] was written in 1457. At that time King René stayed for a while at Blois with his cousin Charles of Orléans, at whose court his son was being educated. Under the influence of a court which paid homage to the ideals of chivalry and beauty, he drafted his romance in which he more or less described himself and his romantic dreams. The spirit of King Arthur and the Round Table, Mandeville's adventurous books of travels, the mediaeval romance of Alexander and especially the *Roman de la Rose* live once more in this biography of the gallant knight Cœur who seeks to gain the lady Doulce-Mercy through his valorous deeds. The allegorical characters representing human qualities, such as the lady Espérance, the dwarf Jalousie, the Vielle Mélancholie, the knight Humble Requête, are, like the corresponding symbolic scenes and objects, the forest of *longue attente*, the well *des pleurs* and the boat *de fiance* in the style of the *Roman de la Rose* and of Charles of Orléans' poetical works. Cœur's stalwart companion is Désir. At the beginning there is a most beautiful scene, in which the God of Love takes possession of Cœur's heart and hands it to Désir. Briefly, the plot of the complicated dream-story is as follows: The lady Doulce-Mercy is a prisoner of the knight Dangier in his castle, and Cœur, accompanied by Désir, sets out to deliver her. In the evening he reaches the house of the ugly dwarf Jalousie who misdirects him through the forest of *longue attente*. The knight solves the riddle of the inscription at the Magic Well and they reach the forecourt of the castle of the knight Courroux for their first combat. Cœur is victorious but falls into an ambush and is taken prisoner. Désir goes for help to the knight Honneur and delivers him. After crossing the plain of the *pensée ennuyeuse* they meet the lady Espérance, who advises them to go by sea to the Island of Love. Having had more adventures on the way, they arrive at last at the *hôpital d'amour*, which they take for a church and at the castle of *plaisance*. René, describing the coats of arms of all the love-sick heroes, from mythical Aeneas and

ill. XII, plates 47–51

31) Vienna, Nationalbibliothek, Cod. 2597.

Paris to his contemporaries, which are in the hospital, remarks maliciously that he also saw the *Cerf Volant*, that is the crest of Charles VII, but hung so high that it was scarcely visible.

There is little original thought in this poem, either in its plot or in its ideas and reflections. All the more extraordinary, therefore, are its seventeen miniature illustrations. They are of the same rich, inspired quality as Fouquet's Chantilly miniatures, and again and again one is struck by their resemblance. In their poetic conception and their passionate sensuality they are superior to any book illustrations made at that date, not excepting the highly developed work of Italian and Flemish illuminators. Like Fouquet, the Master of King René was a staunch adherent of the new realism in painting, as far as design, construction and perspective are concerned. Although no direct traces of Italian influence are to be found in his works, he was doubtless familiar with Italian art, if not from any other source, at least through the Italian illuminated manuscripts in the possession of the King, among which were such outstanding examples as the *Passio* ill. X *Scti Mauricii* illuminated in 1453 by Giorgio Schiavone.[32] The Master of King René, while avoiding the antiquated intersection of planes, is yet able to convey the complete illusion of space. His figures, full of vitality and strength, like his magnificent horses, move with natural ease. His architecture, inspired by the old buildings of Provence, is correctly portrayed, and in his landscapes, the local character and vegetation of a particular region is enhanced by the spacious atmosphere of the universal. Not only was he endowed with a wonderful sense of colour, he was also a master of effects of light and shade. King René's foremost poetic talent lay in his power of describing nature. He knew perfectly how to convey in a few phrases the changing mood and atmosphere of day or night, thus proving himself to be a true disciple of the Italian Humanists. He was fortunate in finding a painter who in that very respect proved to be most inspired and sympathetic, able to convey new impressions by the most daring use of colour. plate 47, 51 The sunrise at the Magic Well, the dusk at the Hermit's cell, the splendour of plate 50 early morning in which Désir and Humble Requête meet, or again on the seaill. XII shore where Cœur embarks, the landing of the knights on the Island of Complate 48 paignie and Amitié are all of sublime poetic beauty. The night scene in which the God of Love takes possession of Cœur's heart can only be compared to Piero della Francesca's Dream of Constantine at Arezzo. The late mediaeval romantic attitude towards nature is here combined in an unique fashion with the artistic

32) Paris, Bibliothèque de l'Arsenal, Ms. 940.

64

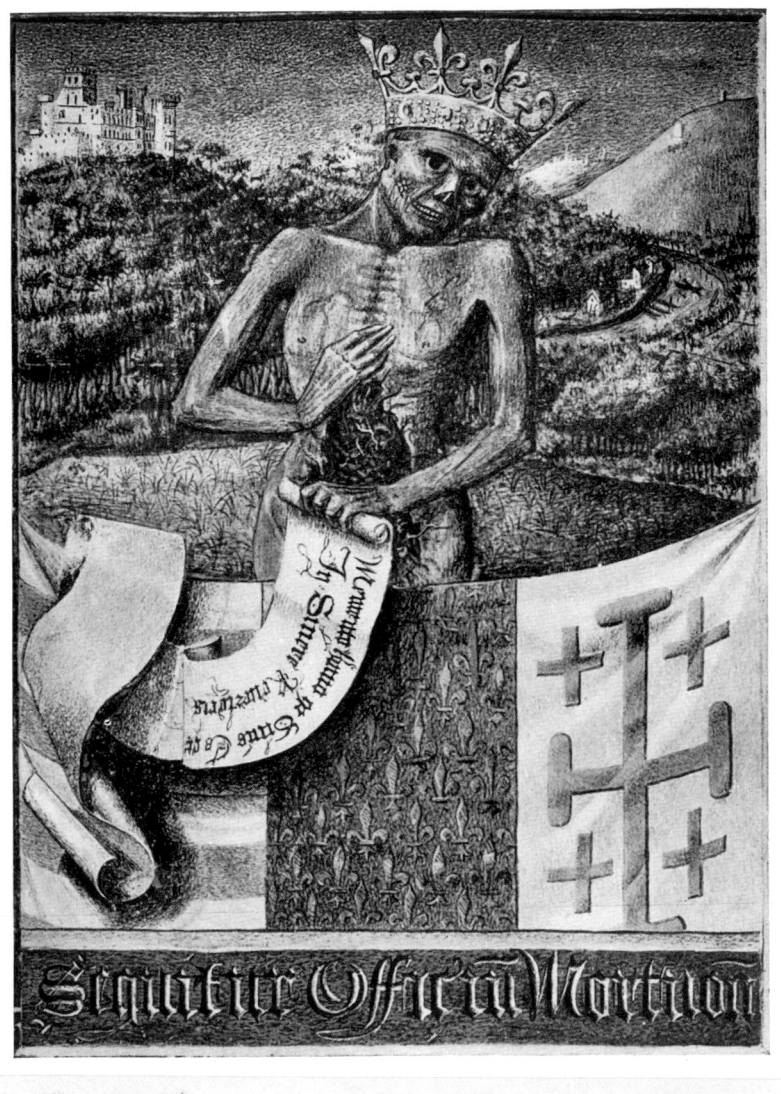

Illustration XI   *Unknown Master: "Le Roi mort"*

spirit of a new age and has at the same time taken on the characteristics of a robust antique paganism which comes as a refreshing relief after the effeminate features of the Christian-erotic mysticism prevalent in the rest of France.

Two more manuscripts of René's were illuminated by the same master. The first is a *Theseïde*, a translation, commissioned by the King, of Boccaccio's first epic poem, dealing with the tragic passion of two Theban princes, Arcitas and Palemon, for the sister of the mythological King Theseus. It is characteristic that in this poem the mediaeval strain is more prominent than the historical-didactic strain in Boccaccio's *Cas des nobles hommes*. The second is a Christian allegorical reflection entitled *Le Mortifiement de la vaine plaisance*, composed after the death of René's first wife. Piety and Repentance are here personified in human form and guide the soul to salvation, while René expresses by means of a story the futility of earthly vanity. The original manuscript of the *Theseïde* with illus- ill. XIII, plates 46, 52 trations by the Master of King René and his assistants is preserved at the Nationalbibliothek at Vienna.[33] Two manuscripts of the *Mortifiement*, which was written about 1454, left his workshop. The superior version—unfortunately fragmentary—which once was in the possession of the Angevins Dukes of Lorraine, is now at the Library of Metz, the other at Berlin in the Kupferstichkabinett.[33a] The latter was, according to court accounts, executed in 1457 ill. XIV for Jeanne de Laval by a partner of Adenot Lescuyer, Court Painter to the Queen of Angers.

In spite of its date, 1468, the miniatures of the manuscript of the *Theseïde* were at first counted among Fouquet's earlier works. They have, however, nothing to do with Fouquet himself nor with any of the manuscripts of that group of painters. On the other hand, some of its illustrations, such as the dedicatory miniature, The imprisoned Princes Arcitas and Palemon espying Emilia in her Garden, and Emilia hawking, show Flemish influence, which is absent from any of the miniatures of Cœur. This rather remarkable fact was the reason why the artist was sought among those Netherlandish miniature painters of the King whose names appear in the documents of his court. Those most frequently mentioned are a certain Barthélemy de Clerc, de Cler or d'Eilz, who stood apparently in great favour, accompanied the King everywhere, and was his *valet* from 1447 to 1470; and a certain Coppin Delf. Yet René and his wife, Jeanne de Laval, paid salaries to a considerable number of miniature painters, and so long as none of

33) Cod. 2617.
33a) Ms. 78 C 5.

the many manuscripts from his libraries, which have been preserved, can be directly connected with one or the other name, their authorship must remain hypothetical.

It is obvious that the Master of King René shows little resemblance to the well-known painters of Provence, either to Enguerrand Charenton or to Nicolas Froment. The only painting on a large scale which shows a very close similarity with his work is strongly influenced by Flemish painting; it is the altar-piece of the Annunciation from Saint-Sauveur at Aix[34] which was painted soon after 1442 for a weaver of that town named Corpici. The Prophet Isaiah, represented here on the left wing, is an enlarged version of the figures of Cœur and Désir. In both the figures of the Prophets, the influence of the Ghent altar-piece and the monumental art of Jan van Eyck is very pronounced, while in the Annunciation of the centre panel, and still more in the representation of Christ as a Gardener on the back, a clear connection with the school of Avignon is to be seen. Unfortunately oblivion has descended upon the painter of this magnificent altar-piece also; the recent identification with the Neapolitan painter Colantonio del Fiore may be dismissed as unfounded. In the Church of the Celestines at Avignon, there was formerly a fresco representing the Holy Sacrament and the Ascension of the Virgin. It was painted, in 1445, for the chapel of Nicolas Rolin, the chancellor of the Duke of Burgundy, and of his son, Jean Rolin. An old copy of this work, lost to us to-day, authorizes us to see in it a certain relationship to the Aix pictures and to the miniatures of the Master of King René. The only tenable theory is that the Master of King René was a native of Provence and not of Anjou. The reasons for this inference are the resemblance of the miniatures to the altar of Aix and the fact that King René settled down at Aix in 1442 and resided chiefly there and at Tarascon during the fourth decade of the century.

The last work of the poet king was *L'Abuzé en Court*, a satire directed against Louis XI. Either it was written after the time of the Master of King René or else no copy of the original manuscript has survived. It deals with a courtier who, abandoned by friends, love, and all worldly illusions, arrives at the hospital, where he is received by *Pauvreté*. Bitter experience inspired this work. In 1474 René was forced to surrender Anjou to Louis XI, who also gained Provence at René's death in 1480. René II, his son, kept Lorraine as his only duchy. His reign did

plates 53, 54

34) Centre part: Aix-en-Provence, Eglise de la Madeleine; upper part of the left wing: Amsterdam, Rijksmuseum; lower part of the left wing: Vierhouten, D.G. van Beuningen coll.; right wing: Brussels, Musées Royaux des Beaux-Arts.

Illustration XII   *Master of King René: Cœur boarding the Ship*

not last long and his artists dispersed after his death. Coppin Delf took service with the French Dauphin, later King Charles VIII, and in 1482 decorated his chapel in the Church of St. Martin at Tours with mural paintings. The unification of France, so skilfully achieved by Louis XI through diplomacy and brute force, applied also to the realm of art.

Just as the centralized power of the French Kings held sway in Tours and from thence radiated out over the whole country, so the school of painting and especially of book illustration, founded by Fouquet, extended beyond the narrow provincial confines of the city, and the so-called *art tourangeau* became essentially the art of the absolutist French Court. How strongly Fouquet influenced the school of court illuminators, is best demonstrated by the fact that fifty years after his death, during the reign of Francis I, his manner, although it had grown feeble, attenuated and lifeless — was still reflected in their work. The two artists who did most to propagate and modify Fouquet's style, thereby founding the School of Touraine in a wider sense, were Jean Colombe and Jean Bourdichon. It is not definitely established whether these two were actually trained in Fouquet's studio, but their style is directly based on his art and, most characteristically, on his later rather than on his earlier manner. On more than one occasion, both artists selected subjects and compositions similar to his. Jean Colombe, a relative of the sculptor Michel Colombe, lived at Bourges near Tours and was older than Bourdichon, who was born in 1457. He is known to have worked as an independent master as early as 1470. But he did not die until 1529, eight years after Bourdichon. As the end of both their careers lies outside the period of this study we shall deal only with their earlier work, up to about ten years after Fouquet's death.

Besides these two, there were without doubt many other imitators or pupils of Fouquet, for there exists a considerable number of illuminated manuscripts closely related to those already mentioned. One of the best and most original of plate 63 these is a Parisian manuscript, the *Livre intitulé de richesse*,[35] illustrated by a still unknown master who worked (judging from the costumes) at the time of Louis XI, that is to say in Fouquet's life-time. In style it shows modifications of Fouquet's manner similar to those found in the work of Colombe and Bourdichon. All trace has been lost of the works of other miniature painters at Tours, whose names are on record and who may possibly have been among Fouquet's pupils — Jean de Launay, Jean Poyet, Jacques de Litemont, Jean Couart, Jean-le-Sage or Allart Folarton who worked for King Louis XI and his queen, or for the city of Tours. Only a signed prayerbook by Jean

35) Paris, Bibliothèque Nationale, Ms. fr. 9608.

Illustration XIII　　　　　　　　*Master of King René: The Liberation of Arcitas and Palemon*

Montluçon[36] has survived. At present, therefore, it is only possible to give rather scanty proof of Fouquet's wide influence, although we can see that its direction and development followed the lines of Colombe and Bourdichon.

The question whether Colombe was not older than has hitherto been supposed, and began to work at an earlier date, arises in connection with a prayerbook at the   ill. II
Staatsbibliothek at Munich,[37] which is said to have belonged to Jacques Cœur. Beneath the picture of a man praying, with which this book of hours begins, is an angel holding a scroll with the inscription "*A vaillans [cuers] riens inpossible,*" the well-known motto of Jacques Cœur. It is significant that the word *cuers* is deleted. Boll, the discoverer of this manuscript, concluded that a later owner of the book did not want to be connected with that infamous name and had therefore overpainted Cœur's coat of arms with his own. All the illustrations of this manuscript, among them an excellent large miniature of the Annunciation and a half-length figure of the Virgin with the features of Agnes Sorel, are in the manner of Colombe and are likely to have been painted before 1451, the year in which Jacques Cœur fell from grace and was arrested and imprisoned until his adventurous escape from France. Considering the date of Colombe's death (1529), this would point to an unexpectedly and improbably early beginning of his career. Caution prompts us to envisage another possibility. The Munich prayerbook may have been executed for one of Cœur's sons, either for the Bishop of Bourges or for Geoffroy Cœur. He may have had it decorated with the memorial portrait and motto of his father. This would not be the only example of this kind: King René also had the picture of his father, Louis II of Anjou, copied from an old portrait, painted for his prayerbook.[38] This would also explain the sitter's youthful appearance and lack of personality.

Like Fouquet, Jean Colombe was rediscovered through a note of François Robertet in one of the famous manuscripts of the old Duke of Berry, whose magnificent book of hours, the *Très riches Heures*, illuminated by Paul of Limburg is   plates 55–57
to-day, along with the Fouquet miniatures, one of the greatest treasures of Chantilly, and was inherited in the course of the 15th century by Duke Charles I of Savoy, a brother-in-law of Louis XI. Duke Charles commissioned the painter Jean Colombe in 1485 to complete this work which Paul of Limburg had left

36) Paris, Bibliothèque de l'Arsenal, Ms. 438.
37) Cod. lat. 10103.
38) Paris, Bibliothèque Nationale, Ms. lat. 1156 A.

75

unfinished, as Jacques d'Armagnac had done in the case of the *Antiquités Judaïques*. Colombe had previously illuminated another unfinished manuscript for the Duke, an *Apocalypse*[39] which had been begun between 1428 and 1435 by two painters at the Court of Savoy, Jean Bapteur of Fribourg in Switzerland and Perronnet Lamy. While at Bourges, Colombe's connection with the distant Court of Savoy had apparently been established by an introduction from Queen Charlotte, the wife of Louis XI and sister of the reigning Duke Charles I. He had painted for her before 1470 the dedicatory miniature to a *Livre des douze Perilz d'enfer* by Pierre Caillemesnil,[40] and a prayerbook as well as some other manuscripts which have disappeared. To accomplish the lengthy work on the *Apocalypse* and the *Très riches Heures*, he went to live for a time at Chambéry, the residence of the Duke of Savoy, and was there given the rank of a *familier et enlumineur de livres*, which means that he was regularly employed by the court that formed the natural link between France and Italy.

It was by no means an easy task which Colombe undertook when he agreed to complete the illustrations of the *Très riches Heures*. Apart from the fact that Paul of Limburg's pictures were of the highest artistic perfection, three of them were half finished and Colombe was compelled to adapt his style to that of the older master. In the calendar picture of September, for instance, the background with the view of the castle was finished by Paul of Limburg, and Colombe had to plate 55 fill in the foreground with the harvesting peasants. Of the November picture Paul of Limburg had only painted the semicircular section of the Zodiac and Colombe supplied the illustration of the month. He probably used here, as for the two other illustrations, an existing sketch by Paul of Limburg, because the attitude of the swineherd is remarkably like one in a fresco by Giovanni Miretto in the Palazzo della Ragione at Padua, with which Paul of Limburg was familiar but which was certainly unknown to Colombe. The third picture which Colombe plate 56 had to finish was that of a procession partially framing a column of text. The left and upper part was finished by Paul of Limburg, the lower part again completed by Colombe after existing sketches. Colombe's independent activity began with the *Ecce homo* for the Hours of the Cross in which the Duke of Savoy and his wife Blanche of Montferrat appear on either side of the framework. In the empty spaces, he painted the Presentation of the Virgin, two pictures of the Vigil of Death, Purgatory and other subjects, making much use of the richly ornament-

39) Escorial, Anc. I. B. 3.
40) Paris, Bibliothèque Nationale, Ms. fr. 449.

76

ed forms of flamboyant Gothic architecture for decorative effect, as for example in the Presentation, which shows the Cathedral of Bourges, in the Requiem, and in the Miracle of St. Anthony in which the Palace of Jacques Cœur is seen in the background.

plate 57

Colombe's love for fantastic, turreted and crenellated Gothic buildings, for overcrowding, and for over-rich ornamentation, is evident in all his manuscripts and is in a sense the expression of his artistic convictions which were orientated towards the past. In a large miniature of a *Romuléon*,[41] illuminated for the Governor of Paris, Charles de Gaucourt, Colombe depicts the identical group of buildings of the Palais Royal of Paris which Paul of Limburg had painted in the *Très riches Heures*, and in another miniature of the same manuscript he depicted the ancient royal castle of Melun-sur-Yèvre. Perhaps the best example of his fantastic creative power is to be found in a single large page depicting the building of Troy[42] which may have been cut from a *Recueil des histoires de Troye* by Raoul Lefèvre of the year 1464. This miniature also shows most clearly the wide difference between Colombe and Fouquet and proves that Colombe is only superficially, in his types, his colours and his technique, a disciple of Fouquet's, and does not share his fundamental convictions. Fouquet's pronounced realism is alien to Colombe, who, like the older masters, created chiefly from his imagination. As his nude figures show, he is largely ignorant of human anatomy; all his portraits are schematic and superficial. He borrows certain features from the art of Fouquet, as for instance the St. Martin in the prayerbook of Louis de Laval, which is taken from the Chevalier prayerbook, but he fails to endow them with new life. With his feeling for pomp and decoration, although influenced by new forms of art, in disposition he is old-fashioned and romantic; even more than Fouquet, he is the born court painter. It is, therefore, not surprising that, as far as we can see, he worked exclusively for the Court and for noble patrons. For the Bastard Louis of Bourbon he painted a manuscript of the Life of Christ; for both the wife of Philippe de Comines and for Adelaide of Savoy a well-known bibliophile, a prayerbook; for Anne de Beaujeu, daughter of Louis XI, and for Duke René II of Lorraine, son of the celebrated King René, a book of hours; for Cardinal Charles of Bourbon (d. 1485) the large dedicatory miniature of a *Vie de saint Louis* and for Louis de Laval he illustrated the *Passages d'outre-mer* by Sébastien Mame-

plate 60

plate 59

41) Paris, Bibliothèque Nationale, Ms. fr. 364.
42) Berlin, Staatliches Kupferstichkabinett, Inc. Nr. 4645.

rot.[43] His largest and in many respects most important work is the book of hours
plates 61, 62 for Louis de Laval[44] which contains the extraordinary total of 1160 miniatures, not
all of them painted by himself, of course, but in collaboration with the craftsmen
employed in his studio. Louis de Laval, Seigneur de Châtillon, Grandmaster
of the Rivers and Forests of France, one of the first eleven Knights of the Order
of St. Michael and a relative of King René's, was a powerful and influential man.
The title-miniature, in which he is represented as an old man—he died in 1489,
aged 78 years—kneeling at his prayer-desk in the usual fashion, was wrongly
attributed to Fouquet. Jean Colombe's manner and technique cannot be mistaken in the portrait figure. It is doubtful whether this manuscript existed in
Fouquet's lifetime, although it is certainly the one in which his influence is
most strongly shown. Anne de Beaujeu, wife of Pierre of Bourbon and Regent
during the minority of Charles VIII, inherited this manuscript in 1489, and
some of the miniatures are repeated also in the book of hours which probably
belonged to this princess and which is one of the most beautiful and most carefully executed of the productions of Colombe.[45] Some features of the miniature
ill. XV, plate 58 representing the Fall of Man recall the realism of the Flemish. In the Annunciation, painted on two pages and introducing the figure of Anne de Beaujeu as
donatrix, Colombe has created one of the most vivid pictures, surpassing even
the similar Annunciation in the book of hours said to belong to Jacques Cœur.

Jean Bourdichon was much closer to Fouquet than Colombe. He became his
successor—as far as one can call anyone successor to such an outstanding artist—
in two respects: in his prestige as an artist and in his position as court painter. As
early as 1478 to 1480, he was paid by the court for various works in the Castle of
Plessis near Tours which Louis XI extended and redecorated: a painted tabernacle, the frame-work for an equestrian statue of St. Michael, executed by Jacques
François, the nephew of Michel Colombe, and the ceiling of one of the rooms
decorated with angels and scrolls bearing inscriptions. Furthermore, being, like
Fouquet, also a panel painter and miniaturist, in 1480 he painted 24 pictures for
the King on parchment in which ships with maidens and sailors were depicted,
and a large view of the city of Caudebec in Normandy on five sheets of parchment

43) Paris, Bibliothèque Nationale, Ms. fr. 177–179. – Formerly Frankfort-on-the-Main, J. Baer & Co.
(1914). – Chantilly, Musée Condé, Ms. 1362. – New York, Pierpont Morgan Library, MS. 677. – Paris, Bibliothèque Nationale, Ms. lat. 10491. – Paris, Bibliothèque Nationale, Ms. fr. 2829. – Paris, Bibliothèque Nationale,
Ms. fr. 5594.
44) Paris, Bibliothèque Nationale, Ms. lat. 920.
45) New York, Pierpont Morgan Library, Ms. 677.

joined together. For the Queen he painted between 1483 and 1484 two miniatures of the life of St. Gregory and two of Notre Dame de Pitié, as well as 19
riches histoires in a manuscript called *Papaliste*, which contained prophecies con-
cerning the Pope. At her death in 1483, he was paid for the portrait which was
hung above her tomb. From the accounts of Margaret of Austria's treasurer, it is
evident that he also worked between 1484 and 1485 for the Burgundian princess,
betrothed to the Dauphin, who was then being educated at the French court.
Finally, he repeatedly painted the portrait of the monk Francis of Paola, whose
power to work miracles inspired the sick King Louis XI with such hopes that,
with great difficulty, he had him brought from Italy, an undertaking only achieved
through the mediation of the Pope. One of these portraits known to us through
copies and woodcuts was later sent to Pope Leo X by Francis I and the remainder

79

were preserved by the Brothers of the Minorite Order of Plessis-les-Tours as late as the 19th century.

In addition to those works which are known to us solely through written records, together with the portraits of Charles VIII as a youth, and of Admiral Malet de Graville,[46] of which copies have survived, Bourdichon also painted a ill. XVI small portrait of Louis XI in profile which is preserved in a private collection in Paris.[47] Though lacking Fouquet's subtle mastery, he depicts the King's features with great realism: his crude ugliness, his hypocritical expression, his aversion from all romantic ideas, and his great cunning. The sallow complexion, the glinting whites of the large slanting eyes with their vague expression are striking and typical characteristics of Bourdichon's portraits.

Bourdichon's activity at court during the last years of Louis XI's reign and the life and atmosphere of the court seem to have left their mark on his development. Deep piety and the superstitious adoration of saints and relics had, since 1478, possessed the lonely monarch—inaccessible in his castles of Plessis and Cléry, where he endeavoured by all manner of means to prolong his life—and generated in those surrounding him a despotic, sombre and mystical cult which contrasted strongly with his otherwise enlightened attitude of mind and his sober and unscrupulous political actions. In reality, Louis XI had treated the Church in France with utter cynicism and had used it for his own ends, a fact which had not been without repercussions on the religious life of his time. The gulf separating the high clergy from the lower orders was wider than ever. At a time when heads of religious orders, such men as Jan Standonck and Jean Raulin, were endeavouring to bring about a reform of monastic life on ascetic lines under the influence of Francis of Paola and the "Brothers of Communal Life" of Windesheim, learned theologians, whether scholastic, nominalist or terminist, were losing their way in endless dogmatic and formalist arguments. Religion (to quote Vossler) only survived in the form of superstition, delusion, fear of death, fanaticism or outward formality. The contrasts between the outward show of religion and the lack of real piety, between the glorification of the supernatural as distinct from genuine mysticism on the one hand, and rational convictions and actions on the other, typical of the period, are clearly expressed in Bourdichon's art. From the beginning, form and colour conflict with one another in his work; the artificial, unreal spirit of the court is apparent in his use of variegat-

46) Leningrad, Hermitage.
47) Formerly Paris, de Ganay coll.

ed colour, which, in contrast to his more or less realistic forms, becomes more and more unnatural. In some of his later miniatures, as for instance the Annunciation to the Shepherds in the prayerbook of Anne of Brittany, or in the Holy Night of the Aragon Book of Hours, he achieves by these means extremely fantastic and impressive effects of light, artificial, but highly imaginative.

Soon after the accession of Charles VIII, then still a minor, and under the regency of Anne de Beaujeu, Bourdichon was nominated *peintre du roi* and *valet*, in 1484, a title held previously by Fouquet. He served in that capacity for 36 years under four kings. The many works which he executed for Charles VIII and his wife, Anne of Brittany, the most important of which, a magnificently illuminated prayerbook for the Queen, and the *Voyage de Gênes* [48] dedicated to her by Jean Marot, interest us only in so far as they direct attention to those earlier works of his which have not yet been fully investigated.

Through a single mistaken attribution, wrong conclusions have been reached which have falsified our whole knowledge of his development. The Bibliothèque Nationale owns a prayerbook with the coat of arms of the Aragons, [49] richly illuminated by Bourdichon, and hitherto assumed to have been made for King Ferdinand I of Naples (d. 1494). As the Abbé Leroquais proved from the text, it had in fact been executed for his son King Frederick III of Naples, who, having been removed from his throne by Louis XII in 1501, had received the Duchy of Maine in compensation and had lived at Tours, Bourdichon's home, from then until his death in 1504. Through this new discovery the theory that the artist had visited Italy now becomes untenable, while the date of this important manuscript must be fixed much later than was formerly supposed, and can, therefore, no longer be considered a comparatively early work of the artist. In this connection several other similar works, such as the prayerbook of Cardinal Alvarez di Toledo in the Biblioteca Nazionale at Naples, the prayerbook in the Rothschild collection and the prayerbook of Charles d'Angoulême, [50] must be dated later.

Probably the earliest known work of Bourdichon is a book of hours [51] which, judging from the coat of arms displayed on it, was ordered by a member of the house of Bourbon-Vendôme or Bourbon-Carency and still shows Fouquet's direct influence. Some of the paintings, as for instance that of the three prophets

plate 71

48) Paris, Bibliothèque Nationale, Ms. lat. 9474. – Paris, Bibliothèque Nationale, Ms. fr. 509.

49) Ms. lat. 10532.

50) Naples, Biblioteca Nazionale, n. 241 I B 21. – Formerly Paris, Edmond de Rothschild coll. – Paris, Bibliothèque Nationale, Ms. lat. 1173.

51) Paris, Bibliothèque de l'Arsenal, Ms. 417.

of the Annunciation with *putti* bearing inscribed scrolls below the picture, a feature which Fouquet loved to use, show indeed such strong resemblance to his style that, in the most recent monograph on Fouquet, all the illustrations were claimed as his. But the style of some of the other pictures, the Flight into Egypt, for example, and the Pope in the Flight from Death, differs from that of Fouquet, and in all of them the technique also is different and more like that of Bourdichon; E. Mâle has rightly identified these illustrations as his work.

Another prayerbook belonging to Catherine of Armagnac[52] is generally recognized as an early work of his which can be dated with a certain accuracy. It bears, besides the initials I. K., the coats of arms of Armagnac and of Bourbon and must have been painted in 1486, as Catherine, daughter of Duke Jacques of Nemours, married Duke John II of Bourbon in 1484 and died two years later in childbirth. Through her sudden death the work was apparently interrupted and some of the shields remained blank; the date of its origin, therefore, cannot be disputed. For this manuscript also he used Fouquet's work as a model and borrowed from him. The figure of Christ, for instance, in the Ascension of the Holy Ghost, is copied with slight variations from the Christ of the Last Judgment in the prayerbook of Etienne Chevalier.

These miniatures, however instructive as evidence of Bourdichon's early creative ability and his relations with Fouquet, are only of secondary importance compared with a single panel-painting which has given rise to long and bitter disputes. plates 64–66 In the Church of Saint-Antoine at Loches is a large altar-piece with the Crucifixion in the centre panel and the Carrying of the Cross and the Entombment on the wings. This altar-piece originally belonged to the Carthusian Monastery of Liget near Loches. It is dated 1485 and is, next to and after Fouquet's Pietà of Nouans, the only large-scale panel-painting of the school of Tours which has been preserved. A close connection existed between the Royal Court at Tours and Loches where the castle furnished by Charles VII for Agnes Sorel stood; she was buried in the church at Loches and it was there that her tomb was erected. The Duke of Alençon was imprisoned at Loches, where he died after his second conviction for treason in the reign of Louis XI who, like Charles VII, had frequently resided there.

Besides the date 1485 on the left wing, there are on the right wing the letters F.I.B. on a rock in the background, next to a kneeling monk. There are two theories to explain these letters. When they were first found, they were held to

52) Formerly Mainz, Busch coll.; later Frankfort-on-the-Main, J. Baer & Co.

Illustration XV   *Colombe: Adam and Eve*

mean *Fecit Jean Bourdichon*, which is the usual interpretation. Later research connected them with the person of the kneeling monk and read them as *Frère Jean
Bourgeois*, basing this theory on existing records which mention that Bourdichon
had painted a picture, now lost, of this Frère Bourgeois, the father confessor of
Charles VII, preaching to the King.

Bourdichon had, however, painted for Frère Bourgeois a prayerbook which still exists,[53] containing two portraits of the owner. As these portraits are very different from the monk of the altar of Loches, and as, further, one is a Franciscan and the other a Camaldolite monk, the second theory must be dismissed as erroneous. The first interpretation of the initials, on the other hand, is strengthened by the stylistic and technical peculiarities of the work. The following characteristics of Bourdichon's art are to be found in the triptych: the symmetrical construction, the rigidity of form and brush-work, the individual way in which the figures are represented and schematized and, in addition, the close dependence on Fouquet. In the composition of the Carrying of the Cross and also in the Crucifixion and the Entombment, there are actual borrowings from the Chevalier miniatures of the corresponding subjects, and from the Pietà of Nouans, but modified in a way which is typical of Bourdichon. The miniature of a Crucifixion in the prayerbook of Margaret of Rohan[54] forms an important link between the altar of Loches and other works of Bourdichon. It is closely connected with the above-mentioned illuminated manuscripts, in particular with the prayerbook of Catherine of Armagnac, while the pose of the executioner at the foot of the cross in this Crucifixion is strikingly like that of Joseph of Aramathea in the Entombment of the Loches altar. The portrait of the Dowager Duchess Margaret of Rohan, widow of Jean d'Angoulême and grandmother of King Francis I, is more decorative than profound in conception and is one of the most characteristic works of Bourdichon, showing a likeness to the holy women of both the triptych of Loches and the prayerbook of Catherine of Armagnac. For the present, these three works would seem to represent the whole of Bourdichon's artistic achievement as a painter of panels and miniatures at the time when he was appointed court painter, that is, about the year 1485. It is difficult to follow his development up to the date of the majority of Charles VIII (1491), for want of accurately dated works, although many are listed in the court accounts, among others, portraits of the King, the Queen and Mademoiselle de Tarentes. Before 1485, payment had been made by the treasury of Charles d'Angoulême, son of Margaret of Rohan, for an Adoration of the Magi, but it is very doubtful if this is identical with the Adoration in the still-existing prayerbook of that prince.[55] This book was illustrated by other

plates 69, 70

plates 67, 68

plate 74

53) Innsbruck, Universitätsbibliothek, Cod. 281.
54) Princeton (N. J.), Princeton University.
55) Paris, Bibliothèque Nationale, Ms. lat. 1173.

artists as well as by Bourdichon, who supplied several pictures for it, and there is no reason to suppose that one of the pictures was paid for separately. The style of this Adoration and of the five other pictures points clearly to a later phase in his development, and, as Duke Charles died in 1497, it seems in fact legitimate to assume that it was painted at a later date.

The chief reason, however, for dating the Angoulême miniatures later, is their close relationship to another triptych of Bourdichon's, which seems, by comparison with the Loches altar, much more advanced and of greater maturity. On account of a certain resemblance to Antonello da Messina, this triptych[56] was plate 73 long thought to be the work of an Italian, until the discovery by Dupont of the real author. Its centre-piece depicts the Virgin and Child, with the Crucifixion in the lunette above; in the wings are St. John the Baptist and St. John the Evangelist and above them the kneeling figures of St. Michael and St. George. The similarity in conception and in certain details between the Virgin of this altar and the Virgin of the Adoration in the Angoulême prayerbook is obvious; to them must be added yet another miniature of the Virgin,[57] in which the pose of the plate 72 Child is the same as in the Naples altar-piece. Compared with the Loches altarpiece it shows a more harmonious symmetry and balance, while its execution is simpler, more confident and of greater clarity. The landscape especially is painted more freely; richer and more subtle, it reminds one strongly, in spite of the realistic view of Tours in the background, of Italian landscapes. Figures and landscape are still more independent of each other than in the Loches altar; the middle distance has disappeared and with it the possibility of developing any action in depth.

This phenomenon is characteristic of the peculiar means of expression which Bourdichon had developed in his maturity and is to be found in all his later works, the Naples altar-piece as well as the Angoulême miniatures. His whole endeavour now culminates in a very strong emphasis on the plasticity and definition of the human figure, that is to say, of the figures of his saints. Fouquet's catholicity, his unity of construction and his dramatic action were alien and uncongenial to Bourdichon and he therefore avoided them. The rules of a new order, of a new ideal of beauty are being developed here, probably under Italian influence. Similar details, a method of representation concentrated on abstract and decorative effects, and a closely related technique also in the use of layers of gold, are to be found in

56) Naples, Museo Nazionale.
57) Private collection in England.

the works of the contemporary Florentine miniature painter Attavante, who, having painted a missal[58] for the archbishop of Dol in 1483, was not unknown in France. There is something statuesque in all the mature works of Bourdichon, closely connected with the harshness of his form and technique. He was therefore, in quite a different sense from Fouquet, the painter of devotional pictures and was much sought after as such. In the year 1490, he received commissions to paint for the Court four panel-pictures of the Virgin, one on clouds, one in glory and two enthroned, which, with the help of the Naples altar-piece and similar representations in numerous prayerbooks of this period, we are well able to imagine. For Bourdichon, more than any other painter, repeated his own motifs, and stuck to the types he had once evolved. A St. Michael, nearly identical with that of the upper left wing of the Naples altar-piece, is found again in the prayerbooks of Frederick III of Aragon and of Charles VIII, and even this figure was not a new invention of his but borrowed from Fouquet's Chevalier prayerbook, from which he also took the David in Prayer and the Job for the book of hours of Frère Bourgeois. A large studio full of the assistants, whom Bourdichon needed to execute his many orders, helped to schematize his art, which was not blessed by an over-rich imagination.

The progressive, creative spirit and wide influence with which Fouquet had endowed the school of Tours thus changed to a rigid conservatism, especially since Tours had lost its importance as a royal residence. New artistic endeavour was appearing elsewhere: at Moulins, the ancestral seat of the Bourbons, under the regency of Anne de Beaujeu and Pierre de Bourbon, in the person of the Master of Moulins, who illuminated among others the Statutes of the Order of St. Michael (1493)[59]; in Paris, and in the regained cities of the Somme, where the inspiration of neighbouring Flanders was fruitful. In spite of this, the reputation of the school of Tours at the end of the century was such that Jean Clouet left Flanders and settled there, beginning a successful career which eventually led to the post of first Court Painter to Francis I.

plates 75–78 Four separate pages of miniatures should be mentioned here as among Bourdichon's finest works. They came into the possession of the Ecole des Beaux-Arts of Paris with the Jean Masson bequest, and were painted about 1490, at a time when the work of Bourdichon was no longer dominated by the influence of Fouquet but showed his own more mature manner. In the Exhibition of 1904

58) Lyon, Bibliothèque Municipale, Ms. 5123.
59) Paris, Bibliothèque Nationale, Ms. fr. 14363

86

Illustration XVI   *Bourdichon: Portrait of Louis XI*

they were catalogued as the *Quatre âges du monde;* lately they have been renamed the *Quatre états de la société*, as they represent Man, first in his primitive state, then as beggar, as craftsman and finally as prince. Their meaning and context has unfortunately been lost with the manuscript of which they formed a part. Their artistic and documentary value is thereby not lessened and their individual significance, rather, is enhanced. When studied on their own merits, they reveal the hand of a master, schooled under Fouquet's influence, who had evolved a strong, highly individual and harmonious style: less rigid than that of Fouquet, but lacking in his creative ability, because less in touch with the life of the common man. It is apparent in these paintings which, with their almost surrealist charm of surface, constitute his best works, that Bourdichon, unlike the great realists, did

87

not seek in Nature the source of his inspiration, but thought and felt in an unreal world of his own creation. From the outset his imagination was curbed by court convention, as was that of nearly all the illuminators of that generation. The transition from the Middle Ages to modern times, so rich in pictorial representation, was over; the driving force from below had ceased and French culture became once more stereotyped and uniform where it was not directly under foreign influence.

The art of Colombe and Bourdichon developed with set rules in the same way as the contemporary art of poetry. It became a complicated interplay of forms and ideals like the verses of a Molinet, a Lemaire, a Jean Marot or any other rhetorician. The spirit of the Renaissance, which had reached France late, was transformed in the atmosphere of court life into dry scholarship, virtuosity and the display of superficial beauty. Art, like poetry, became an intellectual exercise, and the old scholastic tradition of mechanical execution as a substitute for organic development returned in a new guise. The real Humanist Renaissance had no widespread influence in France until after the invasion of Italy. Erasmus, in a letter to Thomas Grey, described the unrealistic, unenlightened spirit of the "barbaric Scotists" which still prevailed in his time (1497) at the University of Paris, in the colleges and therefore among the educated classes of the population. Charles VIII, like the Emperor Maximilian, was dominated by the antiquated ideals of chivalry which his father scorned. Once more the policy of the realm and with it the cultural ideas of the time were completely reversed. Fouquet lived through a period of progress; Bourdichon through a period of reaction.

There was another important reason why miniature painting at that time was pressed more and more into the service of the court. The practice of using woodcuts as book illustrations which had become widespread in the last decade of Fouquet's lifetime was depriving the expensive miniature painter of a large number of middle-class patrons. Only the court and the nobility, who considered the printed book of inferior quality and not worthy of themselves, commissioned handwritten and painted books from the last quarter of the 15th century onwards. The educated commoners, even the wealthy ones, bought the cheaper printed books illustrated with woodcuts. The small exclusive circle of old-fashioned bibliophiles, however, still demanded that richness and magnificence of decoration which Colombe and Bourdichon could supply.

The unrestricted despotism of the Crown, to which reference has been made in the course of these pages, was the cause of the revival of France. It was not

only the basis of French political life but also its supreme aesthetic law. Without it, neither the development of French art nor its ideals of beauty can be understood. Louis XI, a man already thinking in terms of trade and commerce, more positive and realistic in outlook than any other prince of his time, was his own principal state official, dealing personally with everything and endeavouring to give a new impetus to all branches of public life. At the same time, the conception of royal dignity and arbitrary power reached its highest perfection under his reign. In collaboration with the bourgeoisie, he suppressed the last traces of the political independence of the feudal lords; at the same time, however, he took great care that the nobility should retain their rank because it surrounded the throne with an indispensable aura of splendour. The bourgeoisie also lost its importance during his reign; after the once hotly-contested organization of society had become established, functions of the estates under an all-powerful Crown became merely nominal. Like the religious bodies, the guilds were no longer culturally creative; as Vossler expresses it, the spirit of bourgeois initiative had changed into the ambition to secure a position at court. The art of France, which was born of bourgeois genius, was not again patronized by that class until the middle of the 18th century, but was at all times under the patronage of the king and the wide circle of nobility grouped around the throne. Only once again, in the 17th century, when the anarchy of the *Fronde* had created similar circumstances to those at the end of the Hundred Years'War, was the court tradition, but not the ideal of beauty, abandoned for a time in the works of the Le Nain brothers.

Bourdichon's art can only be fully appreciated by bearing in mind this long, unswerving line of development. His statuesque simplifications, the emphasis he gave to his figures and his more or less abstract ideal of form, together with his sense of order, contributed towards the continuity of French painting and helped to prepare the way for the truly absolutist, Humanist art of the court painters of Francis I. It was the logical consequence of increasing dependence on the court, that in the 16th century all branches of French painting should fall into decay, except the three which found employment at court: the arts of book illumination, of portrait painting and of allegorical decoration.

BIBLIOGRAPHY

The entire literature about Jean Fouquet is mentioned in the two following monographs:

> *Cox, Trenchard:* Jehan Foucquet, native of Tours. London (1931).
> *Perls, Klaus G.:* Jean Fouquet. Paris (1940).

For French painting in the 15th century, the Master of King René of Anjou, the Master of Aix, the Master of 1456 and for Jean Colombe and Jean Bourdichon I have used the following most recent works, as well as the literature mentioned therein:

Durrieu, Paul: Chantilly. Les très riches heures de Jean de France, Duc de Berry. Paris 1904.

Durrieu, P[aul]: Jean Bourdichon. In: Thieme-Beckers Künstlerlexikon, IV, 1910, p. 456–457.

Stein, H.: Jean Colombe. In: Thieme-Beckers Künstlerlexikon, VII, 1912, p. 244–245.

Martin, Henry: La Miniature française du XIIIᵉ au XVᵉ siècle. 2ᵉ éd. Paris et Bruxelles 1924.

Smital, O. und E. Winkler: Herzog René von Anjou, Livre du Cuer d'amours espris. Nationalbibliothek in Wien. Handschrift 2597. Bd. 1–3. Wien 1926.

Blum, André, et Philippe Lauer: La Miniature française aux XVᵉ et XVIᵉ siècles. Paris et Bruxelles 1930.

Lemoisne, P[aul] A[ndré]: Die gotische Malerei Frankreichs, 14. und 15. Jahrhundert. Firenze-Berlin (1931).

Labande, L[éon] H[onoré]: Les Primitifs Français. Peintres et peintres-verriers de la Provence occidentale. T. 1. 2. Marseille 1932.

Dimier, Louis: Les Primitifs Français. In: Gazette des Beaux-Arts, 1936, II, p. 35–56, 205–232; 1937, II, p. 217–236; 1938, I, p. 223–232; 1938, II, p. 81–102, 208–236.

(Sterling, Charles:) Chefs-d'œuvre de l'art français. Palais National des Arts. Paris 1937.

Sterling, Charles: La Peinture française. Les Primitifs. Paris 1938. (Bibliothèque artistique.)

Réau, Louis: La Peinture française du XIVᵉ au XVIᵉ siècle. Paris (1939).

Jacques, Charles: La Peinture française. Les peintres du moyen-âge. Paris (1941). (Bibliothèque française des arts.)

Additional works consulted:

Boll, Franz: Jacques Cœurs Gebetbuch in der Münchener Hof- und Staatsbibliothek. In: Zeitschrift für Bücherfreunde, VI, 1902/03, p. 49–68.

Bouchot, Henri: L'Exposition des primitifs français. Paris [1904].

Bouchot, Henri: Bibliothèque Nationale. Inventaire des dessins exécutés pour Rogier de Gaignières et conservés aux Départements des estampes et des manuscrits. T. 1. 2. Paris 1891.

Bouchot, Henri: Les Portraits de Louis XI. In: Gazette des Beaux-Arts, 1903, I, p. 213–227.

Champion, Pierre: Histoire poétique du quinzième siècle. T. 1. 2. Paris 1923. (Bibliothèque du quinzième siècle. 27. 28.)

Champion, Pierre: Louis XI. T. 1. 2. Paris 1927. (Bibliothèque du quinzième siècle. 33. 34.)

Champion, Pierre: François Villon, sa vie et son temps. T. 1. 2. Paris 1913. (Bibliothèque du quinzième siècle. 20. 21.)

Champollion–Figeac: Le Tournois du roi René. Paris 1826/27.

Clément, P(ierre): Jacques Cœur et Charles VII. T. 1. 2. Paris 1853.

Dufresne de Beaucourt, G(aston): Histoire de Charles VII. T. 1–6. Paris 1881–1891.

Durrieu, P[aul]: La Bibliothèque du bon roi René. In: Congrès international des Bibliothécaires et des Bibliophiles. Procès-verbaux et mémoires. Paris 1925, p. 442.

Durrieu, Paul: La Peinture à l'exposition des primitifs français. Paris 1904.

Ganz, Paul Leonhard: Das Wesen der französischen Kunst im späten Mittelalter, 1350–1500. Frankfurt a. M. 1938. (Veröffentlichungen zur Kunstgeschichte. 2.)

Grandmaison, Charles de: Documents inédits pour servir à l'histoire des arts en Touraine. Paris 1870.

Grandmaison, Charles de: Tours archéologique. Paris 1879.

Greene, Belle da Costa, and Meta P. Harrsen: The Pierpont Morgan Library. Exhibition of illuminated Manuscripts held at the New York Public Library. New York 1934.

Hermann, Julius Hermann: Ein unbekanntes Gebetbuch von Jean Bourdichon. In: Beiträge zur Kunstgeschichte. Franz Wickhoff gewidmet. Wien 1903, p. 46–63.

Labande, L[éon] H[onoré]: Notes sur quelques primitifs de Provence. In: Gazette des Beaux-Arts, 1932, I, p. 392.

Lecoy de la Marche, A(lbert): Le roi René, sa vie, son administration, ses travaux artistiques et littéraires ... T. 1. 2. Paris 1875.

Leidinger, Georg: Meisterwerke der Buchmalerei, aus Handschriften der bayerischen Staatsbibliothek ausgewählt. München 1920.

Leroquais, Victor: Les Bréviaires manuscrits des bibliothèques publiques de France. T. 1–5 et planches. Mâcon 1932–1934.

Leroquais, Victor: Les Livres d'Heures manuscrits de la Bibliothèque Nationale. T. 1. 2. Paris 1927.

Lorenzetti, Costanza: I due Codici miniati inediti di Jean Bourdichon in Italia. In: Bollettino d'Arte, V, 1925/26, p. 481–501.

Lyna, Frédéric: Le mortifiement de la vaine plaisance de René d'Anjou. Bruxelles 1926.

MacGibbon, David: Jean Bourdichon. (Glasgow) 1933. (Privatdruck.)

Mâle, Emile: Trois œuvres nouvelles de Jean Bourdichon. In: Gazette des Beaux-Arts, 1902, I, p. 185–203.

Martin, H[enry], et Ph[ilippe] Lauer: Les principaux Manuscrits à peintures de la Bibliothèque de l'Arsenal à Paris. Paris 1929. (Publications de la Société française de reproductions de manuscrits à peintures.)

Montaiglon, Anatole de. In: Archives de l'art français, VII, 1855/56, documents IV.

Müntz, Eugène: Les Arts à la cour des Papes pendant le XVe et XVIe siècle. T. 1. 2. Paris 1878–1879.

Olschki, Leonardo: Die romanischen Literaturen des Mittelalters. Wildpark-Potsdam (1928). (Handbuch der Literaturwissenschaft.)

Olschki, Leonardo: Manuscrits français à peintures des Bibliothèques d'Allemagne. Genève 1932.

Petit Dutaillis, Charles: Charles VII, Louis XI et les premières années de Charles VIII. Paris 1902. (E. Lavisse: Histoire de France. T. IV, 2.)

(Pognon, Edmond:) René d'Anjou. Traité de la forme et devis d'un tournoi. Paris (1946). (Verve, IV, No. 16.)

Prutz, Hans: Jacques Cœurs Beziehungen zur römischen Kurie. In: Sitzungsberichte der kgl. bayr. Akademie der Wissenschaften. Phil.-hist. Klasse. Jg. 1910, Abh. 2.

Prutz, Hans: Kritische Studien zur Geschichte Jacques Cœurs, des Kaufmanns von Bourges. In: Sitzungsberichte der kgl. bayr. Akademie der Wissenschaften. Phil.-hist. Klasse. Jg. 1909, Abh. 3.

Quatrebarbes, Comte (Théodore) de: Œuvres complètes du roi René .T. 1–4. Angers 1844–1846.

Renouvier, Jules: Les peintres et les enlumineurs du roi René. Montpellier 1857. (Extrait des Publications de la Société Archéologique de Montpellier. No. 24.)

Strohmer, Erich v.: Der Meister von 1456 in der Galerie Liechtenstein in Wien. In: Pantheon, XXXI, 1943, p. 25–34.

Vallet (de Viriville, Auguste): Histoire de Charles VII, roi de France, et de son époque 1403–1461. T. 1–3. Paris 1863–1865.

Vitry, Paul: Michel Colombe et la sculpture française de son temps. Thèse lett. Paris 1901.

Voßler, Karl: Frankreichs Kultur im Spiegel seiner Sprachentwicklung. 2. Aufl. Heidelberg 1929.

Wescher, Paul: Das französische Bildnis von Karl VII. bis zu Franz I. In: Pantheon, XXI, 1938, p. 1–11.

Wescher, Paul: Beschreibendes Verzeichnis der Miniaturen, Handschriften und Einzelblätter des Kupferstichkabinetts der Staatlichen Museen in Berlin. Leipzig 1931.

PLATES

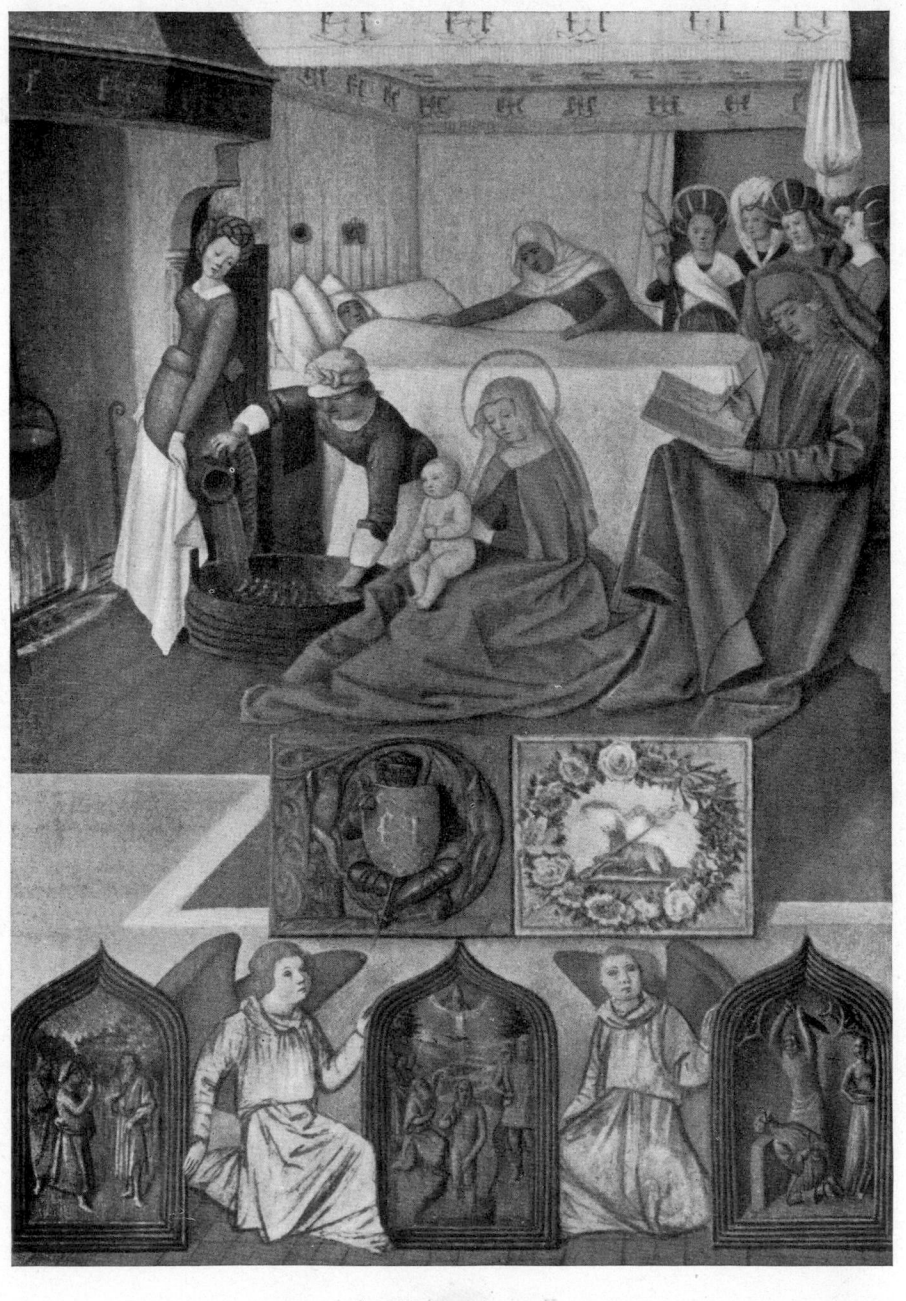

1. *Fouquet:* The Birth of St. John the Baptist

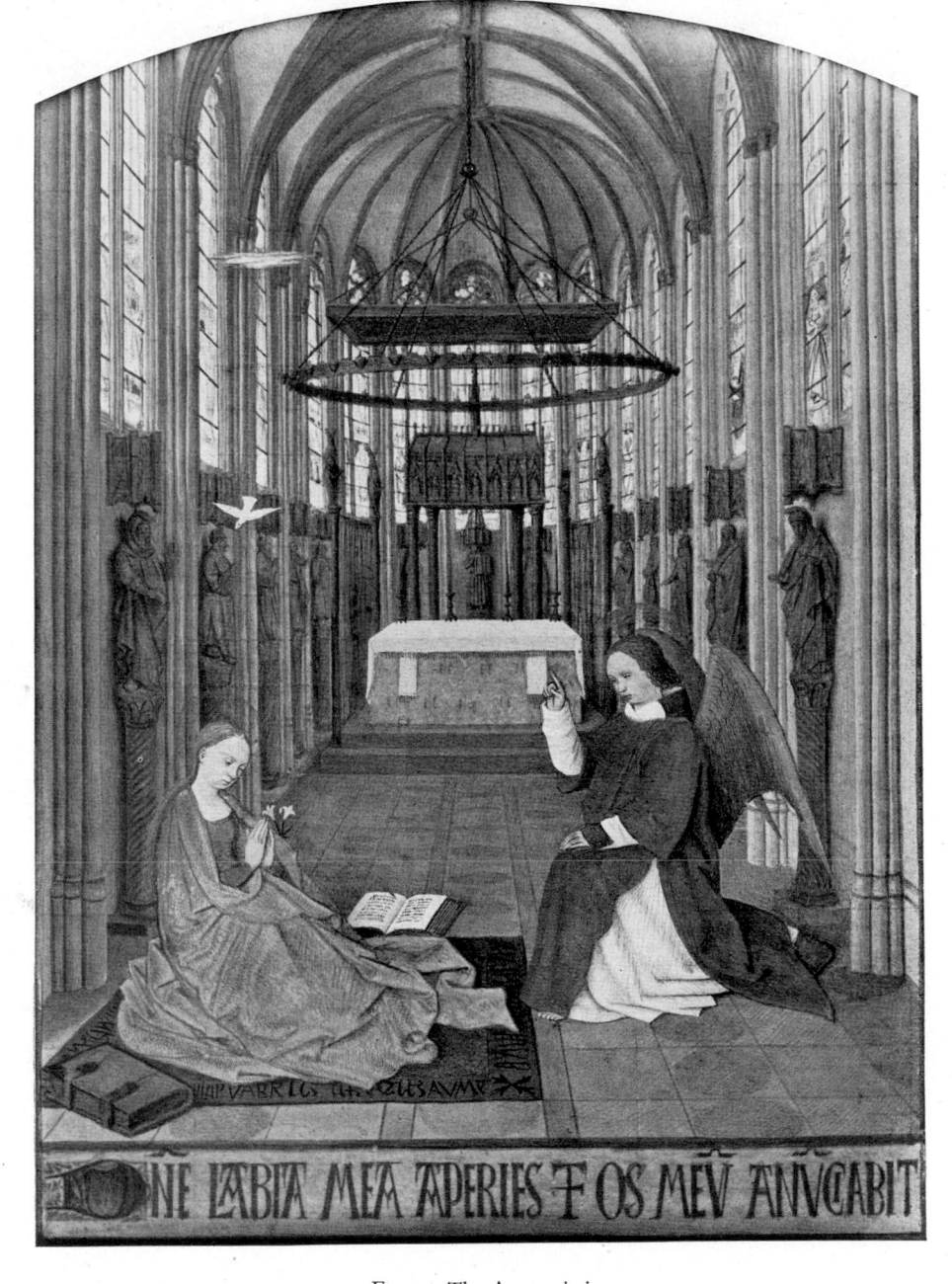

2. *Fouquet:* The Annunciation

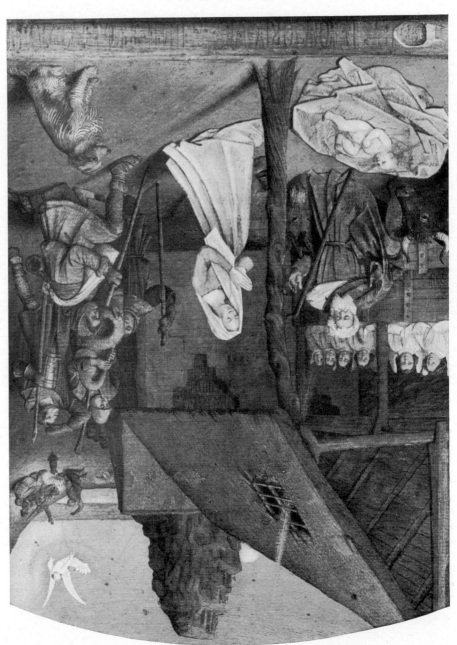

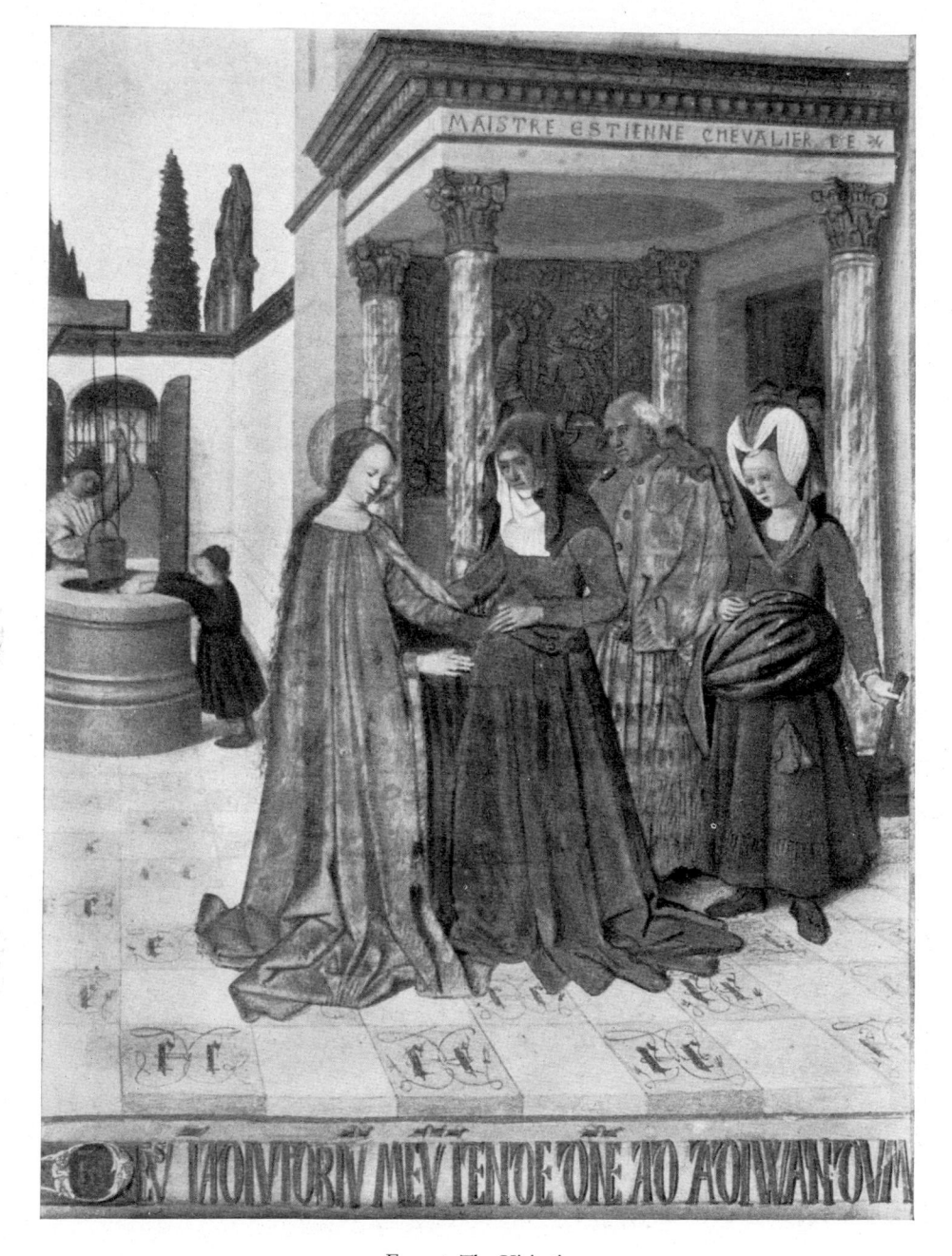

4. *Fouquet:* The Visitation

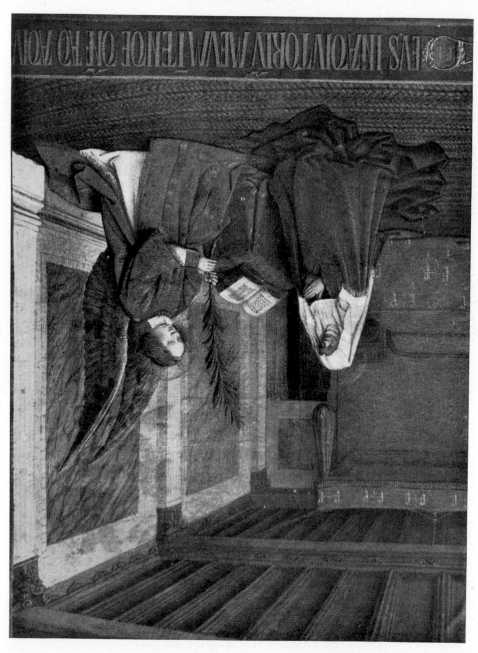

5. *Fouquet:* The Annunciation

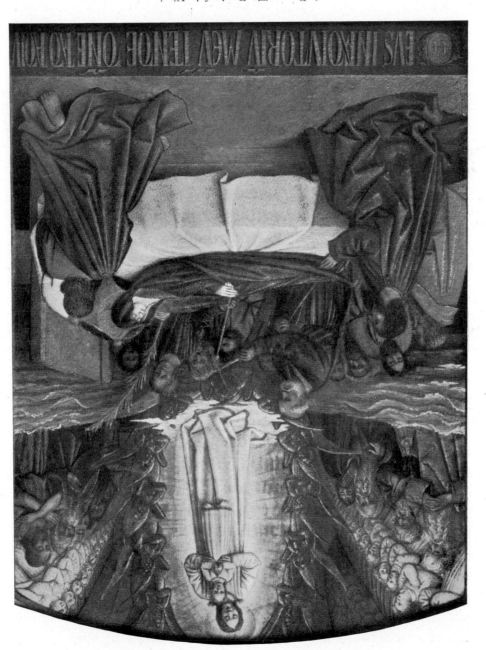

6. *Fouquet:* The Death of the Virgin

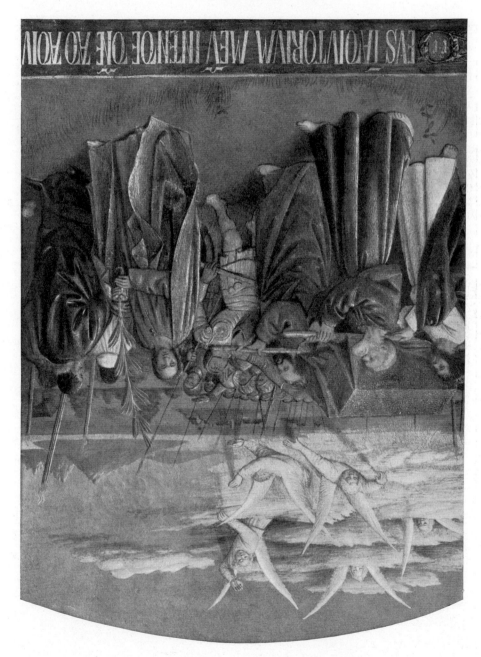

7. *Fouquet:* The Funeral of the Virgin

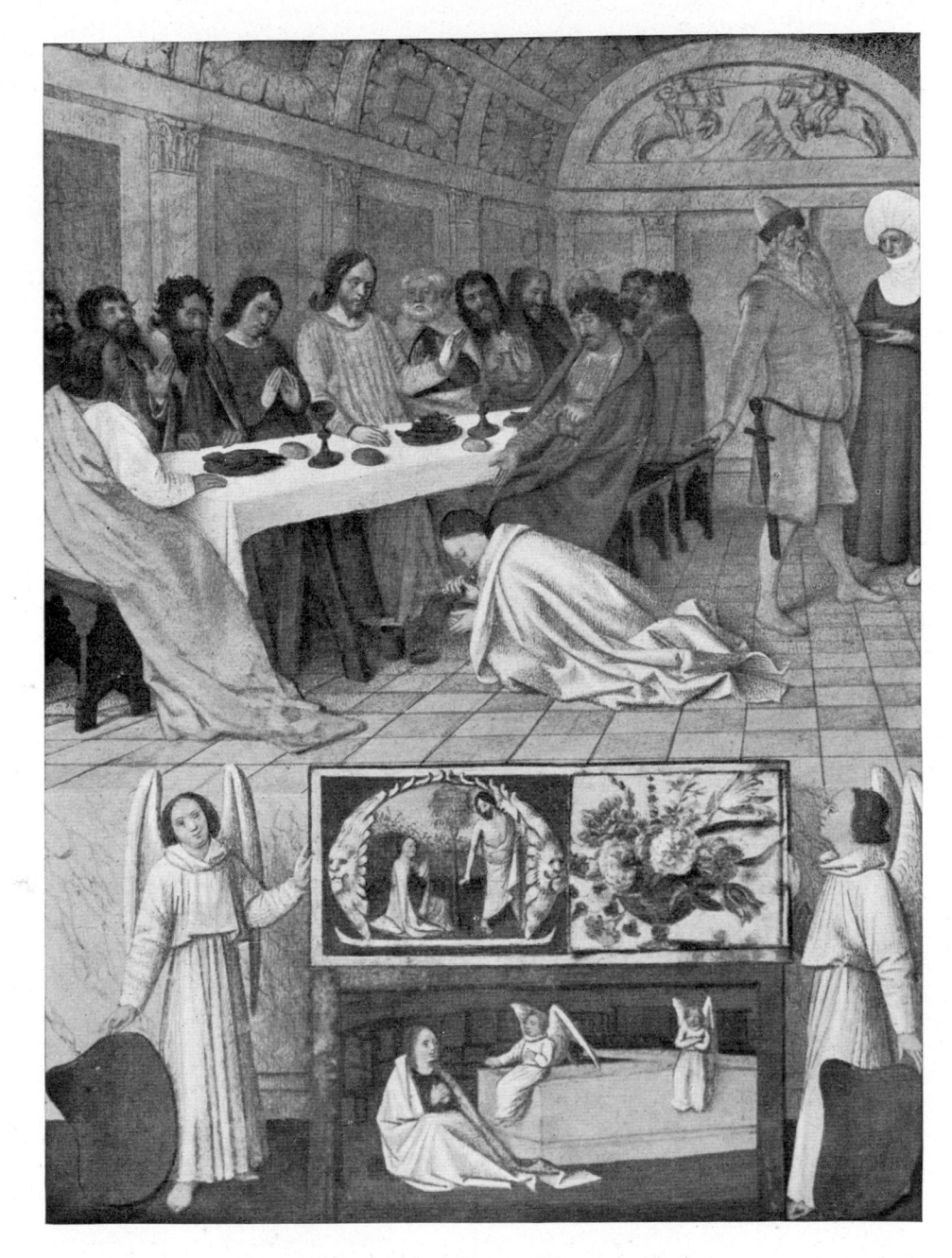

8. *Fouquet:* Jesus at the House of Simon the Pharisee

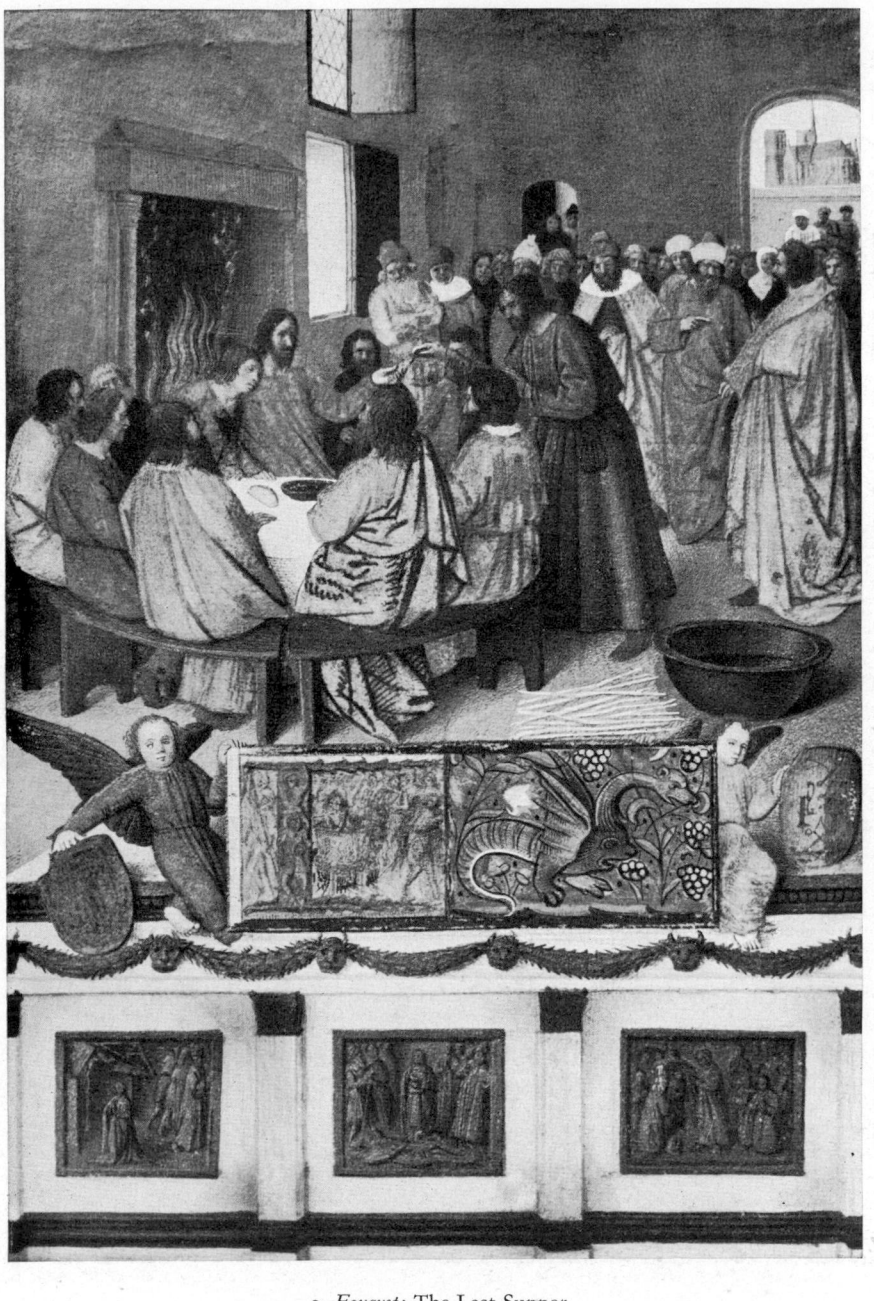

9. *Fouquet:* The Last Supper

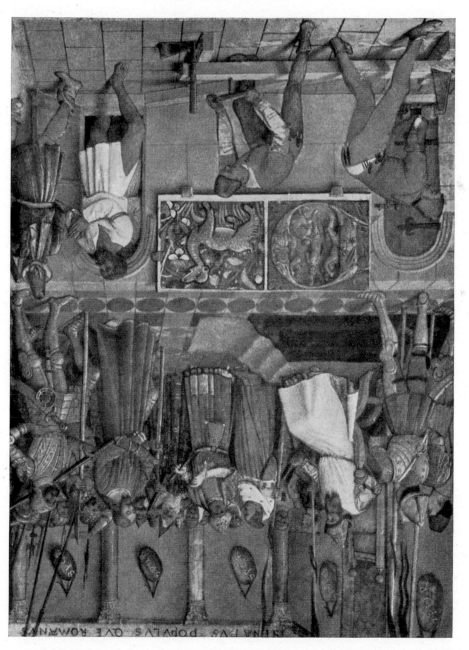

10. *Fouquet:* Jesus before Pilate

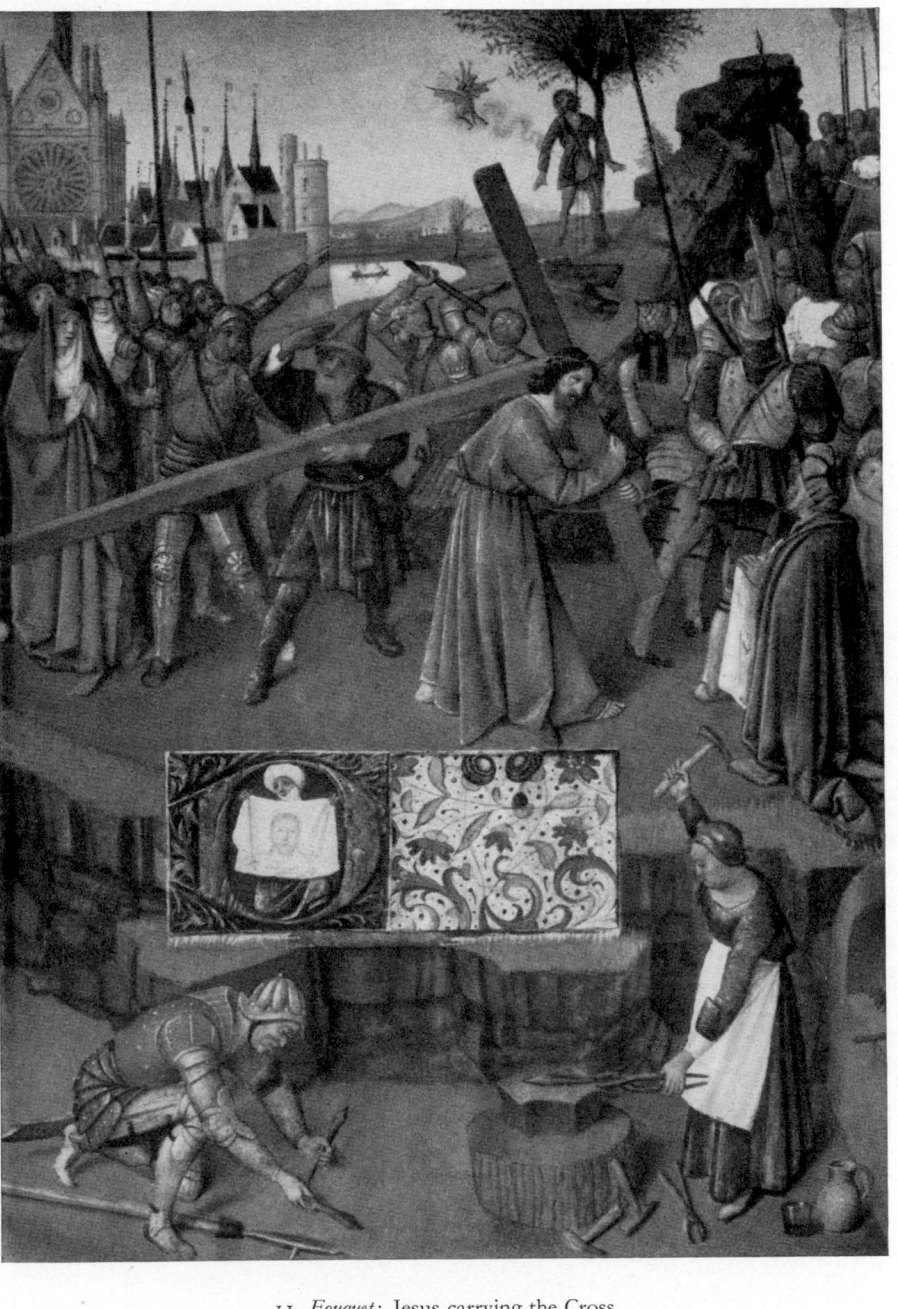

11. *Fouquet:* Jesus carrying the Cross

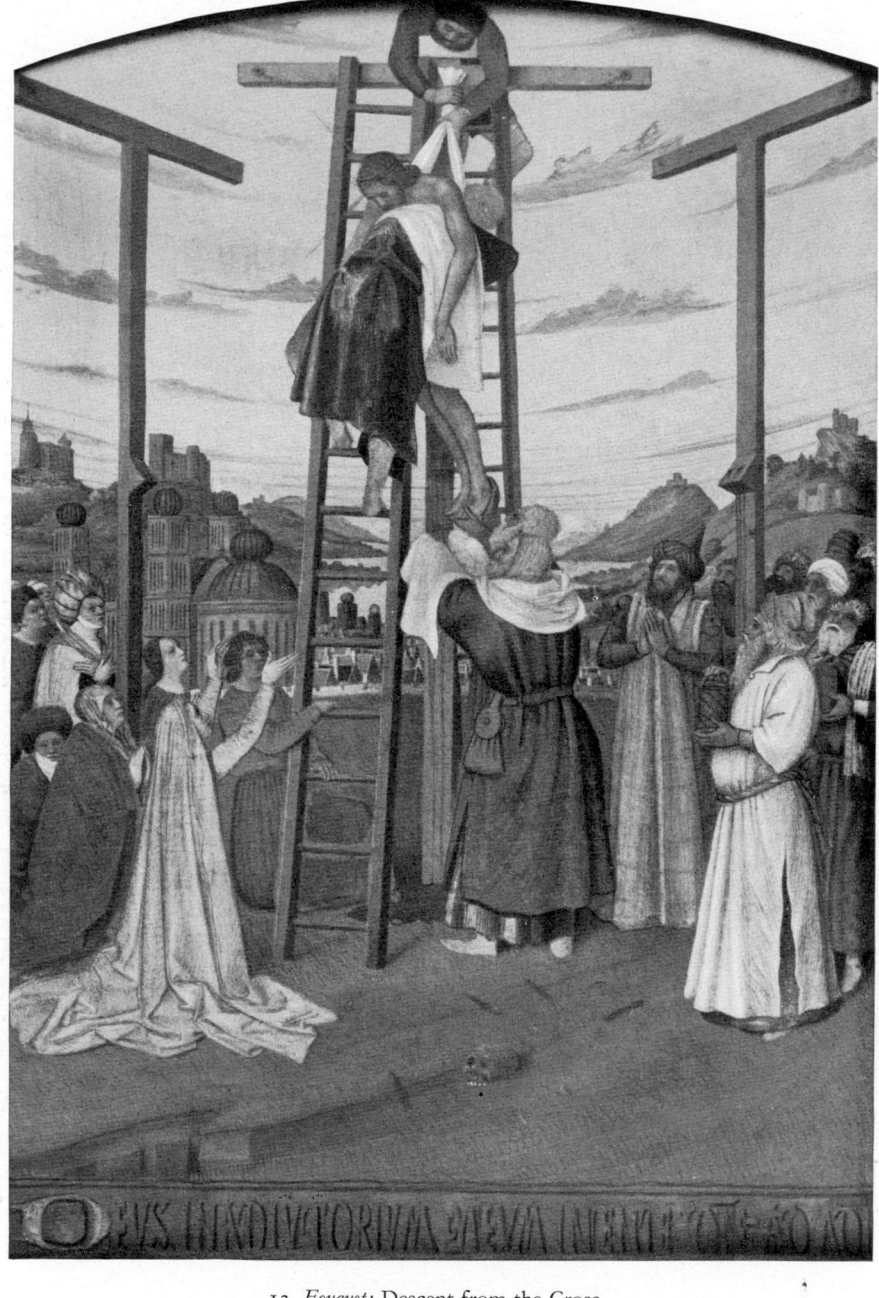

12. *Fouquet:* Descent from the Cross

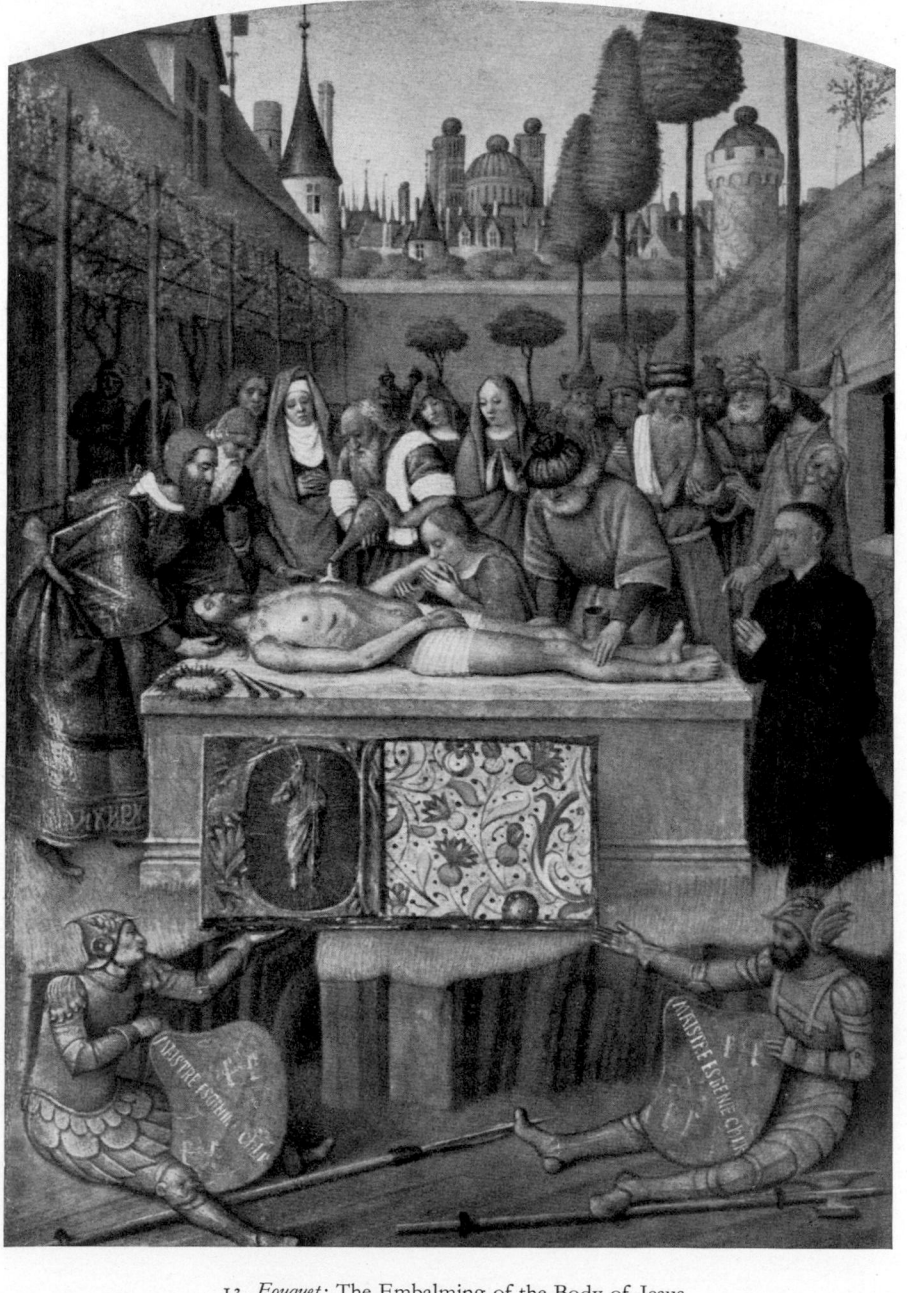

13. *Fouquet:* The Embalming of the Body of Jesus

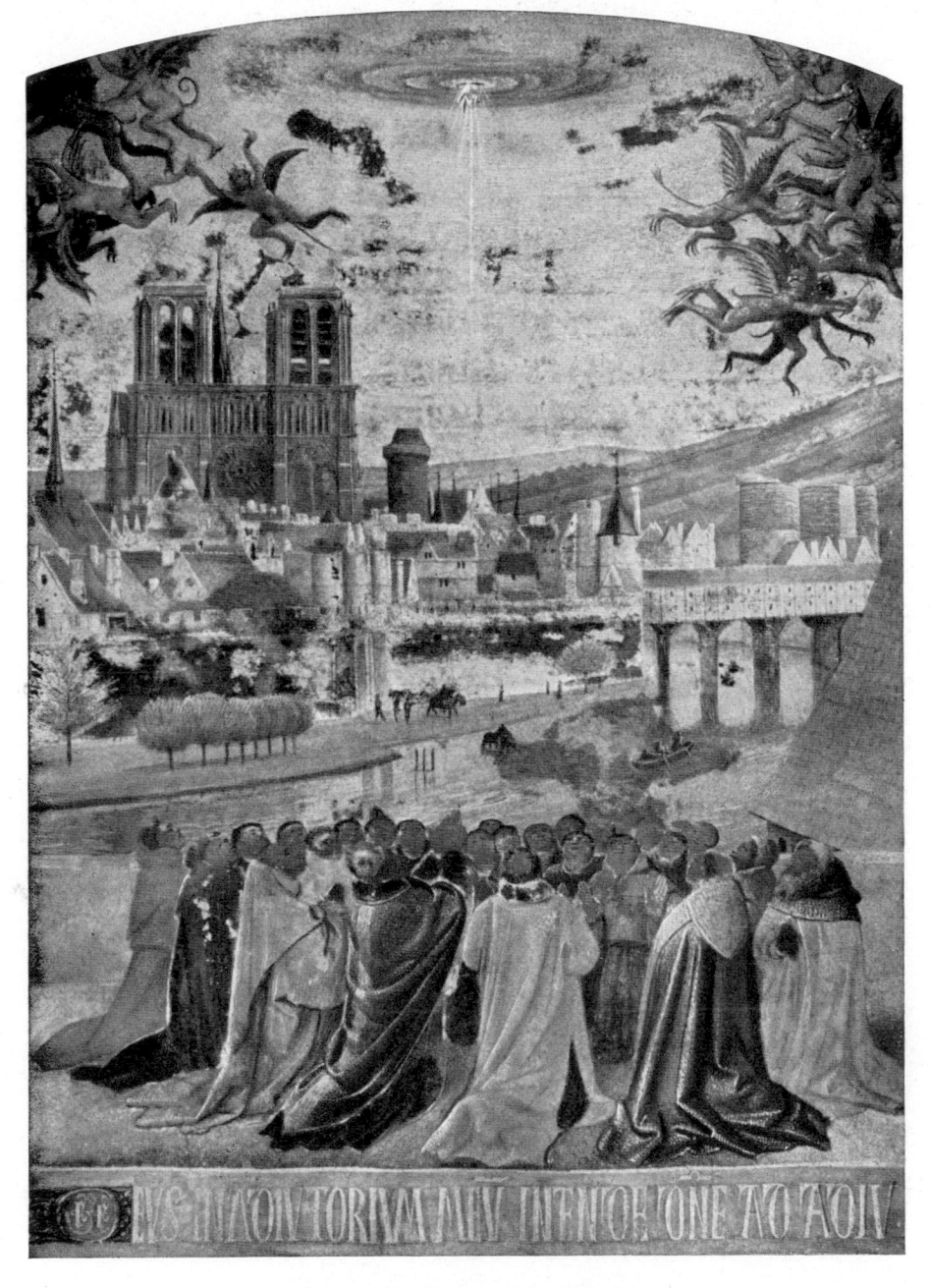

14. *Fouquet:* The Vespers of the Holy Ghost

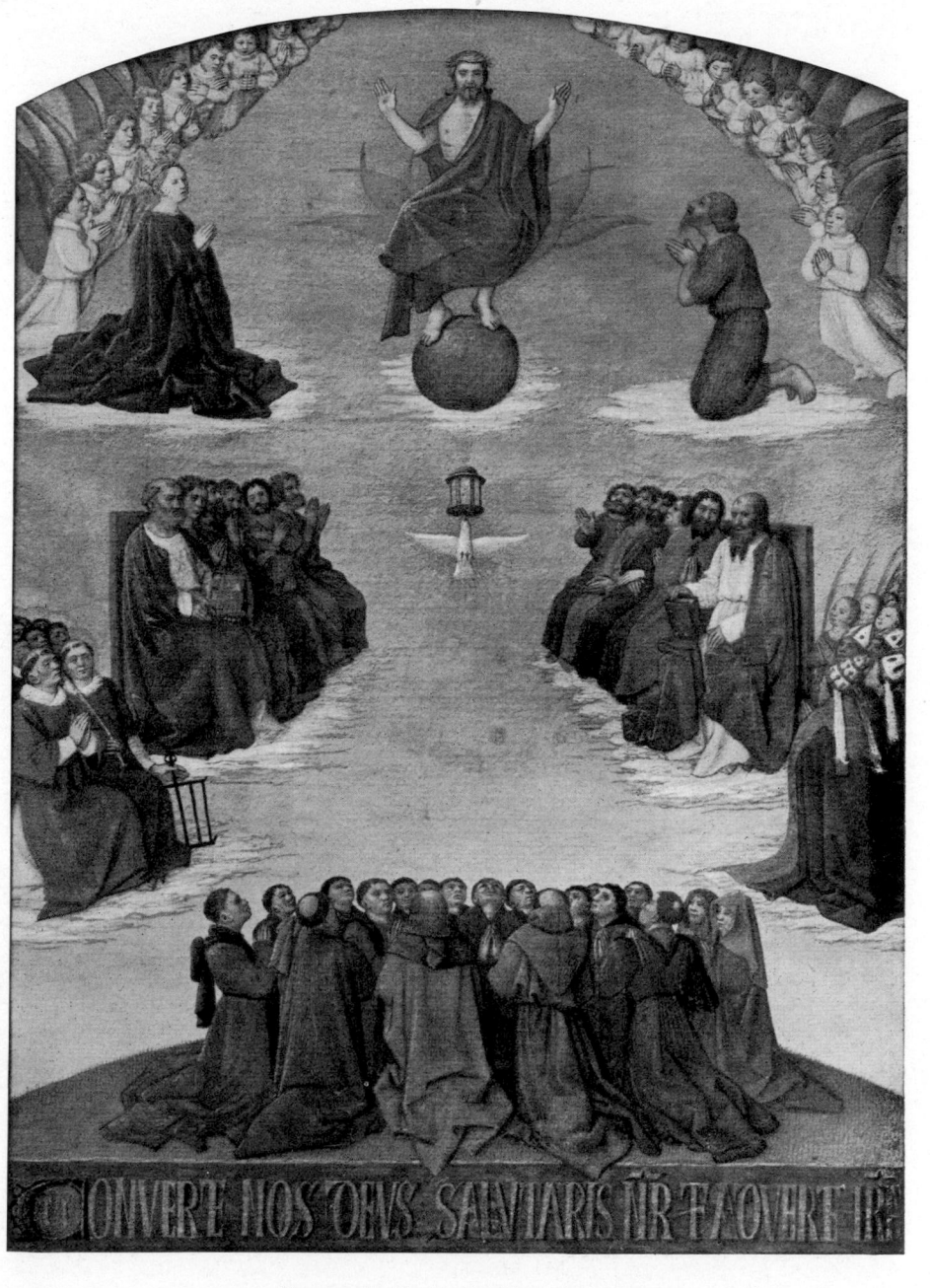

15. *Fouquet:* The Ascension of the Holy Ghost

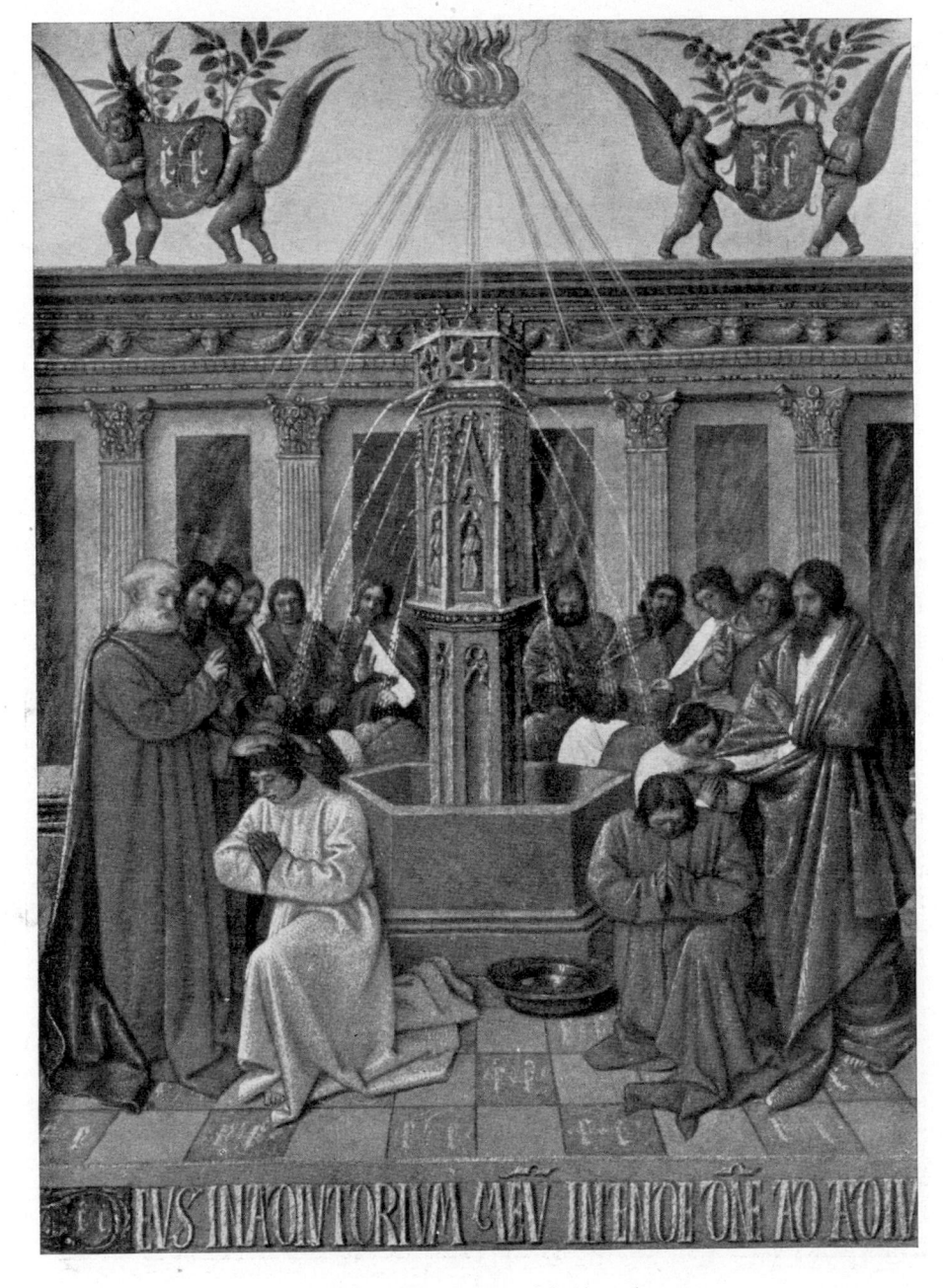

16. *Fouquet:* The Spring of the Apostles

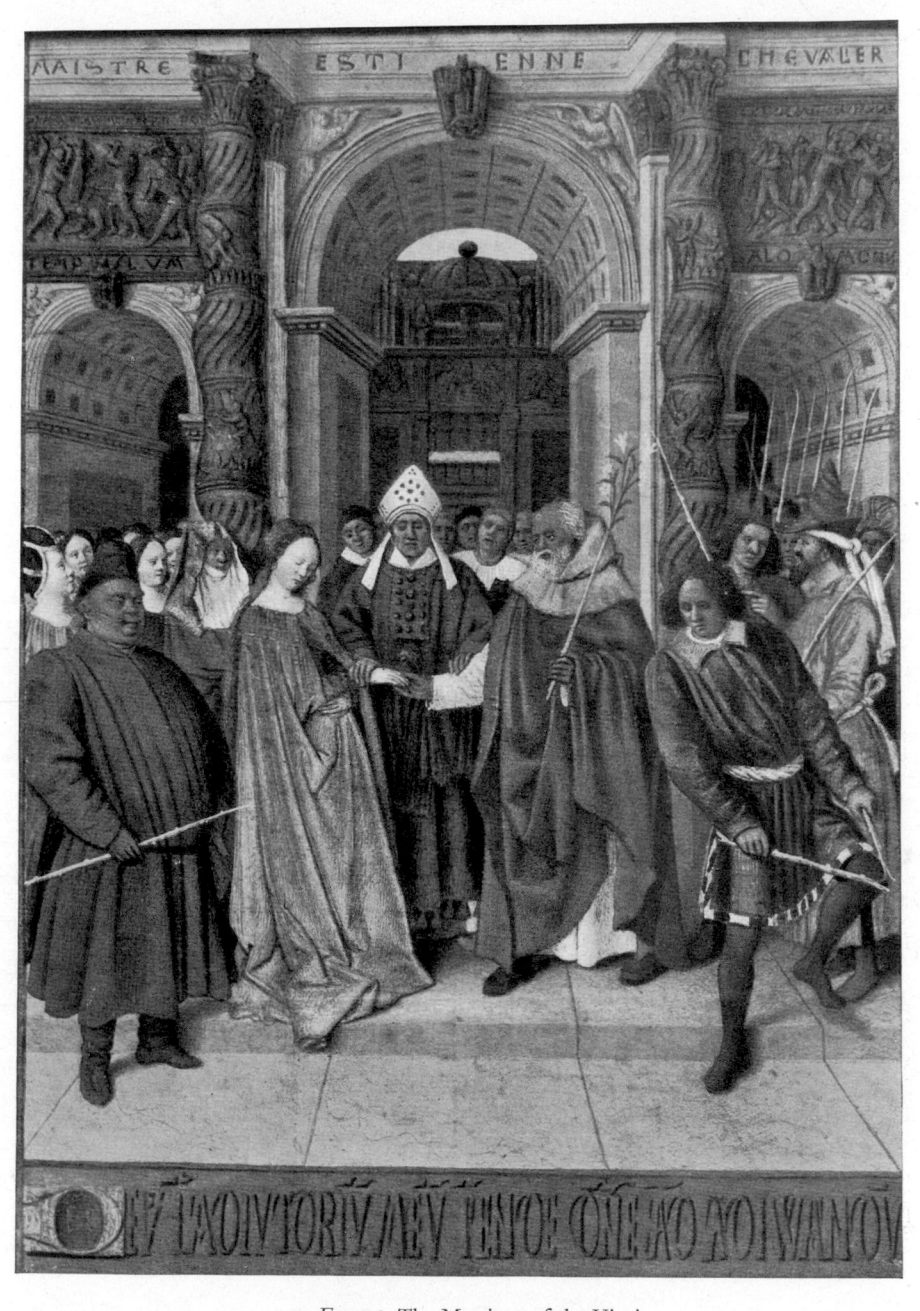

17. *Fouquet:* The Marriage of the Virgin

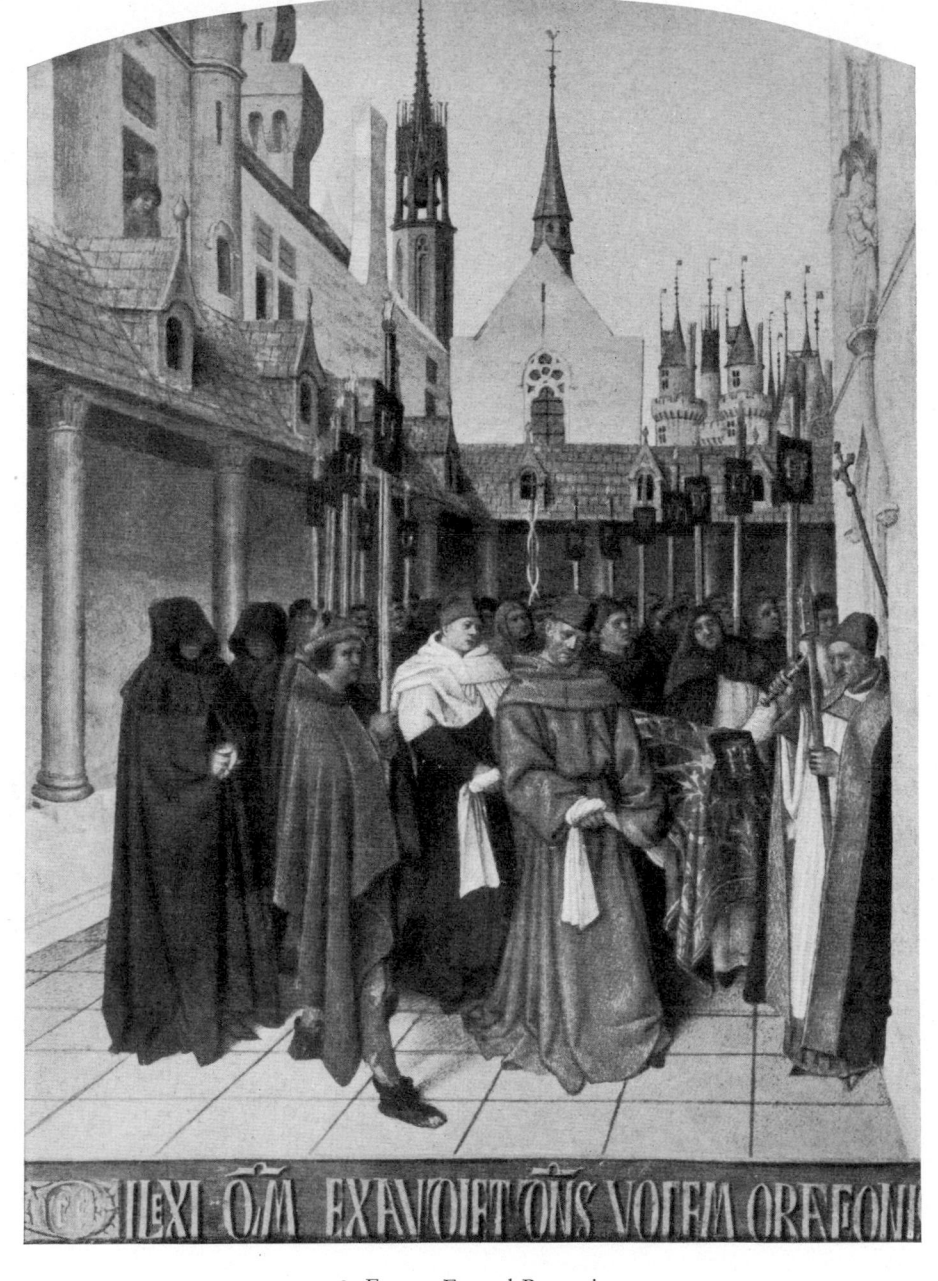

18. *Fouquet:* Funeral Procession

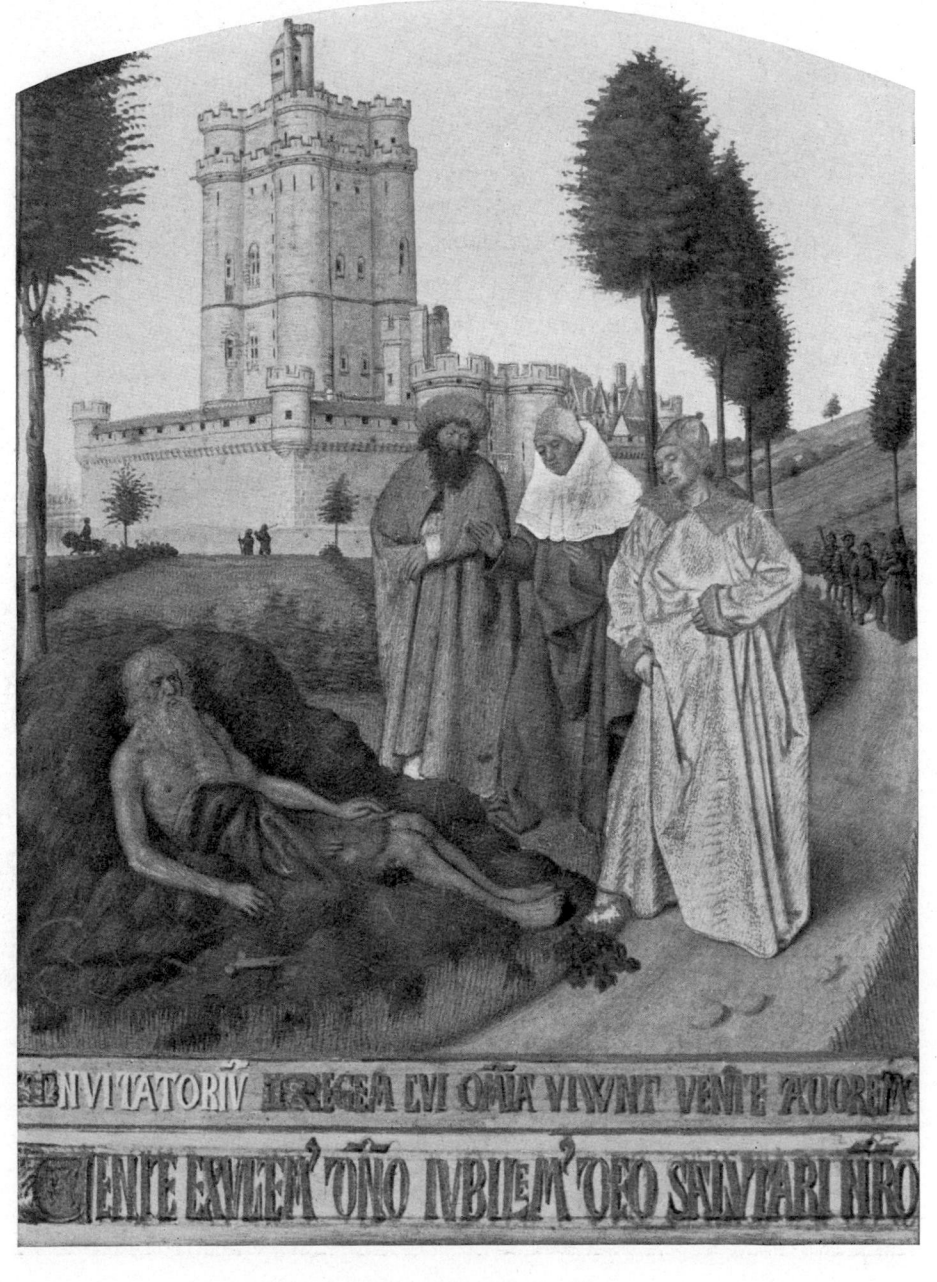

19. *Fouquet:* Job on the Dungheap

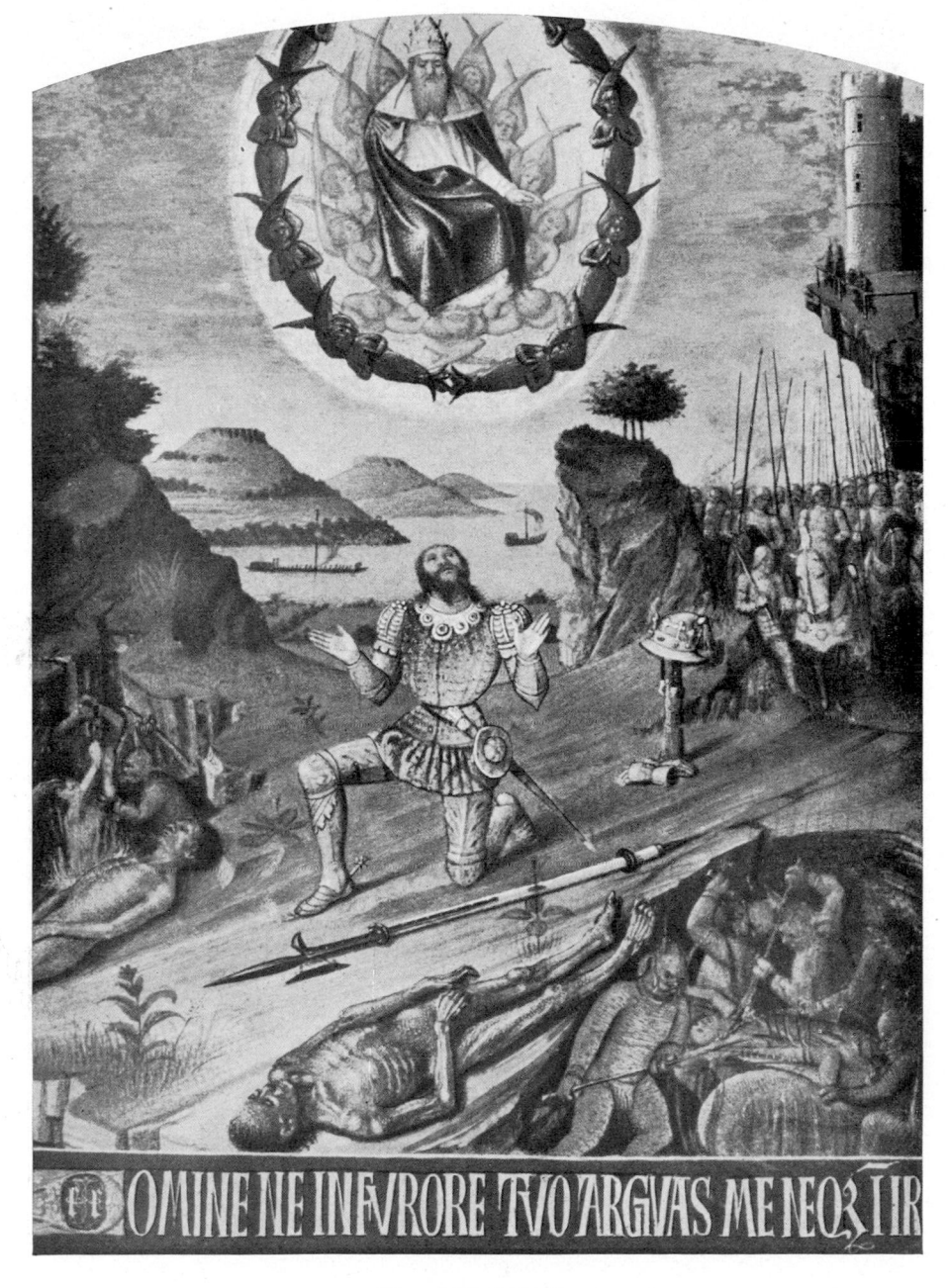

20. *Fouquet:* David in Prayer

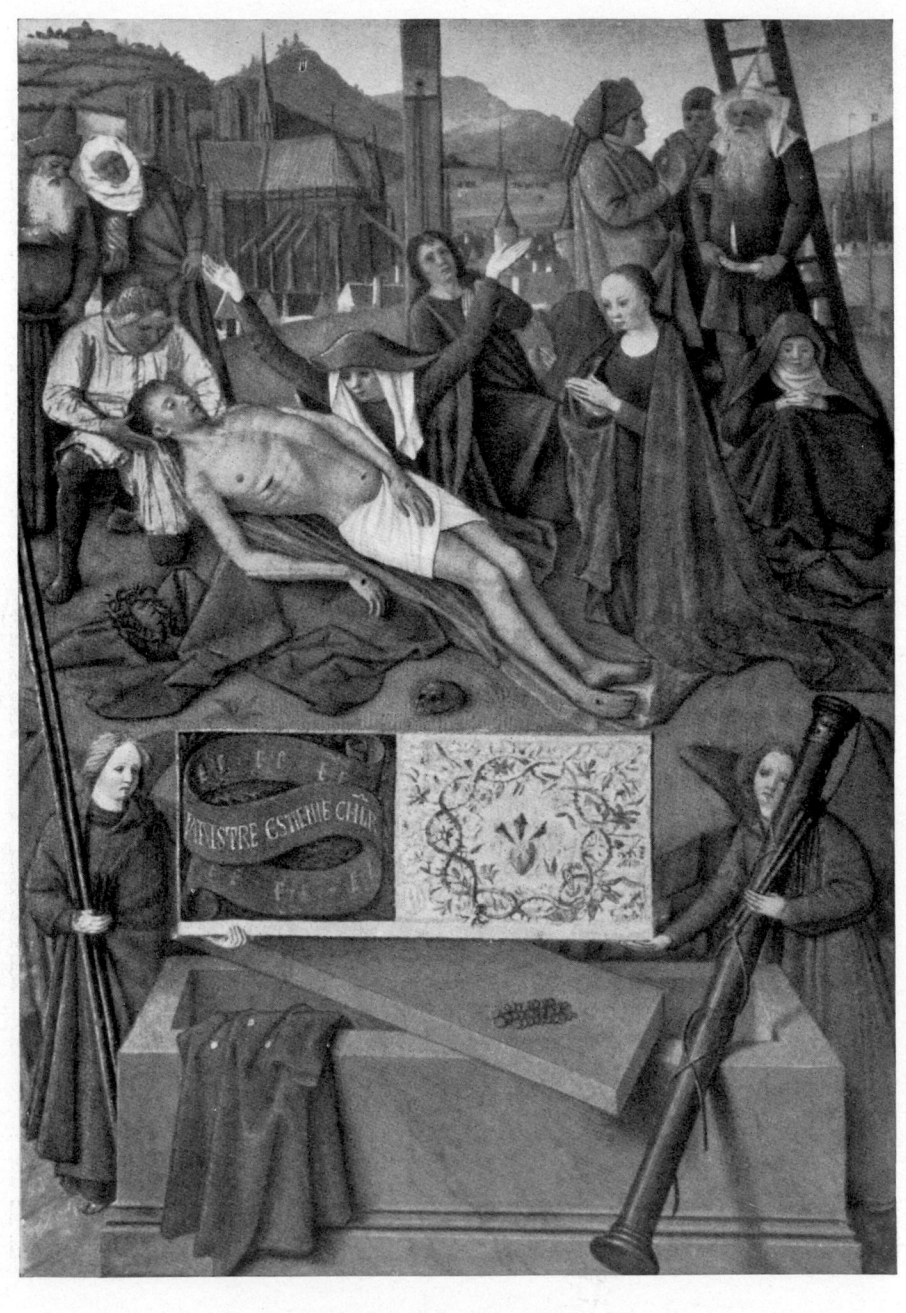

21. *Fouquet:* Stabat Mater Dolorosa

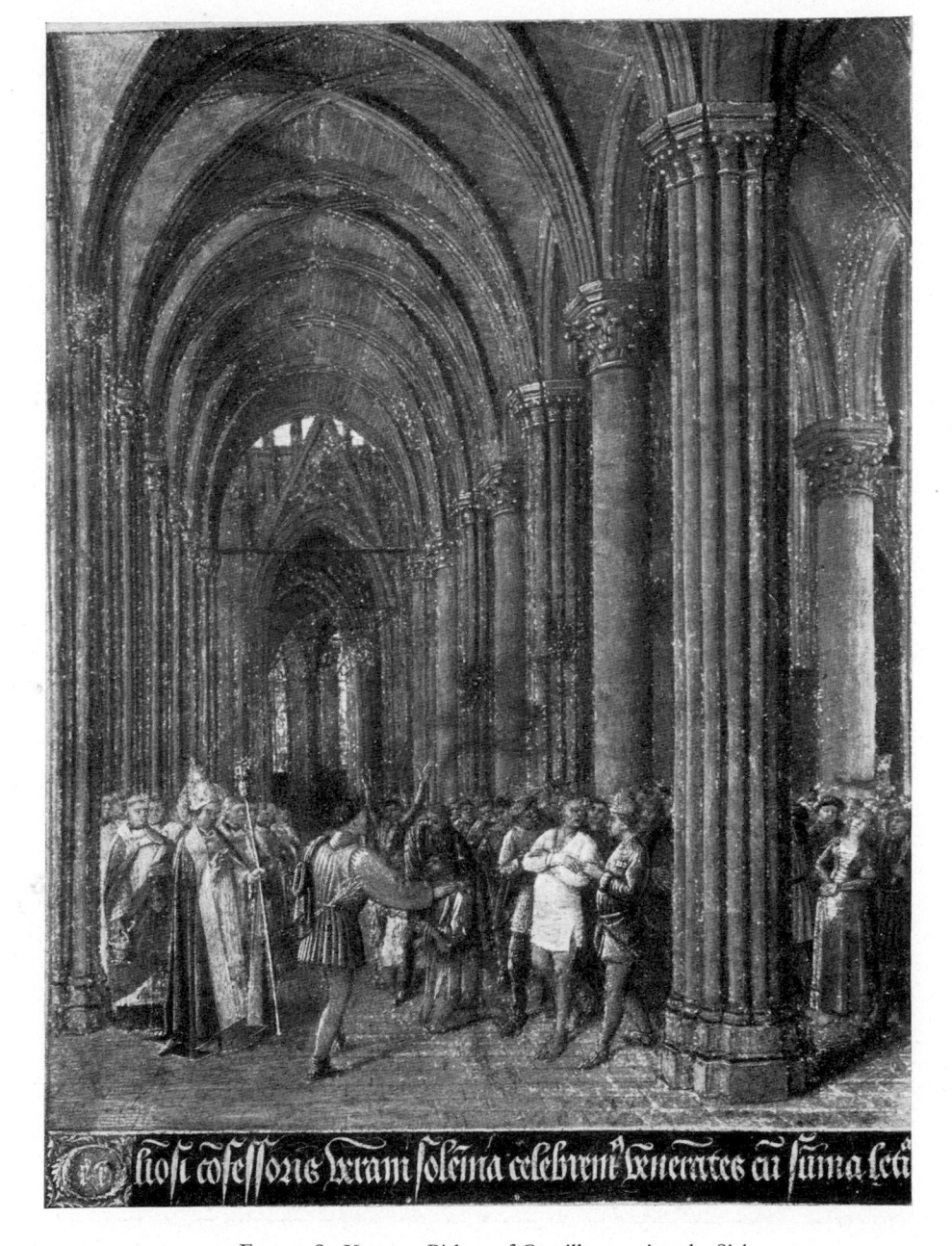

22. *Fouquet:* St. Veranus, Bishop of Cavaillon, curing the Sick

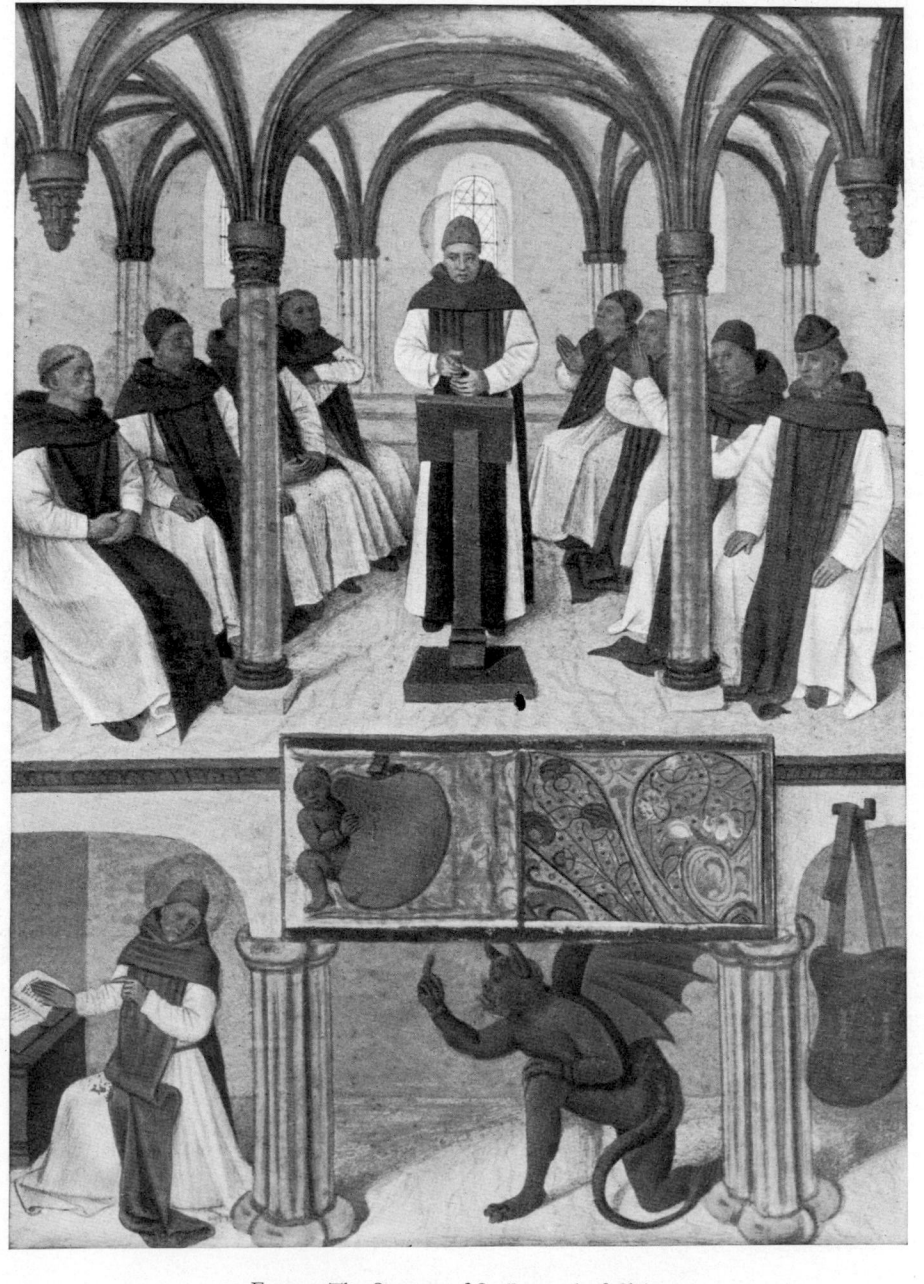

23. *Fouquet:* The Sermon of St. Bernard of Clairvaux

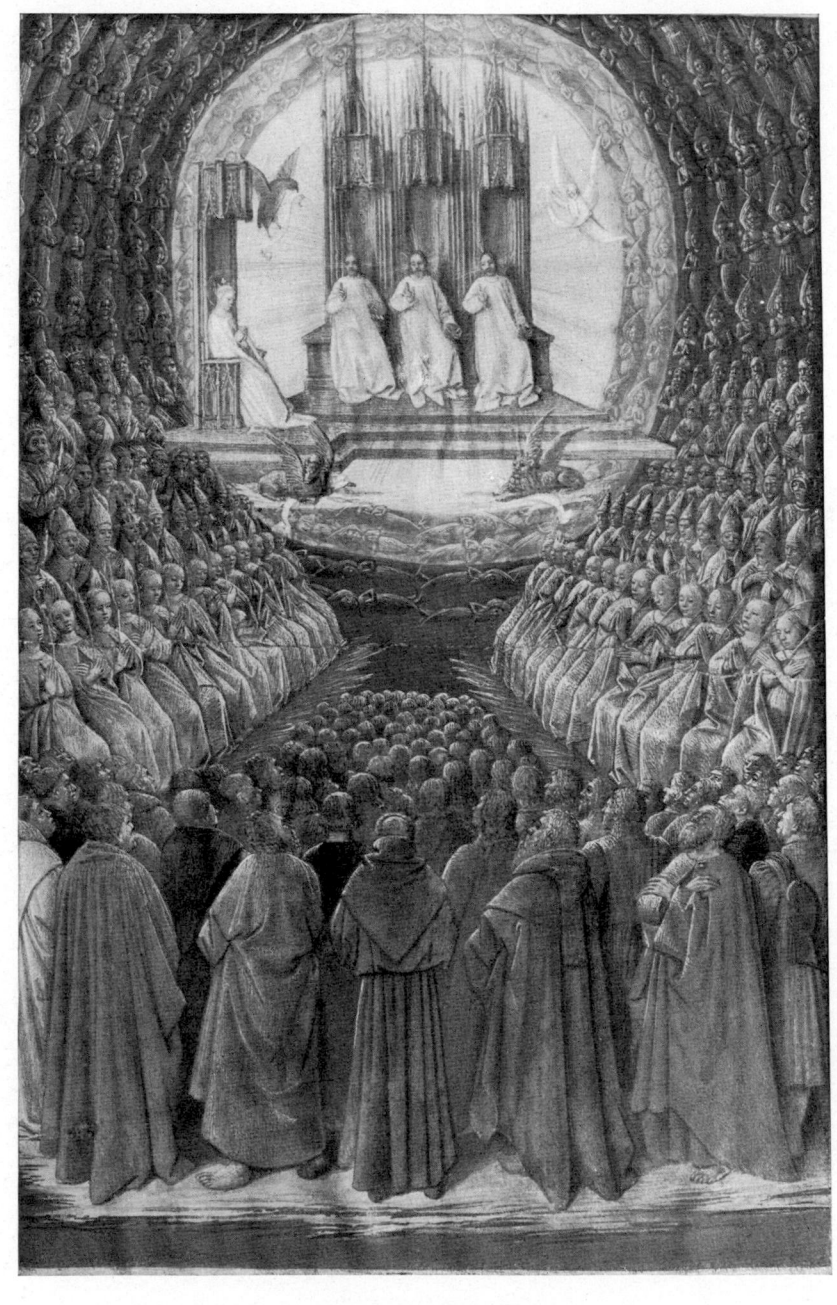

24. *Fouquet:* The Holy Trinity

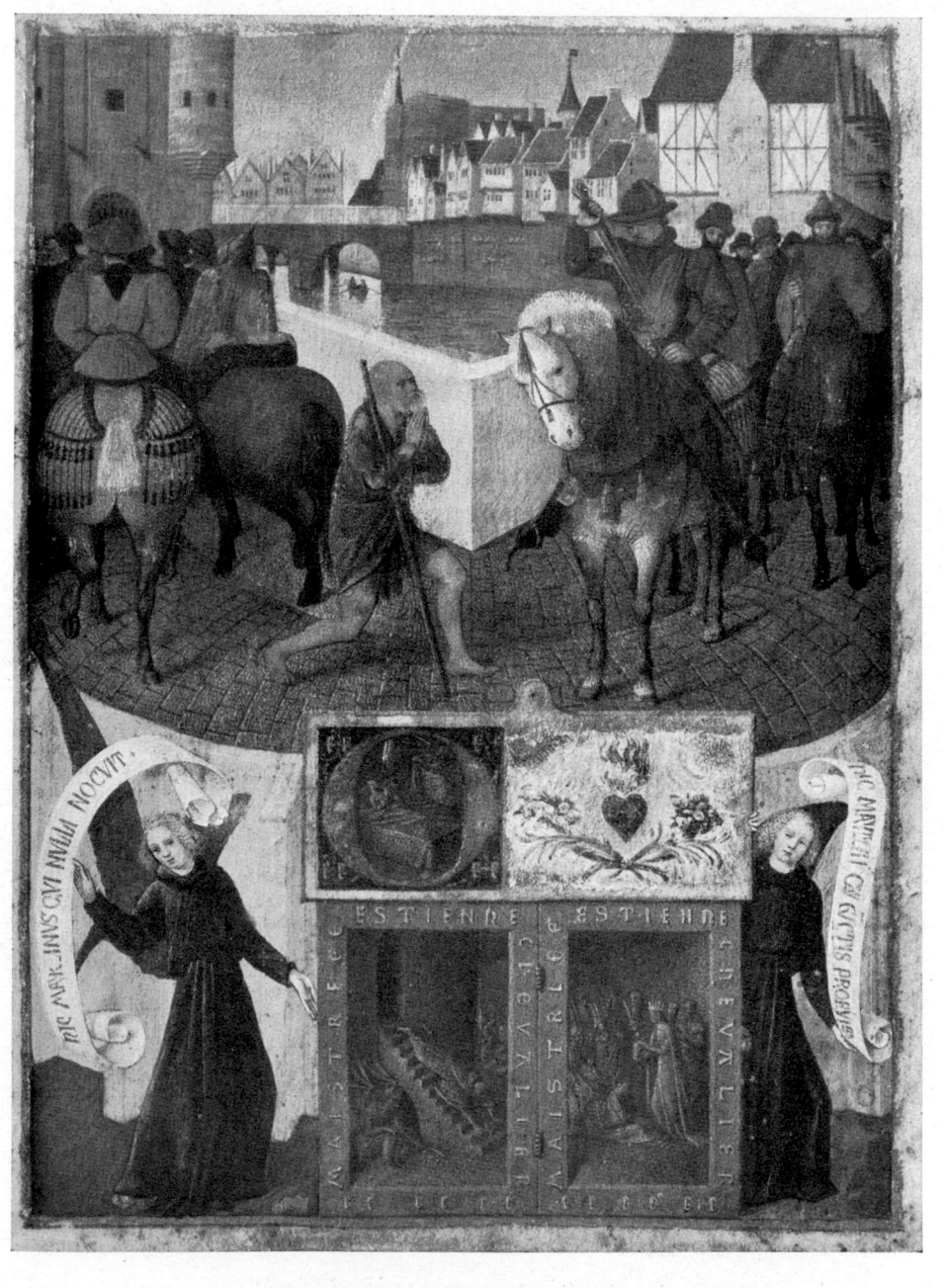

25. *Fouquet:* St. Martin sharing his Cloak with a Beggar

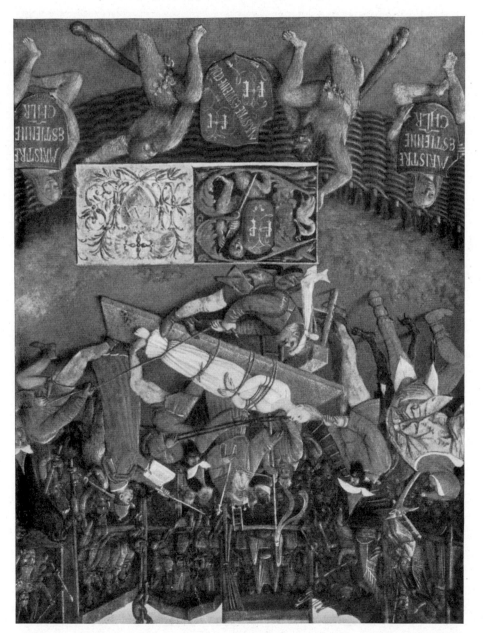

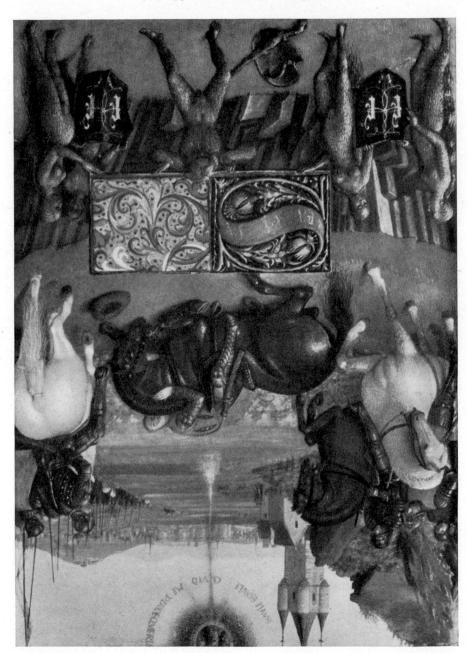

27. *Fouquet:* The Conversion of St. Paul

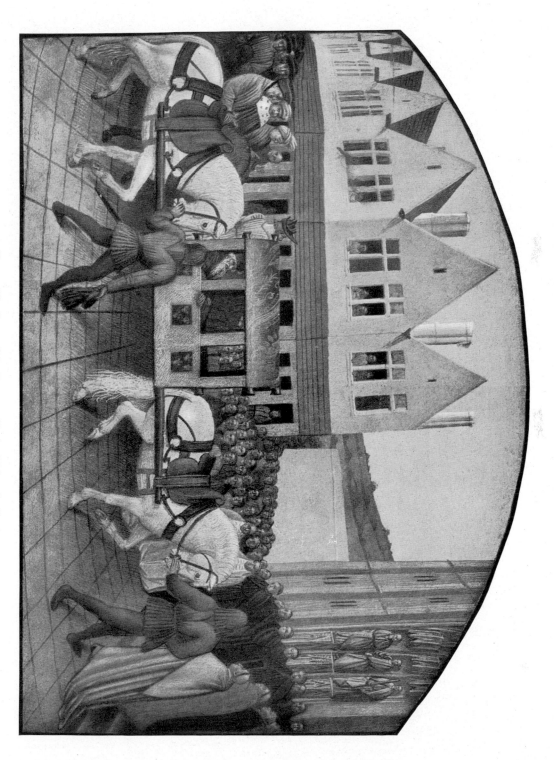

28. *Fouquet*: The Entry of the Emperor Charles IV into St. Denis

29. *Fouquet*: King Charles V receiving the Messengers of the Emperor Charles IV

30. *Fouquet*: The Arrival of the Emperor Charles IV

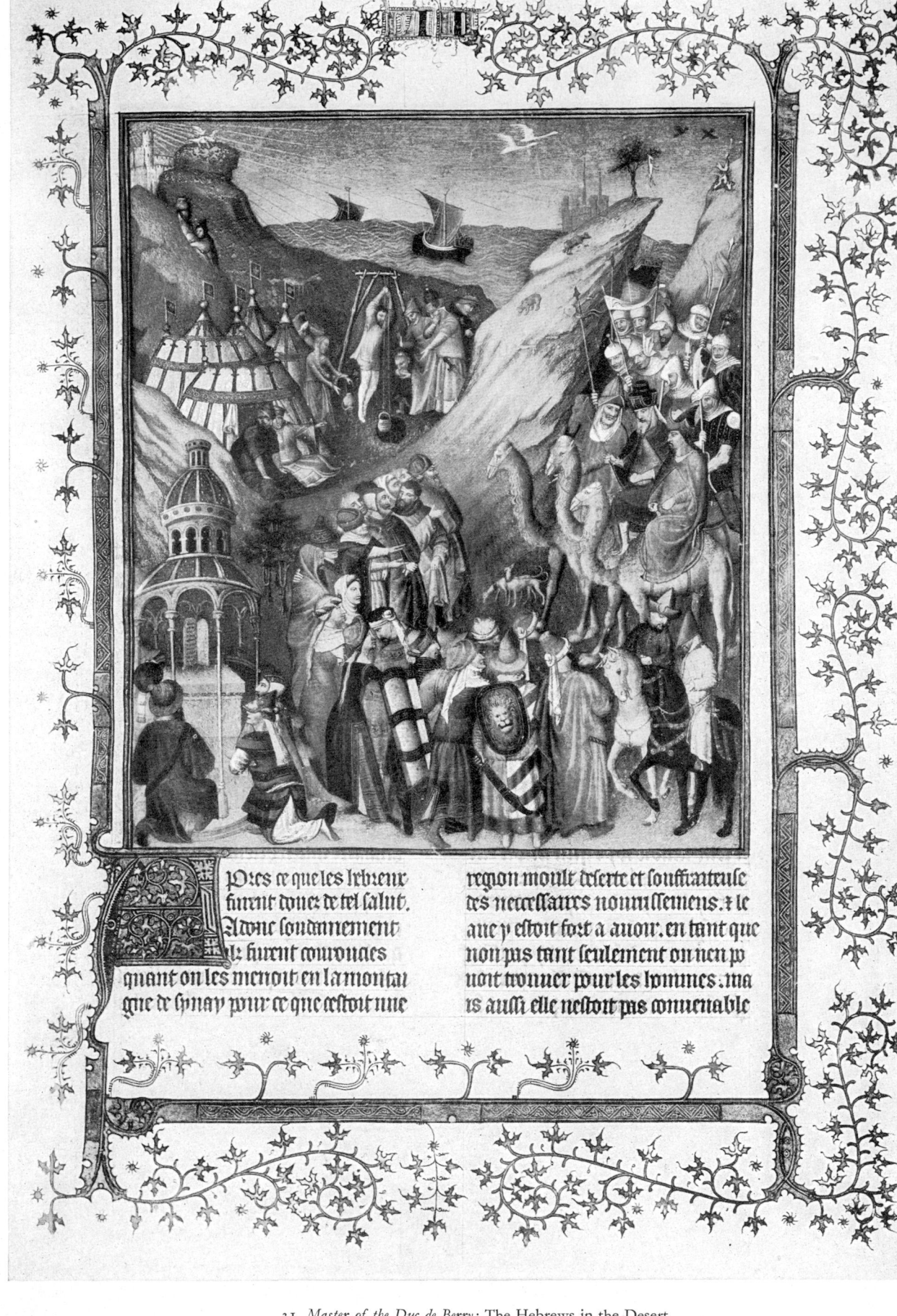

31. *Master of the Duc de Berry:* The Hebrews in the Desert

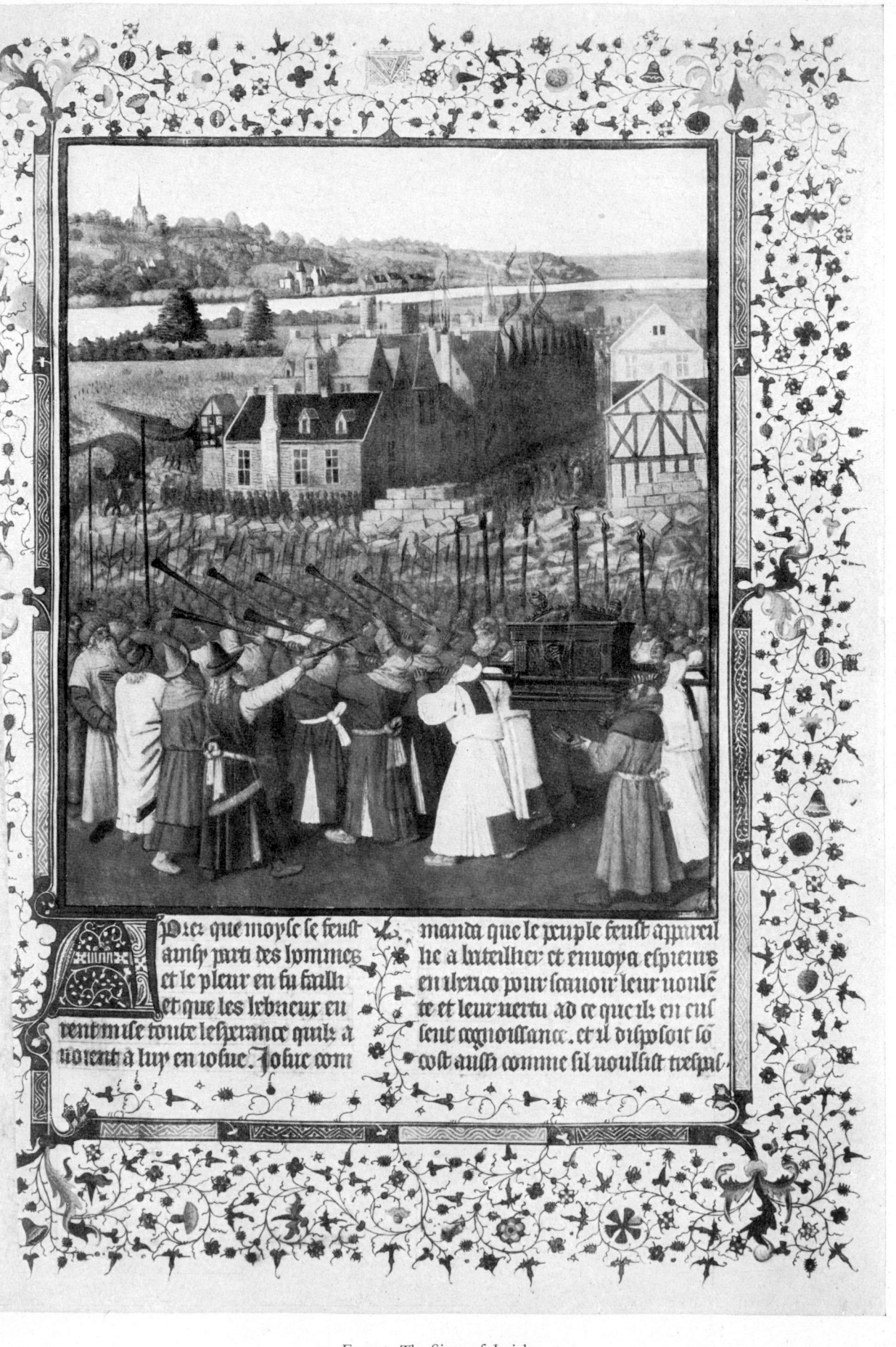

A bataille de quoy nous
auons prile par deuant
fu faicte la iournee que
dauid retourna en sielelech.
en la quelle bataille les amalechnte
furent namais. Et comme il auo

it la demour deur iours en sielelech
il nient un homme la tierre iournee
qui estoit eschappr. et auoit sa robe rom
pue et desciree et la teste couuerte de ce
dres. et auoit li mesismes mis saul
a mort en la bataille quil fist contre

33. *Fouquet:* David lamenting over the Death of Saul

La ant. Erechie roy
de deux lignes. Anou
la tenu quatone ans
le royaume. le roy des
assyriens nomme sennacherub a
tresgrant main mist les tentes cotre

li. et par fort bras prist toutes les ci
tes de iuda et te lemamn. Et ainsi
comme il aloit en iherusalem. Ere
chie ennora legats au deuant de
li. En li promettant quil li obei
roit et quil paieroit les treux trie q

34. *Fouquet:* The Destruction of the Temple

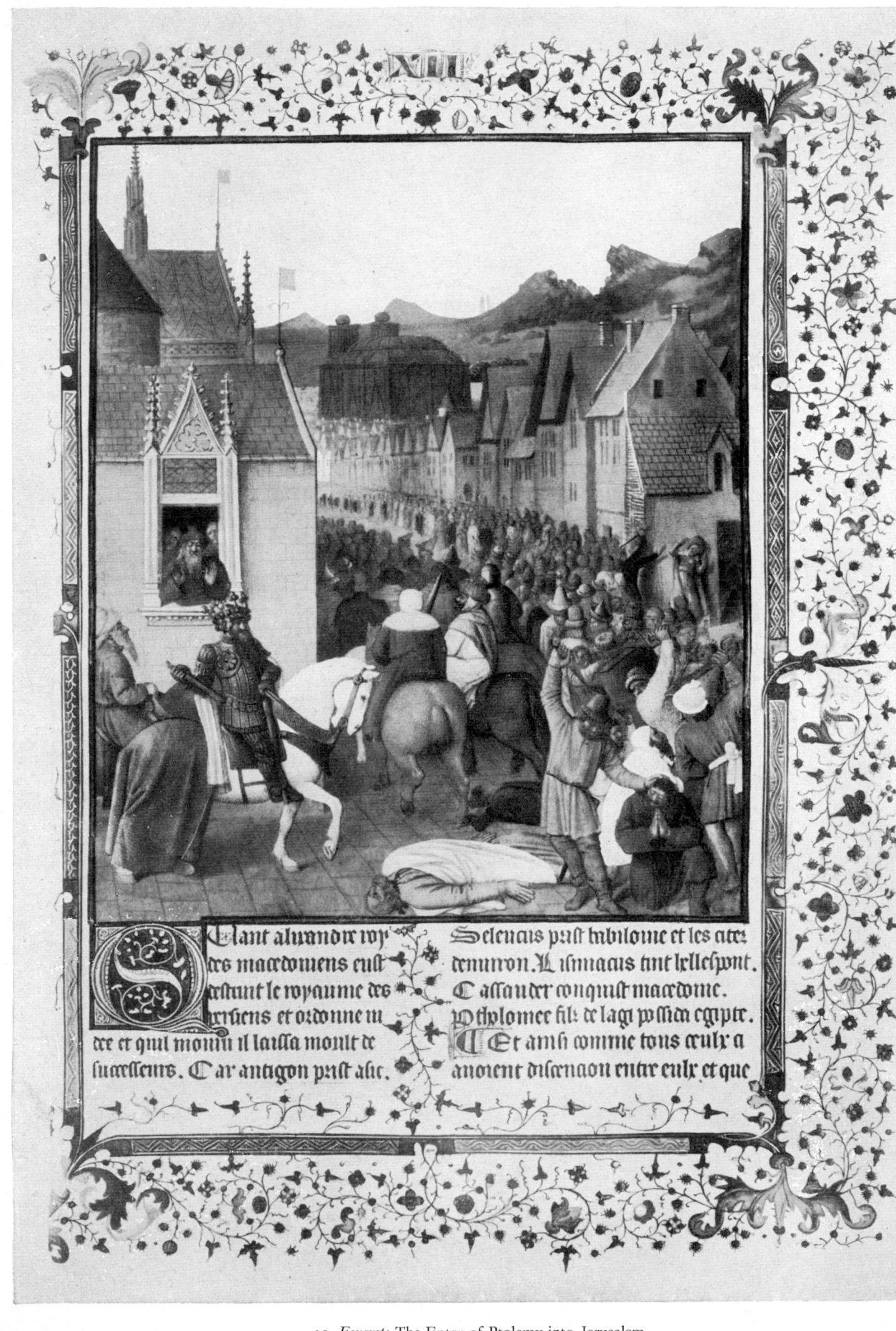

35. *Fouquet:* The Entry of Ptolemy into Jerusalem

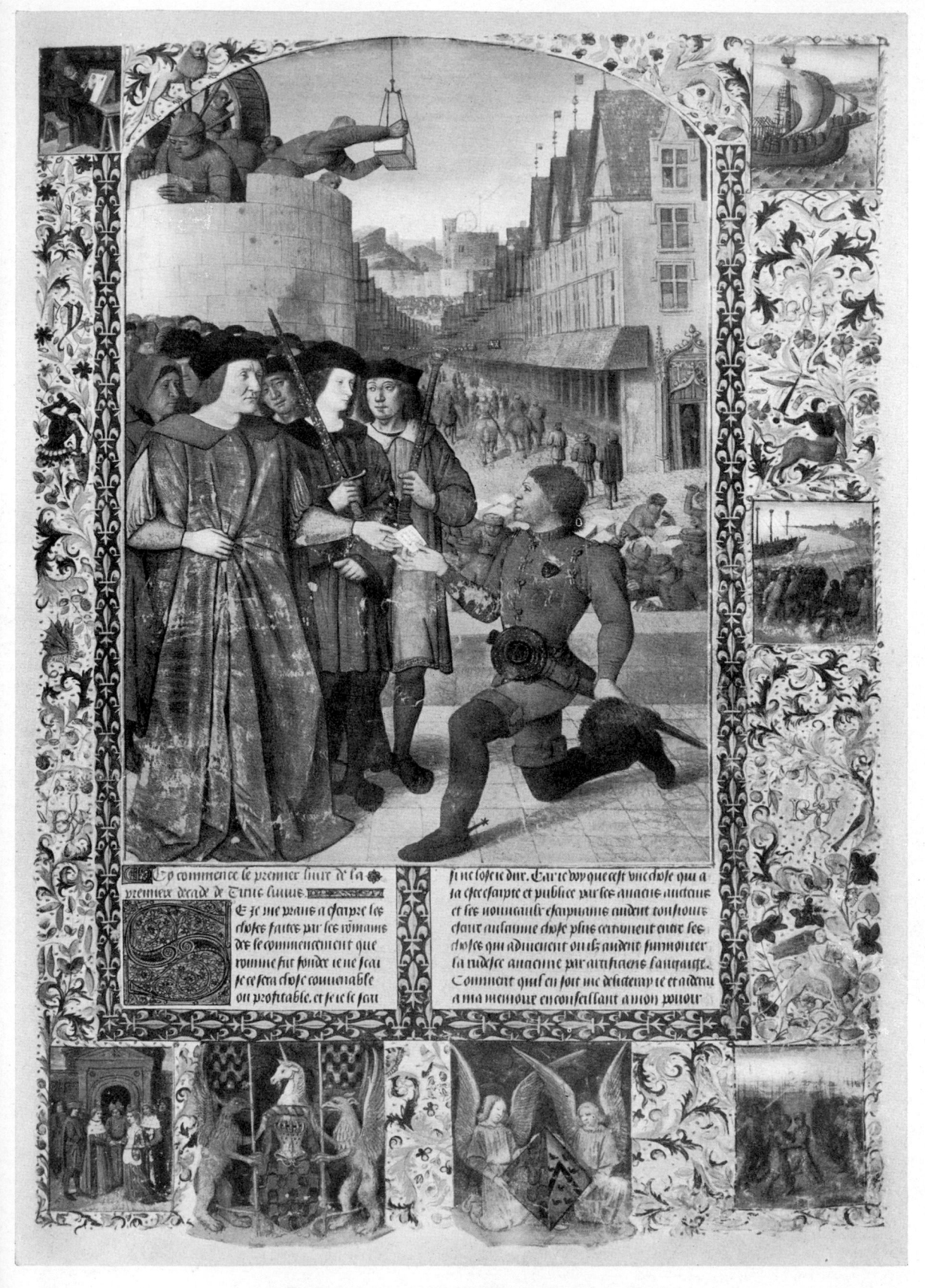

36. *Fouquet and successor:* The Building of the Roman Wall

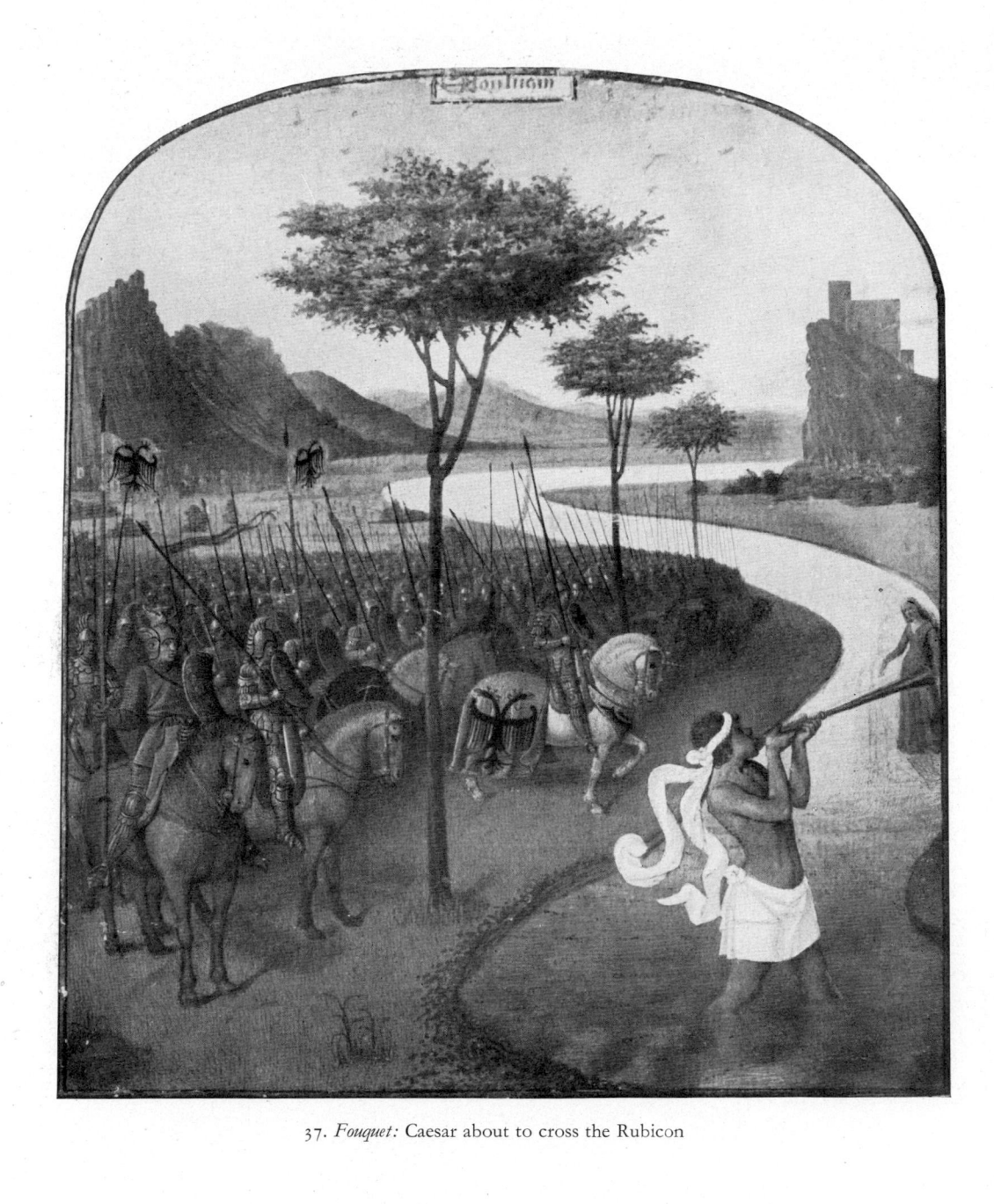

37. *Fouquet:* Caesar about to cross the Rubicon

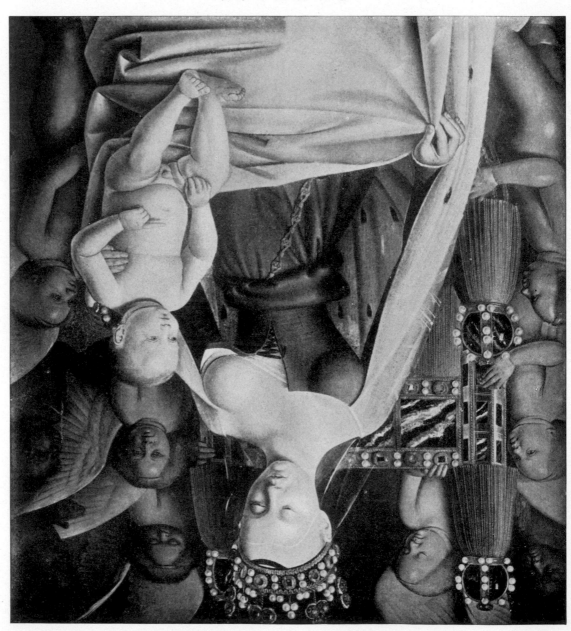

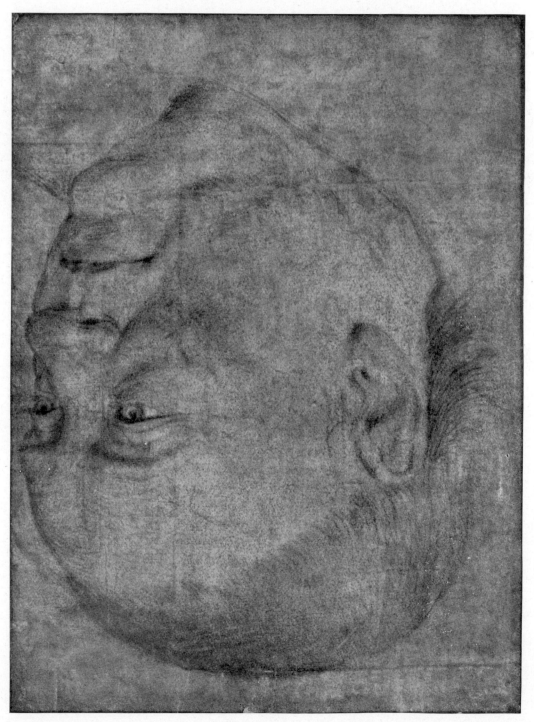

39. *Fouquet:* Study for the Portrait of Guillaume Juvénal des Ursins'

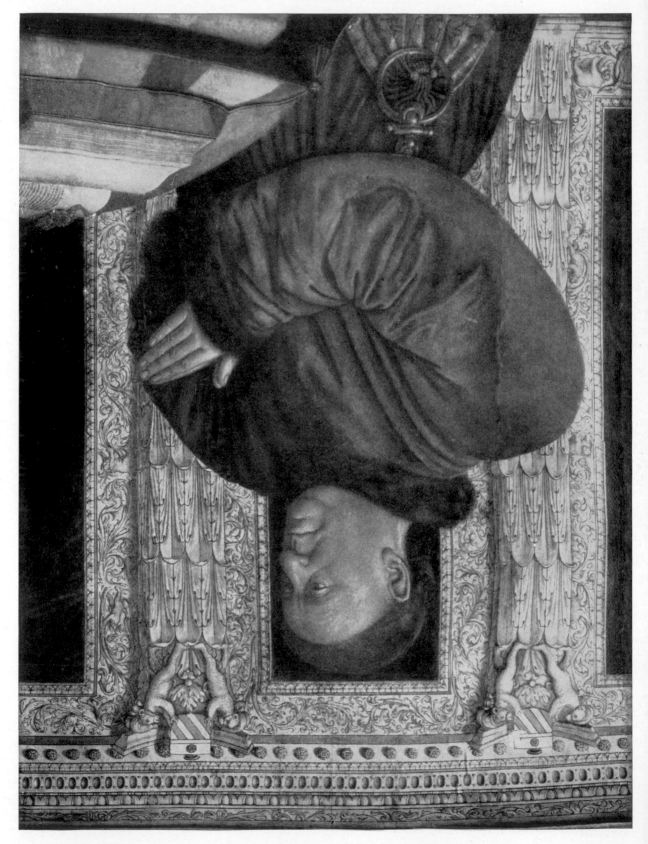

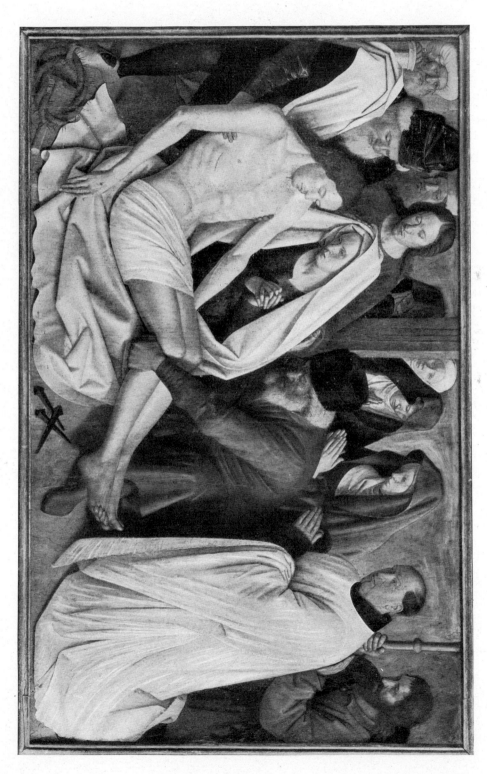

41. *Fouquet:* The Pietà of Nouans

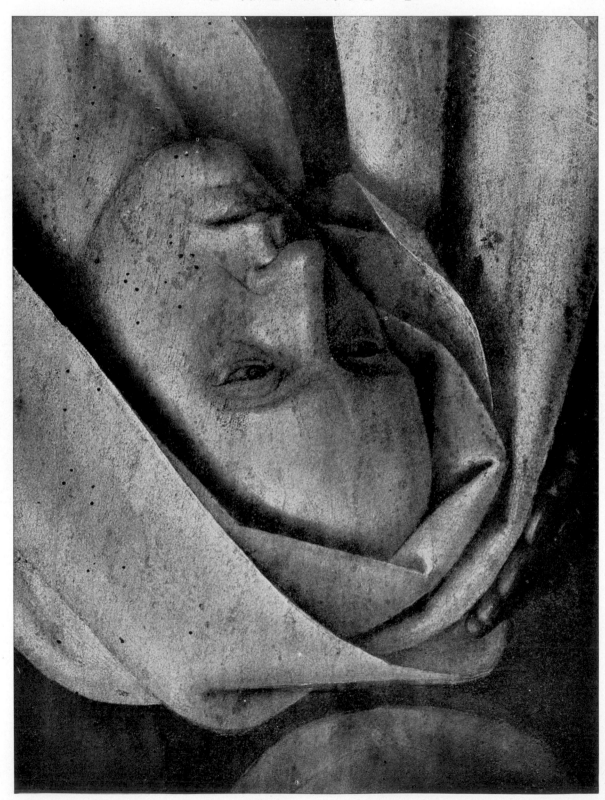

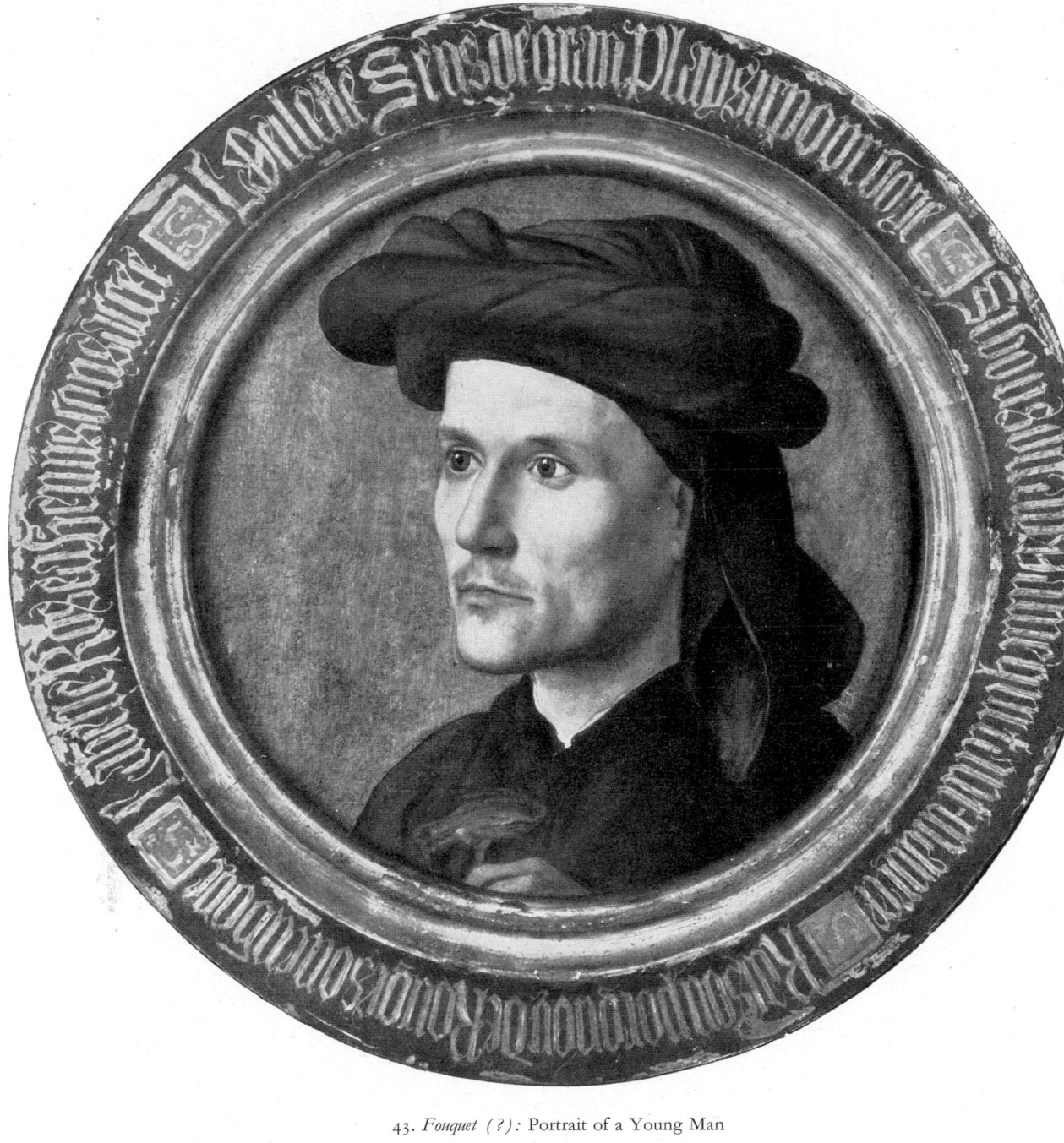

43. *Fouquet (?)*: Portrait of a Young Man

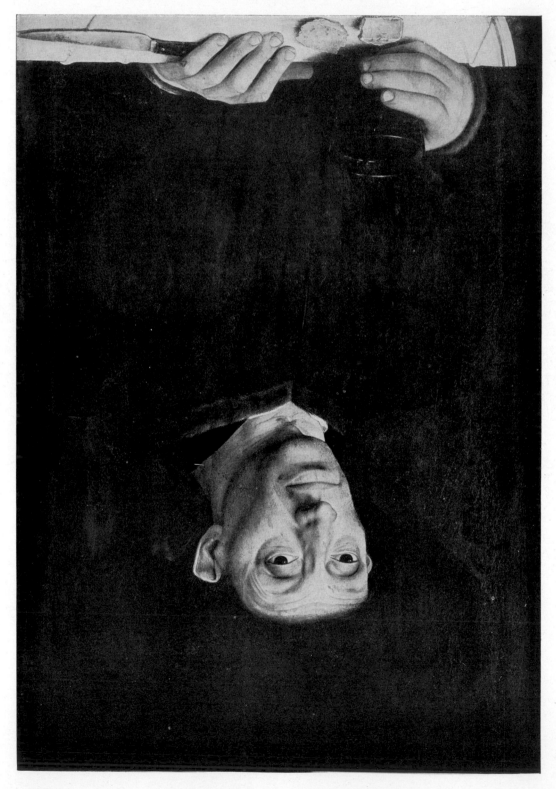

44. *Master of 1456:* Portrait of a Man with a Wine Glass

45. *Master of King René:* The Duke of Bourbon receiving the King-of-Arms of Brittany

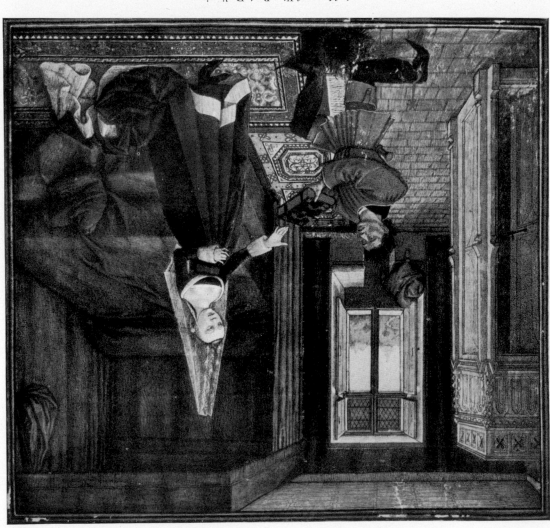

46. *Master of King René:* Dedication

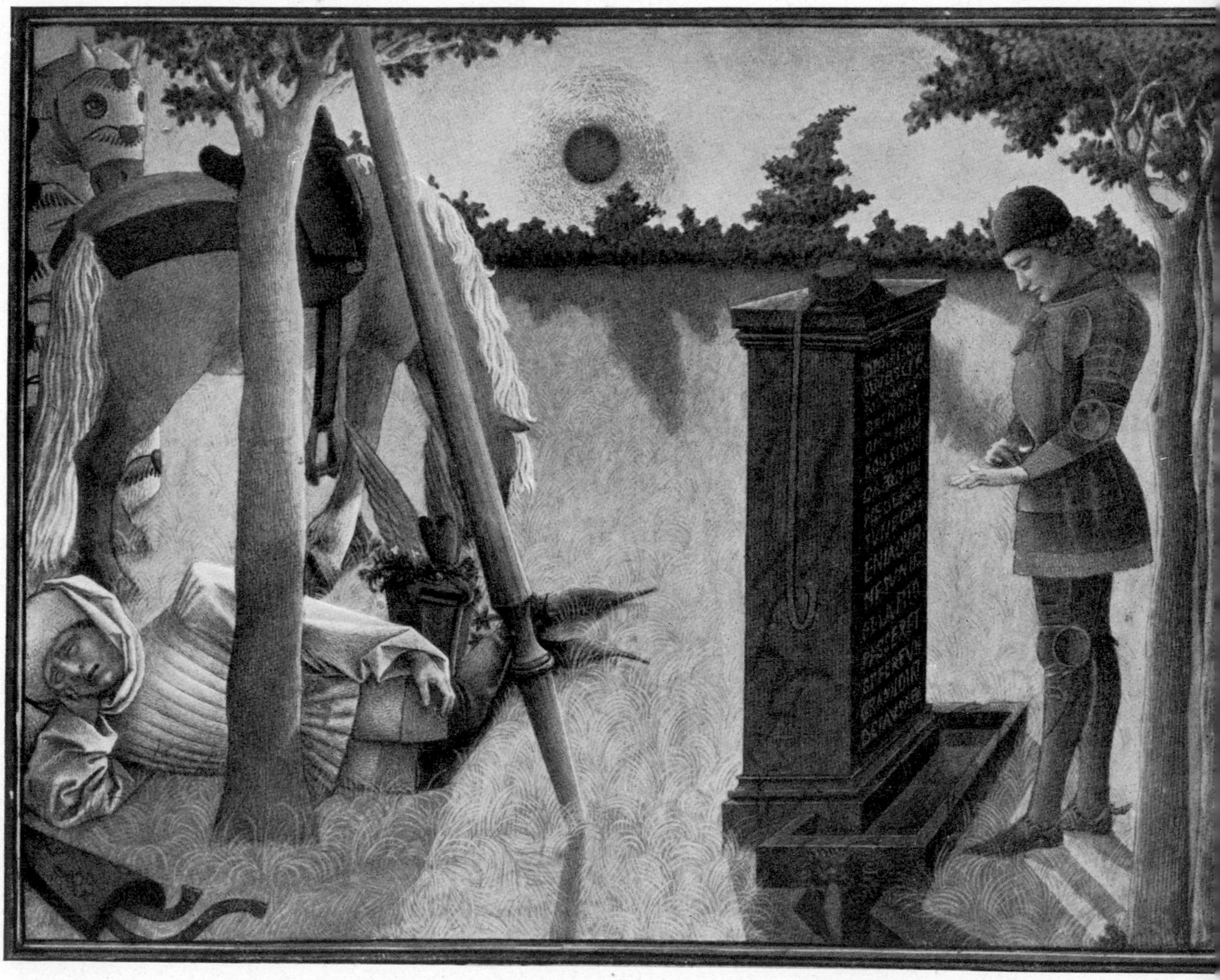

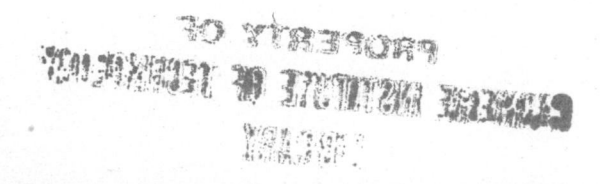

47. *Master of King René:* Cœur and Désir at the Magic Well

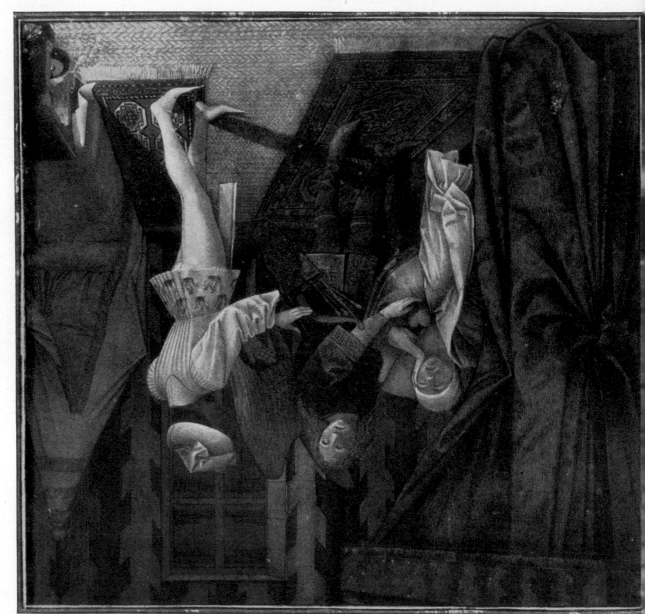

48. *Master of King René:* Love takes Possession of Cœur's Heart

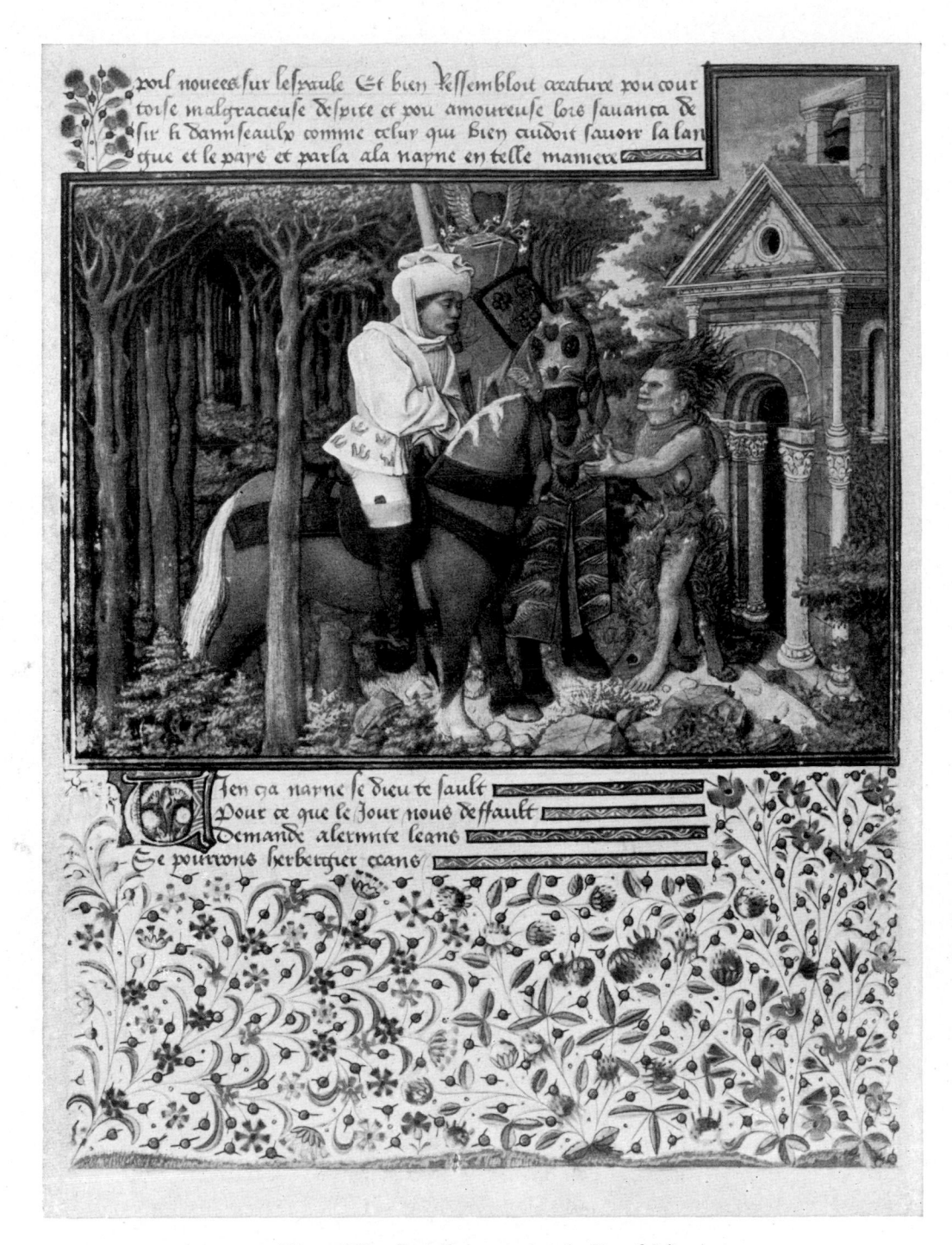

49. *Master of King René:* Cœur meeting the Dwarf Jalousie

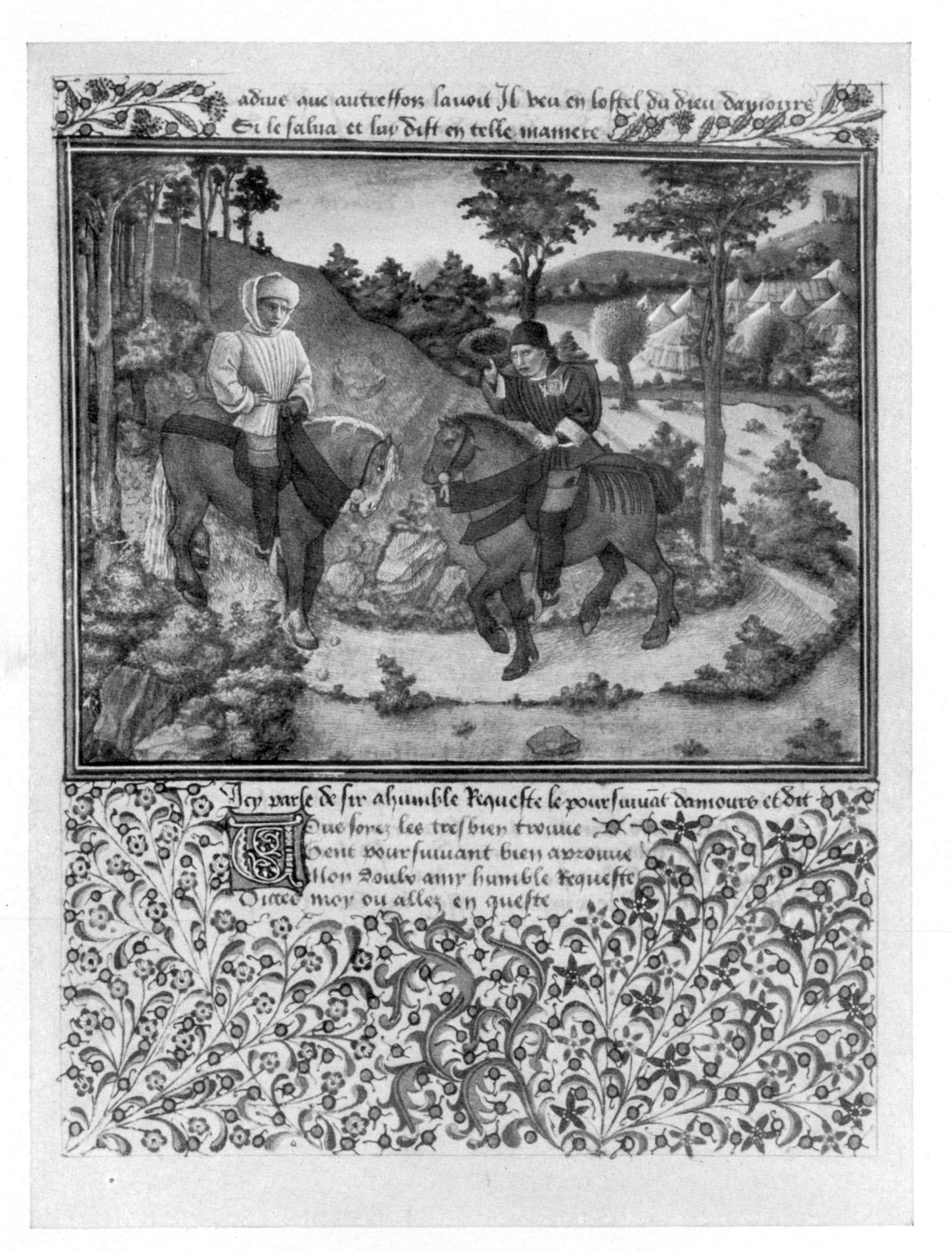

50. *Master of King René:* Désir meeting Humble Requête

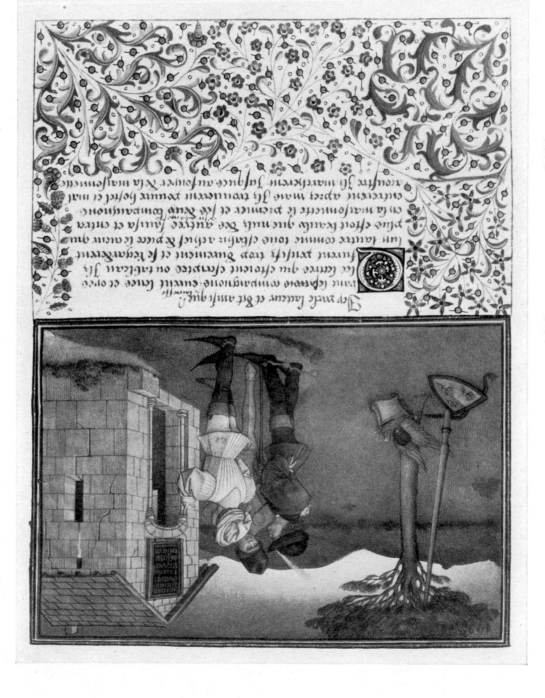

52. *Master of King René:* Arcitas and Palemon espying Emilia in her Garden

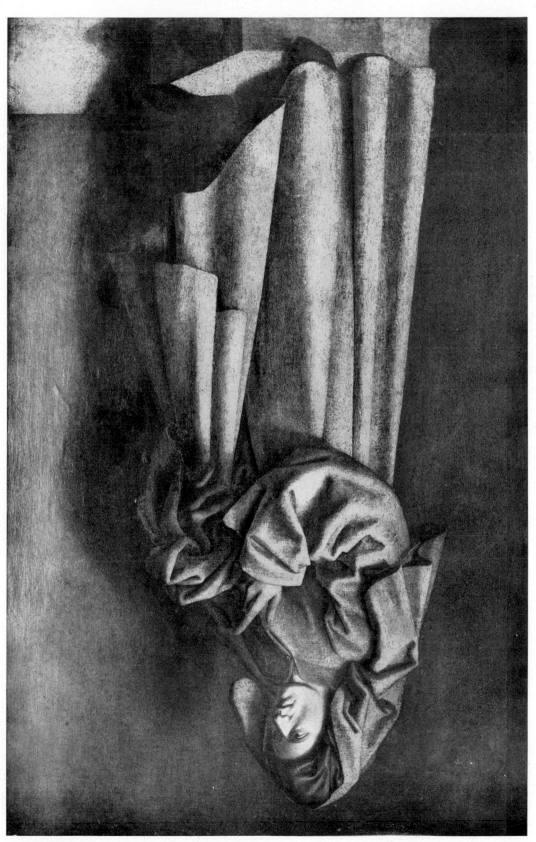

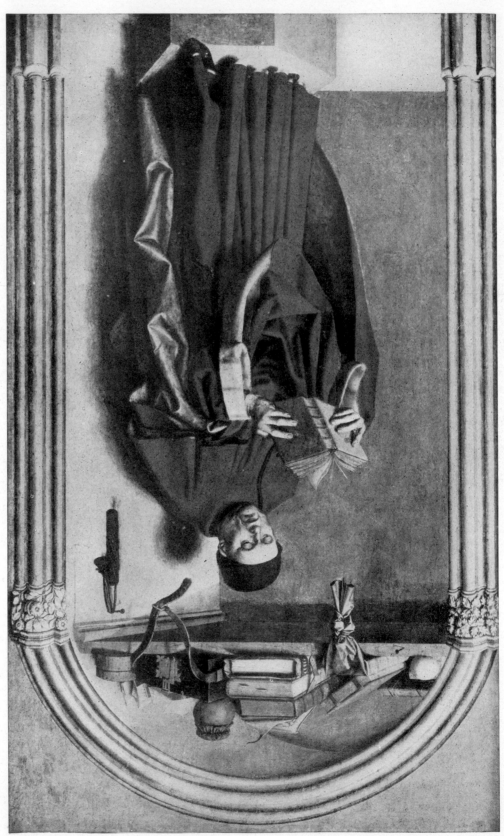

54. *Master of the Annunciation:* The Prophet Jeremiah

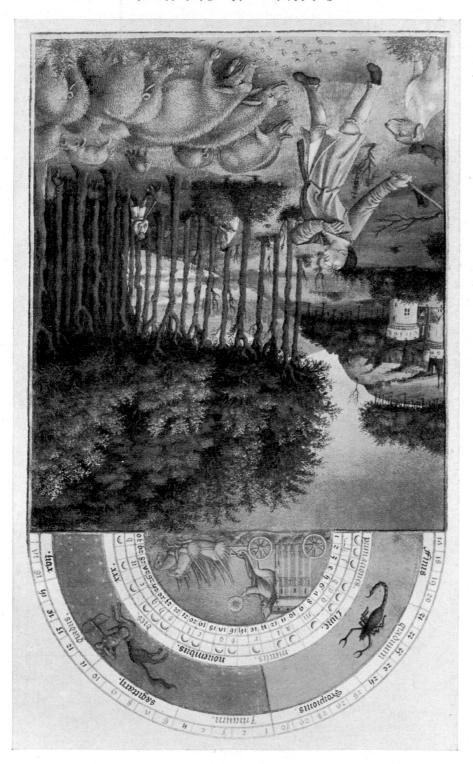

56. *Paul of Limbourg and Jean Colombe:* Procession of Supplicants against the Plague

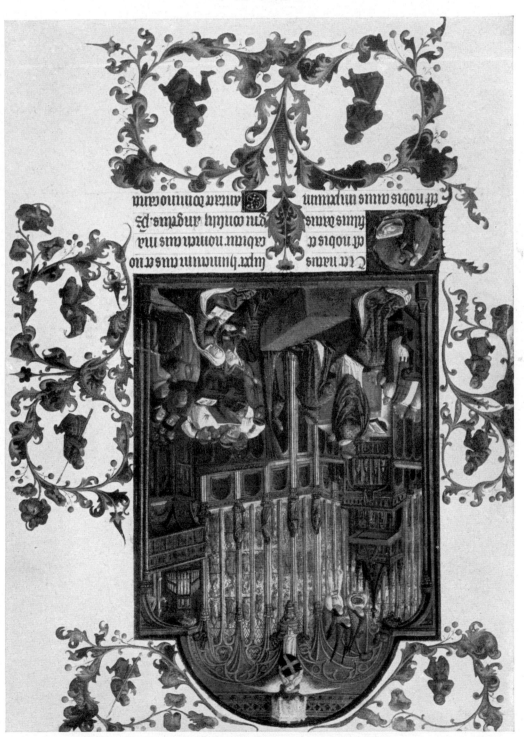

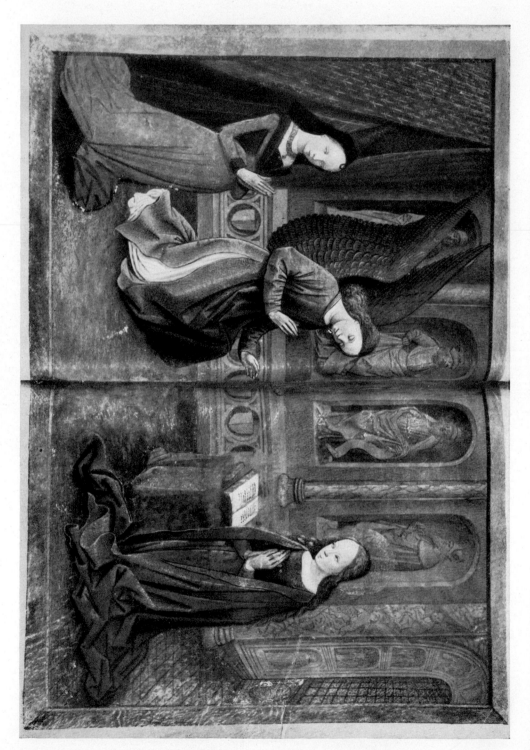

58. *Colombe:* The Annunciation

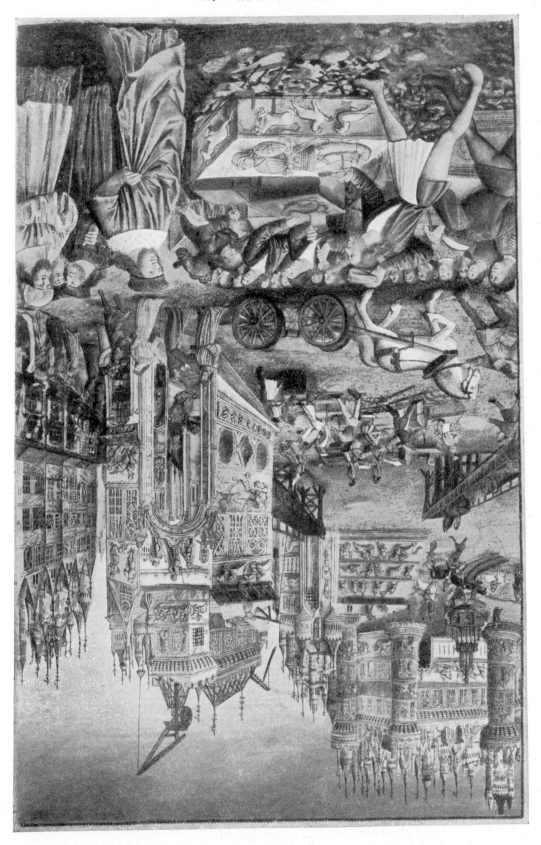

mcr.anisi que Sapion passoit
en auffrique deuers Sypsiar. a
vint par cas dauenture quen cestlu
propre temps estoit a seribal bout
te sore despaigne entre ou port auer
vu ness. et descendit primier en
terre. Et Sapion et lesine apres. et
sen asertit au roy. Auquel sem
bla chose de moust grant honneur
Que les duc. de deux tresprissans
peuples en cestlu temps estoient
arine en vng mesmes jour dema

dint paw et son amour. Le roy les
imuita tous deux a son palais. Et
comme ilz feussent soubz vng
toit. Le roy essaia de les amener
a prisement ensemble. afin que
la discorde qui estoit entreuls sap
paissast. Et Sapion lui respondit
quil nauoit point sume prince co
tre Aseribal. La quelle se peust finer
parlant auec lui. Et que de sa chose
publicque ne pouoit fair aultre
chose. sans le commandement du

60. *Colombe:* Masinissa receiving Scipio Africanus and Lelius

61. *Colombe:* St. Veronica

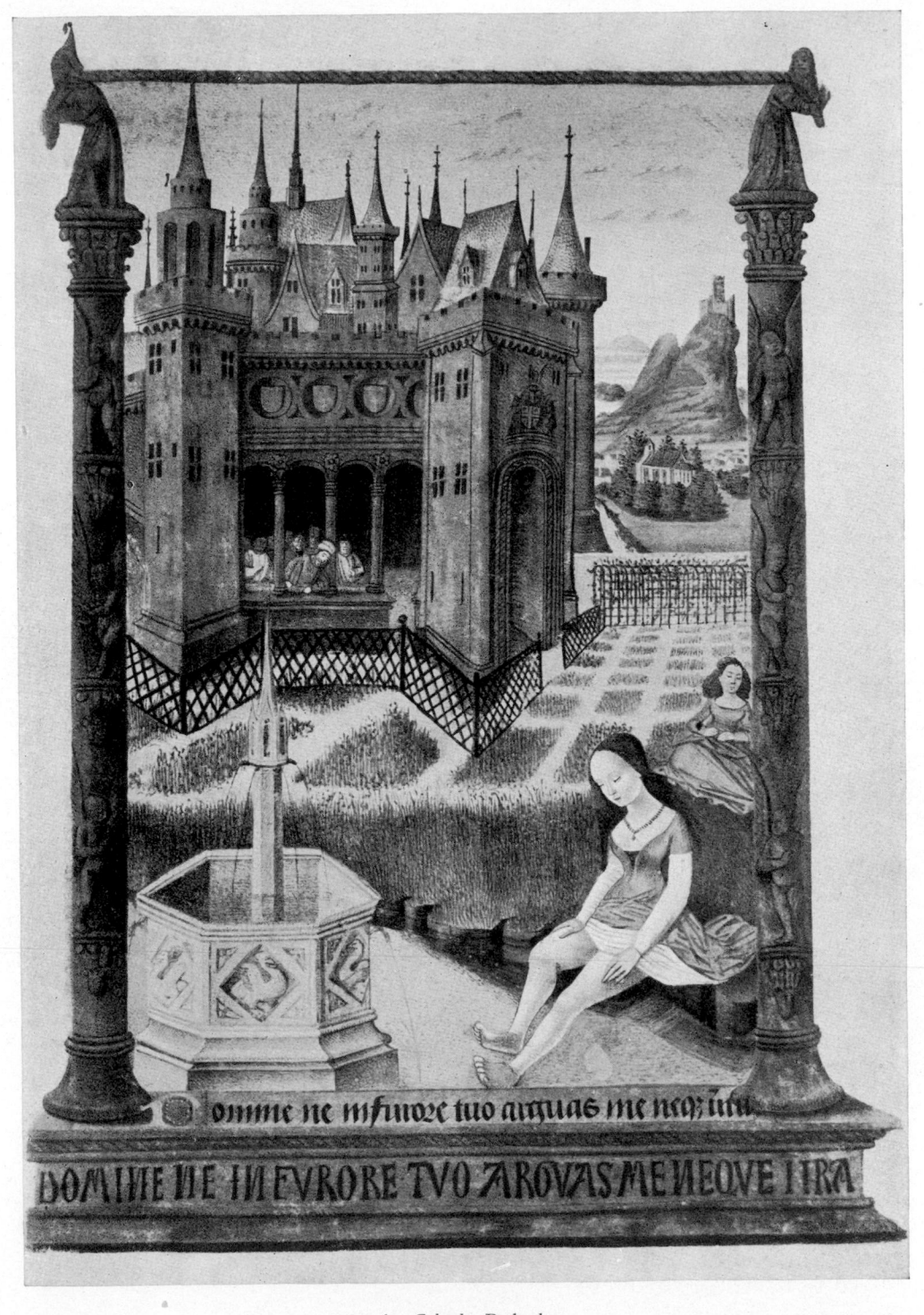

62. *Colombe:* Bathseba

Ey commence le liure Intitule de
Richesse. Et premierement comment
Richesse empesche souuent le sau
uement

Ostre sauueur ihu
rist en son euuan
gile ou vix chapre
de saint mathieu
Ie vous dy veablemt
que vng riches homs difficalement
ou a peines entrera ou royaume
des acilx. Et en cest mesmes cha
pitre dit il consequemment que
vng chameaux entrerent plus legie
rement ou passeroit par le trou

dune aguille que vng riche nentir
roit ou royaume du acl. Translat

Ces deux auctoritez icy ont bien
mestier de exposicion pource que
quant a la premeir il est bien a
noter que nre sauueur ne dit
mie que ce soit impossible dung
riche homme estre sauuez mais dist
que cest difficale. Car cest bien diffi
cale de posseder richesses et de trop esta
en lamour dicelles estriyez et detenuz
et non estir en lamour dicelles estri
et pource dist saint augustin en le
pistre quil escripsi ad paulinu. Les
choses terriennes sont plus amees

63. *School of Fouquet:* Banker in his Office

64. *Bourdichon:* Crucifixion – Centre panel of the Triptych of Loches

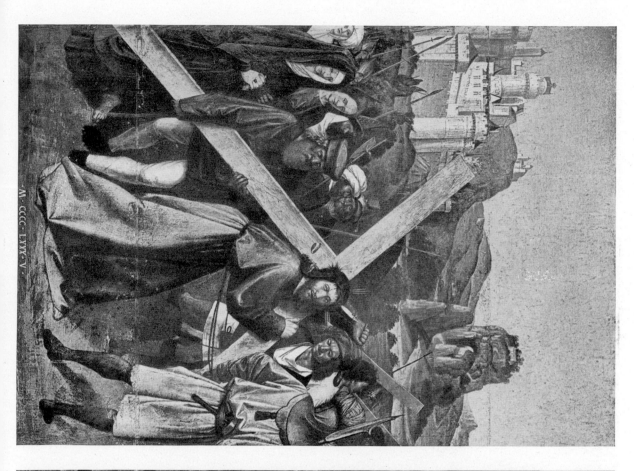

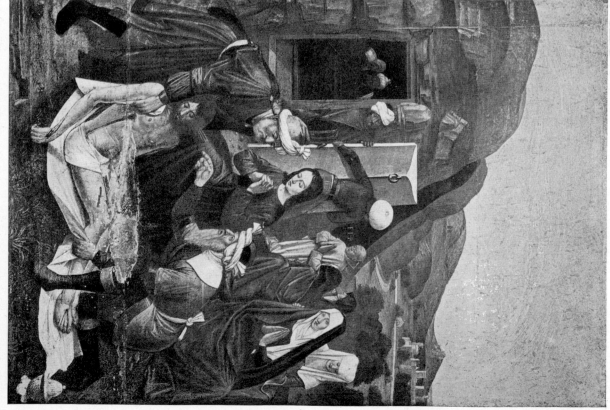

67. *Bourdichon*: Margaret de Rohan

68. *Bourdichon*: Crucifixion

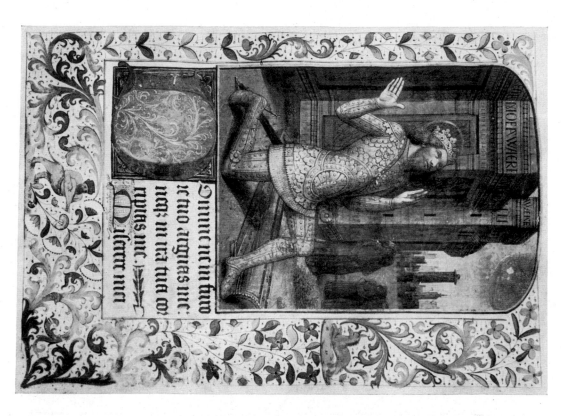

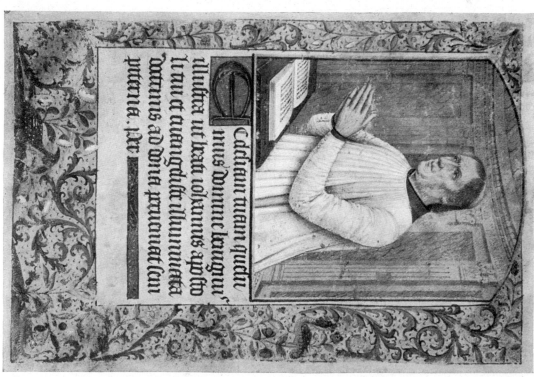

71. *Bourdichon*: Three Prophets

71. *Bourdichon*: Three Prophets

72. *Bourdichon*: Virgin and Child

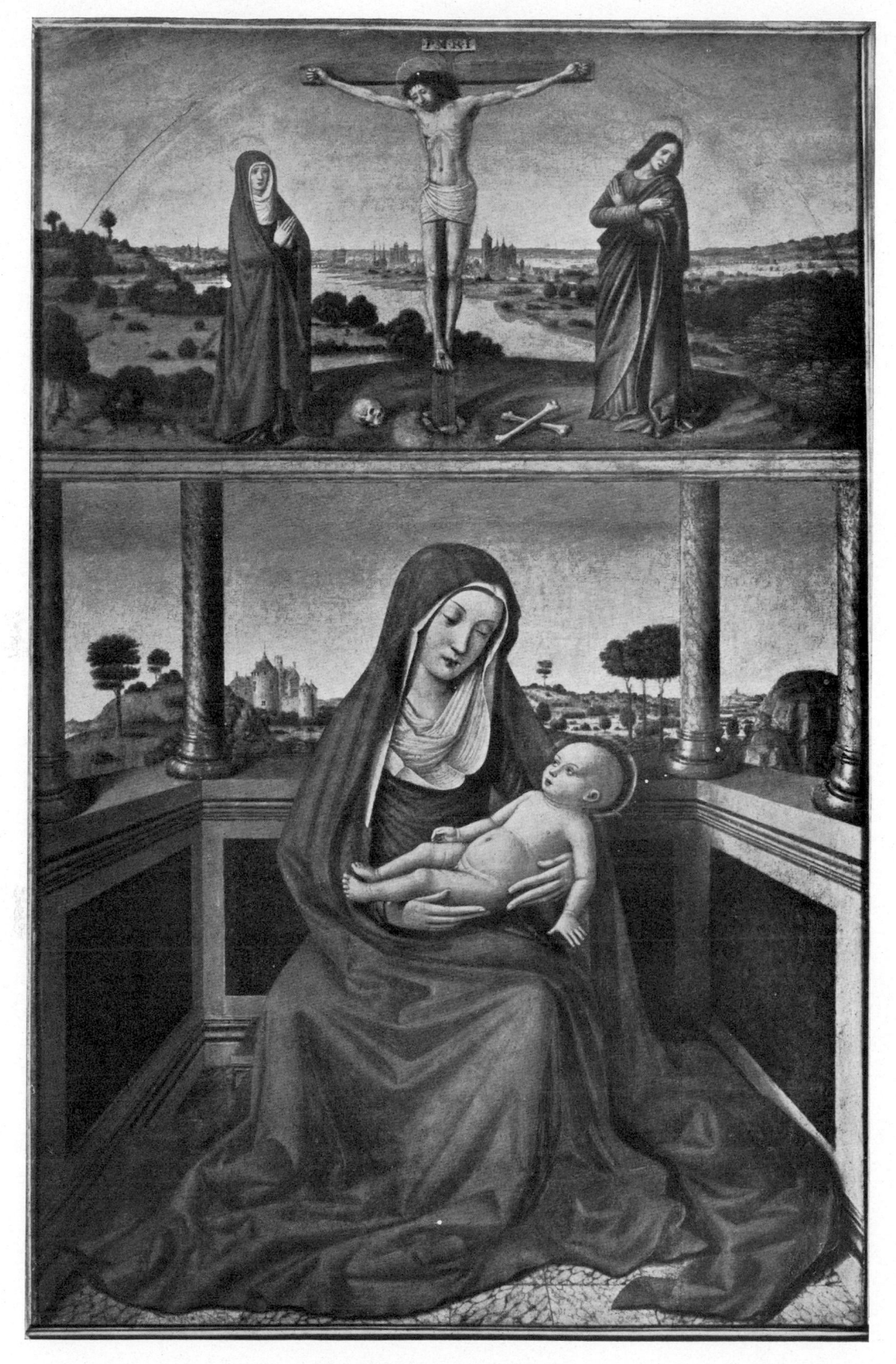

73. *Bourdichon:* Virgin and Child – Calvary

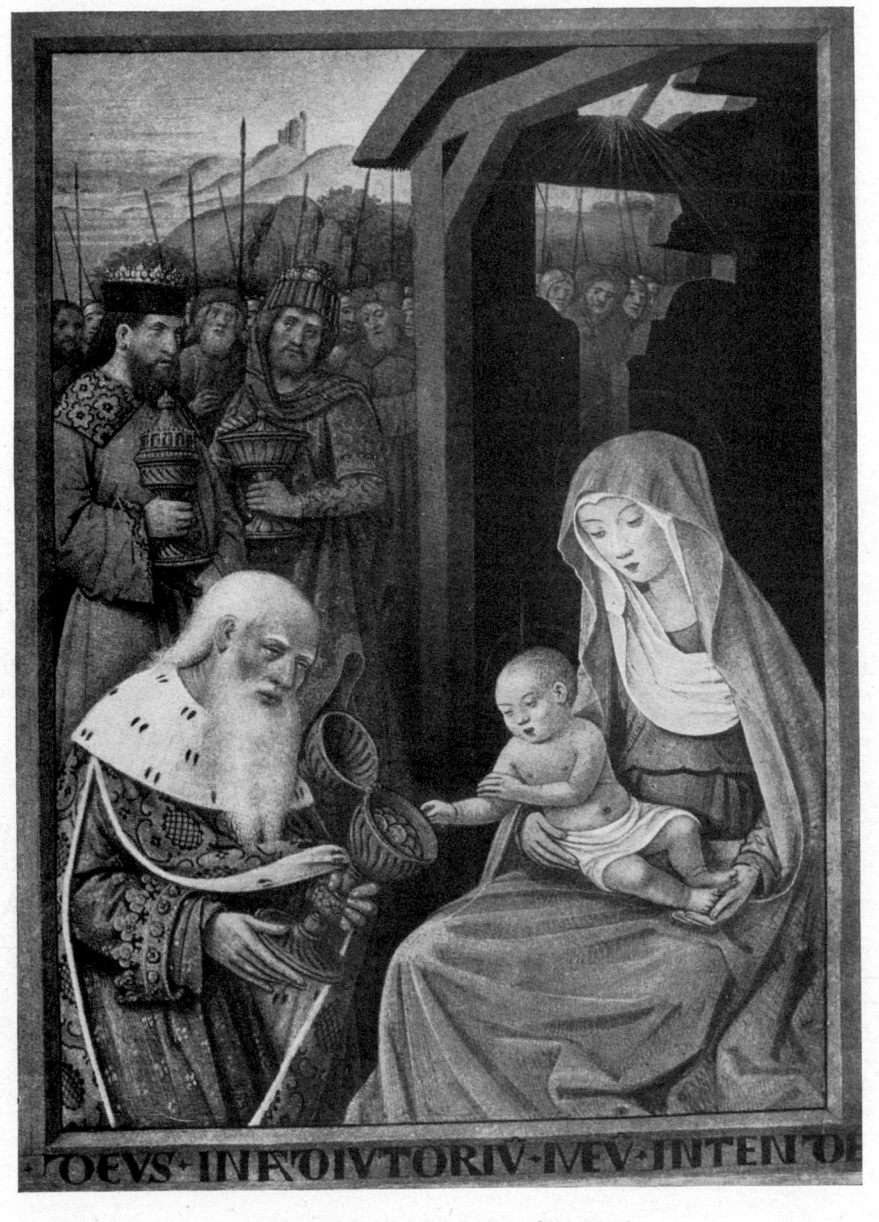

74. *Bourdichon:* The Adoration of the Magi

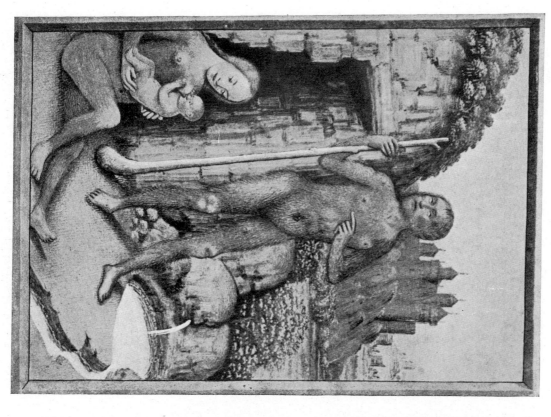

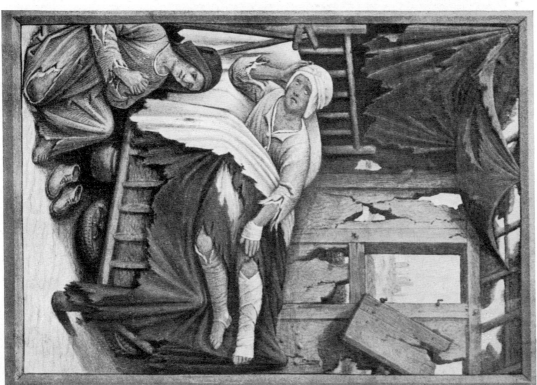

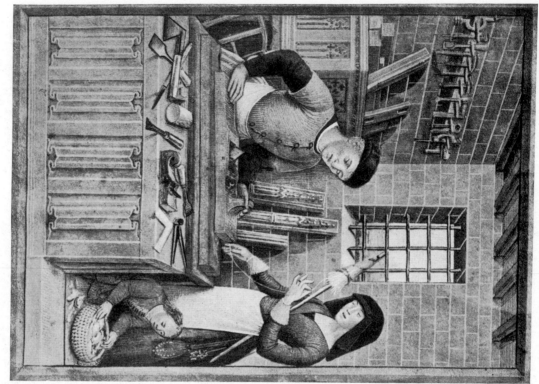

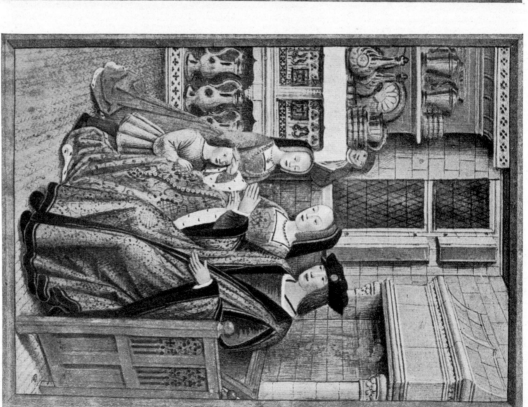

NOTES TO THE ILLUSTRATIONS

Illustrations in the text

Illustration I. St. Margaret, who according to the Golden Legend mastered and so tamed demons that they followed her like lambs, was, besides St. Catherine, Joan of Arc's favourite saint. Just at that time the French court had entered into negotiations with the Pope regarding the rehabilitation of Joan, the saviour of France. By representing St. Margaret, not in the usual fashion as a crowned saint with a dragon, but as a simple shepherdess who was met by the Roman knight Olybrius not far from the walls of the city, Fouquet gave at the same time a picture of the life of Joan of Arc, the country girl from Domrémy, as described for his contemporaries in the *Chronique de la Pucelle*.

Illustrations III and IV. These two miniatures originally spread over two pages, facing each other. This is evident from the frieze, the panelling, the pattern of the floor and the carpet, all of which continue over both pictures. The frieze of *putti*, which also appears on Plate 16, seems to originate from impressions which Fouquet received from works of Luca della Robbia in Florence or elsewhere. The juxtaposition of the entirely Renaissance background and the Gothic cathedral door, which in its turn ends in a Renaissance niche, is characteristic of the two sources from which Fouquet received his inspiration.

Illustration VI. The trial of the Duke of Alençon at Vendôme which began in 1458 was not only a political act directed against the person of the Duke but was designed to strike a blow at the feudal lords as a class. It was therefore staged with the greatest possible pomp in the presence of all the high dignitaries and ambassadors of other countries under the chairmanship of the chancellor Juvénal des Ursins. Duke Philippe of Burgundy, as First Peer of France, had as his representatives his King-of-Arms Jean Lefèvre and the counts Simon de Lalaing and Jean de Croy. In spite of his glorious record, his position as a Peer of France and his close connection with the house of Orléans, the Duke, whom the *Pucelle* had once called her *Beau duc*, was found guilty of treason and *lèse-majesté* and sentenced to many years of detention.

One detail in this representation is remarkable; the magnificent tapestries with the winged stags as standard-bearers, which form such a decorative background to the scene, come from the palace of Jacques Cœur at Bourges and are mentioned in the inventory which was prepared after his arrest and the confiscation of his property.

Illustration VIII. This portrait shows above all the suspicious, incalculable personality of Charles VII and, despite his dilatoriness, the often surprisingly sly intelligence with which he knew how to master people and situations. We receive the same impression from Pierre Sala's description of the meeting between the King and the false Joan of Arc, Jeanne des Armoises: In 1436, taking advantage of the widely spread superstition that Joan of Arc had been miraculously saved, an adventuress, a country girl from the region of Metz, who must have had a certain likeness to the real Joan of Arc, pretended to be the *Pucelle*, found supporters among the knights and finally managed to gain admission to the King's presence. As before, when the real Joan was first admitted to the court, the King held himself in the background and put a richly

97

clad courtier in his own place. Friends had given her a description of the King beforehand and she made straight for him. Charles VII greeted her with the words: *"Pucelle ma mie, soyez la très bien venue, au nom de dieu, qui connait le secret qui est entre vous et moi."* As she knew nothing of this secret, she fell on her knees, confessed and asked for mercy.

Illustration IX. A recent cleaning has removed the hat of the man which was a later addition. For the position of the hands in this picture and in the one in the Louvre (Plate 44) compare the Portrait of a Man by Jan van Eyck at Cibiu, Brukenthalisches Museum.

Illustration X. The manuscript of Jacopo Marcello which he sent to the seneschal of King René, Giovanni Cossa, contains four miniatures in all: A portrait of Marcello in profile, a convention of the Order *du Croissant* (of the waxing moon), a statue of St. Maurice, the patron saint of this order, and a view of part of the ducal palace in Venice, which is carried on the back of an elephant. I have come to ascribe these miniatures to Giorgio Schiavone, a native of Dalmatia and a pupil of Squarcione, by reason of the identity of style of the Marcello portrait and the only signed miniature portrait of this artist in the Jacquemart-André collection in Paris. As Schiavone's presence in Squarcione's workshop cannot be proved before 1456 it must be one of his earlier works.

Marcello distinguished himself as military leader of the Venetians, particularly in the war against Milan, and King René made him his first general in his war against the Aragonese. He died in 1484 at Gallipoli. His portrait had also been painted by Bellini and had been seen by Marcantonio Michiel in the Marcello collection as late as 1525. (Cf. Jacopo Morelli, *Notizia d'opere di disegno*, Bologna 1884, p. 170.)

Illustration XIII. The antiquated character of the Master of King René, inspite of all progress in detail as compared with Fouquet, is revealed in this representation by the proportions of figures and buildings which are also seen again in the plates 49–51. Here we still find the remains of a conception of space, already surpassed by Fouquet, which is derived more from imagination than from observation; the figures, therefore, are depicted too large.

Illustration XIV. The scene represents *l'Ame dévote* in a ramshackle house with two female figures which personify Repentance and Contrition. The miniatures of the Berlin manuscript are stylistically closer to the René Master and the miniatures in the manuscript of Metz (also probably carried out by him) than are the complicated similar pictures in the manuscript of the Morgan Library (MS 705) and Chantilly (Ms. 1477).

Illustration XVI. In the dedicatory miniature which Jean Colombe painted for Charlotte of Savoy in the *Livre des douze Perilz d'enfer*, Louis XI is also depicted, much younger, but on the whole very like this picture, which it also resembles in conception and technique. It would therefore be possible to ascribe this picture to Colombe, whose work often shows a strong resemblance to Bourdichon's. On the other hand, panel paintings by Bourdichon only are known and none by Colombe and records tell us that the former painted a portrait of the King. I would therefore maintain for the time being, as I have done before (Pantheon, XXI, 1938, p. 5), that Bourdichon is the author of this picture, in spite of Charles Sterling's opinion to the contrary *(La Peinture française*, Paris 1938, p. 138*)* and in spite of a certain harshness of technique.

Plate 2. Perspective views of the whole interior of Gothic cathedrals were especially popular in Flanders since the time of Jan van Eyck. They are not only to be found in his book of hours for Duc Jean de Berry (Milan, Principe Trivulzio coll. Cf. notes to plate 22) and in the Madonna in a Church (Berlin, Kaiser-Friedrich-Museum), but also in Rogier van der Weyden's Altar of the Sacraments in the Museum at Antwerp, painted for Jean Chevrot, and in the Presentation of Christ by an unknown French-Burgundian master in the Louvre. This is one of the clearest indications that Fouquet had been in contact with Burgundian and Flemish art, most probably during his time at Paris.

Plate 4. The idea of the colonnade and the view of a landscape can with some certainty be traced to a Florentine source, where it is to be seen, among other instances, in Fra Angelico's Annunciations in the monastery of San Marco at Florence, in the Church of Jesus at Cortona and in the Prado Museum, and also in an early Annunciation by Alessio Baldovinetti at Borgo San Lorenzo di Mugello, as well as in an Annunciation by Domenico Veneziano, now in the Fitzwilliam Museum at Cambridge. (Cf. Ruth Wedgwood Kennedy, *An early Annunciation by Alessio Baldovinetti*. In: Art in America, XXVIII, 1940, p. 139.)

Plate 6. The Death of the Virgin is rarely depicted in this form and similar representations are known only from Italian paintings, as for example one by the *Maestro dal Bambino Vispo* (Chicago, Art Institute) or one of Bartolomeo Vivarini (formerly London, Charles Butler coll.).

Plate 14. The background of this scene shows an evidently accurate view of the Ile de la Cité at Paris, with Notre-Dame, the Sainte-Chapelle, the old tower of the Archevêché and the Petit Pont, as seen from the left bank of the Seine at about the point where today the Rue Dauphine ends and the Pont-Neuf begins. The miniature, though partly damaged by the passage of time, shows Fouquet's great skill as a painter of landscape, thus making the loss of the calendar all the more to be deplored. Within the series of miniatures this picture forms a kind of pendant to the Ascension of the Holy Ghost (plate 15), since it shows the same scheme of composition with the same group of figures in the foreground. On the front and back of the page appear the initials of Etienne Chevalier. The miniature was only recently discovered, together with that reproduced on plate 22, when it came up for auction in December 1946 at Sotheby's, in London; it was in the possession of Louis Fenoulhet, a descendant of an old *émigré* family of Huguenots.

Plate 16. The Spring of the Apostles unites two motives which are usually treated separately; the Sending forth of the Apostles and the Fountain of Life as it is best known from the Ghent Altar and from Jan van Eyck's Fountain of Life in the Prado Museum. (Cf. Evelyn Underhill, *The Fountain of Life*. In: The Burlington Magazine, XVII, 1910, p. 99.) The Spring of the Apostles is therefore a symbolic representation of the radiating power of Christianity, the only life-giving source of earthly existence.

In this picture, as in illustrations III and IV, the mixture of Gothic and Renaissance elements is worth noticing. Similar Renaissance backgrounds are to be found in Fra Angelico's fresco of the Virgin with Saints in the monastery of San Marco at Florence and the fresco of St. Lawrence before the Emperor in the Vatican.

Plate 17. The prominent, iconographically interesting figure of the man breaking the rod in the foreground is taken from Italian Renaissance art where—from Orcagna's relief in Or San Michele at Florence to Raphael's Sposalizio (Milan, Brera)—he is as familiar as he is alien to Northern art. His origin is in a legend, invented by the apocryphal commentators of the gospel, and based on a custom of Roman legal practice.

Plate 19. The inspiration for this magnificent miniature of Fouquet may be traced to the *Vigiles des Morts* or *Neuf leçons de Job* in which Pierre de Nesson gave a free version of the biblical story of Job, probably written about 1424 as a kind of book of consolation for his lord Duke Jean de Bourbon, who died a prisoner of the English. The poem contained one of the many reflections on the transitory glory of earthly things, so popular at that time: "*Car, quant je seré en terre | Je seré povre pourriture | De tenebreuse terre, obscure | Pour dedans pourrir en serre.*" Before Fouquet, another miniature painter from the workshop of Haincelin had painted the scene of Job on the Dungheap in another copy of this poem (Bibliothèque Nationale, Ms. fr. 578), and there also exists a miniature of that subject, by the Master of the *Roman de la Rose*, in a manuscript of poems by Nesson, Chartier and others which is kept in the Kupferstichkabinett at Berlin (Ms. 78 C 7).

The three monumental figures of Job's friends, as well as some figures in the Funeral Procession (plate 18) remind one of the *Pleurants* which were being executed at that time, 1450–53, by Paul Mosselmann and Etienne Bobillet for the tomb of the Duc de Berry at Bourges. The tower in the background is part of the Castle at Vincennes.

Plate 22. The scene is the interior of Notre-Dame in Paris, and Fouquet here obviously follows the example of Jan van Eyck, who was the first to represent a perspective interior of a Gothic cathedral, in an exactly similar way in the Requiem of the Breviary for the Duc de Berry (Principe Trivulzio coll., Milan. Cf. notes to plate 2). The miniature is seriously damaged and the colour has peeled off in spots in many places. The text on the reverse side (previously obverse, with the page number fol. 185) contains a petition to St. Hilarius of Poitiers, as well as the beginning of the "*Anthene de saint vrain.*" The page belongs, as do the miniatures in plates 22-27 to a part of the *Memoriae of the Saints*.

Plate 25. According to the legend, St. Martin had helped King Chlodwig of the Franks to conquer King Alaric of the Goths. When Charles VII had moved to Bourges and Tours and France had been liberated, the Church of Saint-Martin was dedicated to him and he was specially worshipped there. It is therefore not surprising that the king himself is here painted as St. Martin. In 1430 Charles VII ordered a new and precious reliquary for his remains which took the goldsmith Jehan Lambert ten years to make and for which he received the sum of 300 *écus*. It was taken to the church in procession in 1454, in the presence of the Chancellor Juvénal des Ursins and probably also of Fouquet. In 1453 the gate of Saint-Martin was built close to the church and can be seen on the left side of this miniature. Shortly before, the main streets of Tours had been paved with stones, and this at that time still uncommon feature is also depicted in Fouquet's obviously naturalistic picture.

Plate 27. The masterly use of the triangle in the construction of this picture is worth noticing. It is formed by the fallen horse of Paul lying on the ground, the horsemen left and right, who serve as cornerposts and at the same time give the direction of the perspective towards the vanishing point, and the Holy Trinity forming its apex. The wild men at the base of the picture

are perhaps more than mere ornaments, in so far as they indicate that St. Paul was a heathen before his conversion.

Plates 34 and 35. Before 1440 Eustache Mercadé of Corbie wrote the *Mystère de la Vengeance* which in the late 15th century inspired, among other things, a series of designs for tapestries, preserved at the Museum at Reims. In it, with the love for symbolic comparisons peculiar to the Middle Ages, he told of the misfortunes of Pilate and the Jewish people when their country was destroyed by Vespasian. The stories of Flavius Josephus and Fouquet's illustrations were therefore not only of historic interest but were also enjoyed for their religious significance as counterpart to the Passion of Christ.

Plate 37. In the Kupferstichkabinett at Berlin is a manuscript of J. Mielot's *Romuléon* (Ms. 78 D 10) illustrated with many pen and wash drawings in which a successor of Fouquet about 1470–80 repeated in broad lines Caesar's crossing of the Rubicon. The trumpet-blower, whose antique figure may have been inspired by a Roman statue or bas-relief which Fouquet had seen in Italy, was carefully copied. The female figure on the other side of the river, the symbol of the city of Rome, appeared, according to the legend, to predict the success of Caesar's venture.

Plate 38. To prove the theory that this Madonna with the bared breast was a portrait of Agnes Sorel, mistress of Charles VII, we have mentioned, among other examples, the pictures of royal mistresses from the 16th century as preserved in the Cook collection at Richmond, the Museum at Dijon and the Sabina Poppaea of the Musée d'Art et d'Histoire at Geneva. According to Corio, a small book was found on the battlefield of Fornovo in which the numerous mistresses of a French knight were painted in a similar fashion *al naturale* and L'Estoile records in his diary of 1610 that Monsieur and Madame de Sully had had their portraits painted in the nude as Adam and Eve. Brantôme reports similar instances from the time of Henri III and the custom may well have originated with Charles VII who was also the first to establish the practice of a recognized royal mistress. The use of the figures of saints for profane representations was current in the 15th century and there is much to be said in favour of Huizinga's opinion that this was one of the signs of decadence of the dying Middle Ages.

Plates 39 and 40. Guillaume Juvénal des Ursins, Baron de Trainel, was the younger brother of the more remarkable Jean Juvénal, Archbishop of Reims, author of the *Histoire de Charles VI* and of a number of important *Rémontrances*. He was born on the 15th of March, 1400. His father was head of the merchants' guild of Paris, and, especially in the last years of the reign of Charles VI, a man of great political importance. Brought up to become a civil servant, Guillaume Juvénal was made a royal councillor at the early age of twenty-three, was knighted in 1429 at the *Sacre* at Reims, became *lieutenant* of the Dauphiné, *bailli* of Sens and finally, in 1445, chancellor with the help of his brother. The latter office he held until the death of Charles VII. When Louis XI ascended the throne he was deprived of his office and even imprisoned for a time; in 1465, however, he was recalled to his old post of chancellor and held it until his death in 1472. To compete successfully with the ancient nobility, the commoner Juvénal des Ursins had adopted the coat of arms with the bear of the Roman Orsinis, after Jean Juvénal himself during his mission to Italy in 1448 had obtained the authority to do so from the Orsini family and the Pope.

Plate 43. The old inscription round this picture reads: "*Si vous diray Dame qui tant mayree | Raison pourquoy de Rouge son envoyr | La belle Rose a Venus consacree | L'œilette Sens de gran Playsir pour voir.*"

Besides this legend the initial S is repeated four times in the frame. The turban which the man is wearing in his portrait was fashionable in this form from about 1440 to 1470, that is in Fouquet's time.

Plate 45. King René's book on tournaments is entitled *Traictié de la forme et devis comme on fait les tournois* and is dedicated to Charles VII. It does not describe a tournament which had actually taken place but an ideal one, combining the most outstanding customs of chivalry in France, the Netherlands and on the Rhine from the 14th century onwards. René's fictitious story relates that the Duke of Brittany challenged the Duke of Bourbon, by sending his King-at-Arms to him. In this, the third illustration of the Paris manuscript, the King-at-Arms presents the coats of arms of eight candidates for election from among the knights of Brittany.

Among the pictures which are executed in pen and ink, watercolour and gouache, is one depicting the accident which caused the madness of Charles VI. At a tournament the King had disguised himself as one of the wild men and his clothes caught fire during the torchdance. Various views of streets and of the tilting place, drawn in strict perspective, are worth noticing in this, probably the earliest, manuscript of the Master of King René.

Plate 46. The manuscript of the *Theseïde*, according to the calligrapher's note, was dedicated in 1468 by King René to "*Jehanne fille et sœur des Roys de France*," the daughter of Charles VII, and she is therefore portrayed in the dedicatory miniature.

Plate 53. The upper part of the Isaiah panel—the left wing of the Altar of the Annunciation of Saint-Sauveur at Aix—not shown on this plate—is in the Rijksmuseum at Amsterdam. It shows, like the corresponding panel of Jeremiah (Plate 54), a shelf with books above the figure. The central panel alone remained in its home at Aix-en-Provence but was transferred from its original position above the tomb of the Corpici family in Saint-Sauveur to the Eglise de la Madeleine. Besides this altar-piece, only one other picture in the Cleveland Museum of Art at Cleveland (U.S.A.) has so far been ascribed to the same master. It is the portrait of an old man, perhaps also the head of a prophet *(Mélanges Hulin de Loo, 1931, p. 123, and illustration)* and Louis Demonts *(Revue de l'Art ancien et moderne, 1923, I, p. 257–80)* again pointed to a connection between this altar-piece and the St. Jerome of 1436 in the Museum at Naples, whose author is held to be Colantonio del Fiore, an otherwise unknown Neapolitan painter.

Plate 58. The Annunciation scene is carried out on three whole pages of the manuscript preserved in the Morgan Library. The Annunciation in the Garden, which is represented in the Annunciation of the book of hours for Louis de Laval as an episode in the background, appears in this manuscript as a separate third page.

As always in Colombe's work, the portrait figure in the foreground is not endowed with any individual features, and the manuscript itself provides no particular evidence for assuming that it was, in fact, carried out for Anne de Beaujeu. The extremely rich illustrations of this prayer-book—107 full-page pictures—and the costume of those represented would in any case lead one to believe that it was made for a personage of ducal rank. (Compare also ill. XV.)

Plate 60. Charles de Gaucourt (d. 1482), who commissioned this manuscript, was *lieutenant général pour le roi* of Paris at the time when Comte de Saint-Pol was executed there in 1475, and several well-known manuscripts were formerly in his library, notably the *Cité de Dieu* of St. Augustin in two volumes, illustrated in 1473 by the so-called Maître François (Paris, Bibliothèque

Nationale, Ms. fr. 18/19). The old Palais Royal in the Cité of Paris, of which the Sainte-Chapelle (seen on the right) is preserved unaltered, stood on the site of the present Palais de Justice.

Plate 61. The head of Jesus on Veronica's napkin, and a second very similar head in the same prayerbook of Louis de Laval, is nearly identical with the one in the prayerbook of Dame de Baudricourt (formerly P. Durrieu coll.) ascribed to Fouquet. Other miniatures by Colombe, as for example the *Trois morts et trois vifs* in the *Très riches Heures* of the Duc de Berry, also show considerable likeness to those of that prayerbook. If the miniatures in the prayerbook of Dame de Baudricourt are really by Fouquet and not by Colombe, they prove again his direct influence on the latter.

Plate 62. A different picture of Bathsheba is in the prayerbook of Jacques Cœur, folio 80, and in that of Anne de Beaujeu, today in the Pierpont Morgan Library, New York.

Plate 71. Judging from the motto of the coat of arms, *Bien ay cause*, François de Vendôme (d. 1495), Knight of the Order of St. Michael, was the first owner of this manuscript. Besides the twelve small pictures of the months, it contains thirteen large and six smaller miniatures. The prophets in this illustration belong to the Annunciation depicted on the opposite page of the manuscript.

Plate 73. The elaborate arrangement of the architectural construction shown in this altarpiece seems to have been typical of Bourdichon's compositions at that time, as he received payment in 1490 for another panel of the Virgin: "*Notre Dame mise en ung tableau avec trois rois, la lune sous ses pieds et un tabernacle par dessus. Au bas dudit tableau trois paiges qui tiennent trois chevaux et au plus bas trois histoires.*"

LIST OF ILLUSTRATIONS

Illustrations in the Text

Frontispiece. *Fouquet:* Self-portrait. Enamelled medallion. Diameter 3 in. Paris, Musée du Louvre, No. 465.—See text p. 52.

I. *Fouquet:* St. Margaret. Miniature from the *Livre d'Heures d'Etienne Chevalier.* 3½ × 4¾ in. Paris, Musée du Louvre.—See text p. 36 and 97.

II. *Colombe:* Jacques Cœur. Miniature from the so-called *Prayerbook of Jacques Cœur.* Munich, Bayrische Staatsbibliothek, Cod. lat. 10103.—See text p. 75.

III and IV. *Fouquet:* Etienne Chevalier and his Patron St. Stephen.—The Madonna. Miniatures from the *Livre d'Heures d'Etienne Chevalier.* 6½ × 4¾ in. Chantilly, Musée Condé.—See text p. 36 and 97.

V. *Fouquet:* Etienne Chevalier and his Patron St. Stephen. Left wing of the Diptych of Melun. Panel-painting. 36¼ × 33 in. Berlin, Deutsches Museum, No. 1617.—See text p. 48.

VI. *Fouquet:* The Trial at Vendôme in 1458. Title miniature of the Munich *Boccaccio.* 13⅜ × 11 in. Munich, Bayrische Staatsbibliothek, Cod. Gall. 369.—See text p. 43 and 97.

VII. *Fouquet:* Gontran giving his Kingdom to his Nephew Childebert. Miniature from the *Grandes Chroniques des Rois de France.* 3⅞ × 4⅛ in. Paris, Bibliothèque Nationale, Ms. fr. 6465.—See text p. 43.

VIII. *Fouquet:* Portrait of Charles VII. Panel-painting. 33½ × 28¼ in. Paris, Musée du Louvre, No. 289.—See text p. 51 and 97.

IX. *Master of 1456:* Portrait of a Young Man. Panel-painting. 18⅛ × 15¼ in. At present Vaduz, Galerie Liechtenstein.—See text p. 55 and 98.

X. *Giorgio Schiavone:* The Venetian Senator Jacopo Antonio Marcello. Miniature from a Latin manuscript of the Passion of St. Maurice by Marcello. 7⅞ × 5¼ in. Paris, Bibliothèque de l'Arsenal, Ms. 940.—See text p. 56, 64 and 98.

XI. *Unknown Master: Le Roi mort.* Miniature from the *Prayerbook of Duke René of Anjou.* London, British Museum, Ms. Egerton 1070.—See text p. 60.

XII. *Master of King René:* Cœur boarding the Ship. Miniature from the *Livre du cuer d'amours espris* by King René of Anjou. 11⅜ × 8⅛ in. Vienna, Nationalbibliothek, Cod. 2597.—See text p. 63.

XIII. *Master of King René:* The Liberation of Arcitas and Palemon. Miniature from the *Theseïde* of King René of Anjou. 10¼ × 7⅞ in. Vienna, Nationalbibliothek, Cod. 2617.—See text p. 67 and 98.

XIV. *Master of King René: Ame dévote.* Miniature from a *Mortifiement.* 4⅛ × 4⅛ in. Berlin, Staatliches Kupferstichkabinett, Ms. 78 C 5.—See text p. 67 and 98.

XV. *Colombe:* Adam and Eve. Miniature from the *Prayerbook of Anne de Beaujeu.* 5¼ × 3⅝ in. New York, Pierpont Morgan Library, MS 677, fol. 47 v.—See text p. 78.

XVI. *Bourdichon:* Portrait of Louis XI. Panel. 8⅝ × 5⅞ in. Formerly Paris, de Ganay coll.—See text p. 80 and 98.

1–27. *Fouquet:* 1. The Birth of St. John the Baptist. 2. The Annunciation. 3. The Nativity. 4. The Visitation. 5. The Annunciation. 6. The Death of the Virgin. 7. The Funeral of the Virgin. 8. Jesus at the House of Simon the Pharisee. 9. The Last Supper. 10. Jesus before Pilate. 11. Jesus carrying the Cross. 12. Descent from the Cross. 13. The Embalming of the Body of Jesus. 14. The Vespers of the Holy Ghost. 15. The Ascension of the Holy Ghost. 16. The Spring of the Apostles. 17. The Marriage of the Virgin. 18. Funeral Procession. 19. Job on the Dungheap. 20. David in Prayer. 21. Stabat Mater Dolorosa. 22. St. Veranus, Bishop of Cavaillon, curing the Sick. 23. The Sermon of St. Bernard of Clairvaux. 24. The Holy Trinity. 25. St. Martin sharing his Cloak with a Beggar. 26. The Martyrdom of St. Apollonia. 27. The Conversion of St. Paul. (Also text ill. I, III and IV.)

Miniatures from the *Livre d'Heures d'Etienne Chevalier.* Average size $6\frac{1}{4} \times 4\frac{3}{4}$ in. Chantilly, Musée Condé (Plates 1–13, 15–19, 21, 23, 24, 26, 27); New York, Robert Lehman coll. (Plate 14); London, British Museum, Add. MS. 37421 (Plate 20); New York, Wildenstein & Co. (Plate 22); Paris, Musée du Louvre (Plate 25).—See text p. 36 and 99.

28–30. *Fouquet:* 28. The Entry of the Emperor Charles IV into St. Denis. 29. King Charles V receiving the Messengers of the Emperor Charles IV. 30. The Arrival of the Emperor Charles IV. (Also text ill. VII.)

Miniatures from the *Grandes Chroniques des Rois de France.* $6\frac{1}{4} \times 9$ in.; $5\frac{5}{8} \times 4\frac{1}{4}$ in.; $5\frac{1}{2} \times 4\frac{1}{8}$ in. Paris, Bibliothèque Nationale, Ms. fr. 6465.—See text p. 43.

31–35. *Master of the Duc de Berry:* 31. The Hebrews in the Desert. *Fouquet:* 32. The Siege of Jericho. 33. David lamenting over the Death of Saul. 34. The Destruction of the Temple. 35. The Entry of Ptolemy into Jerusalem.

Miniatures from the *Antiquités Judaïques* by Flavius Josephus. Translated by Laurent de Premierfait. Average size $8\frac{1}{4} \times 7\frac{1}{2}$ in. Paris, Bibliothèque Nationale, Ms. fr. 247 and Nouv. Acq. 21013.—See text p. 44 and 101.

36. *Fouquet and successor:* The Building of the Roman Wall. Miniature from the *Histoire Romaine* of Livy. Translated by Pierre Bersuire. $12\frac{5}{8} \times 8\frac{7}{8}$ in. Paris, Bibliothèque Nationale, Ms. fr. 20071.—See text p. 47.

37. *Fouquet:* Caesar about to cross the Rubicon. Miniature from a *Histoire ancienne jusqu'à Jules César et des faits des Romains.* $17\frac{5}{8} \times 13\frac{1}{8}$ in. London, Henry Yates Thompson coll.—See text p. 47 and 101.

38. *Fouquet:* The Virgin and Child of Melun. Right wing of the Diptych of Melun (see also text ill. V). Panel-painting. $37\frac{5}{8} \times 33\frac{5}{8}$ in. Antwerp, Musée Royal des Beaux-Arts, No. 132.—See text p. 48 and 101.

39. *Fouquet:* Study for the Portrait of Guillaume Juvénal des Ursins. Drawing. $10\frac{1}{2} \times 7\frac{5}{8}$ in. Berlin, Staatliches Kupferstichkabinett, No. 4367.—See text p. 51 and 101.

40. *Fouquet:* Guillaume Juvénal des Ursins. Panel-painting. $36\frac{1}{4} \times 29$ in. Paris, Musée du Louvre, No. 288.—See text p. 51 and 101.

41 and 42. *Fouquet:* The Pietà of Nouans. Panel-painting. $57\frac{5}{8} \times 92\frac{5}{8}$ in. Nouans (Touraine), Eglise paroissiale.—See text p. 52.

43. *Fouquet (?)*: Portrait of a Young Man. Panel-painting. New York, Arthur Sachs coll.—See text p. 53 and 101.

44. *Master of 1456*: Portrait of a Man with a Wine Glass. Panel-painting. 24⅜ × 17¾ in. Paris, Musée du Louvre.—See text p. 55.

45. *Master of King René*: The Duke of Bourbon receiving the King-of-Arms of Brittany. Miniature from the *Book of Tournaments* of King René of Anjou. Paris, Bibliothèque Nationale, Ms. fr. 2695.—See text p. 60 and 102.

46 and 52. *Master of King René*: 46. Dedication. 52. Arcitas and Palemon espying Emilia in her Garden. (See also text ill. XIII.) Miniatures from the *Theseïde* of King René of Anjou. 10½ × 7⅞ in. Vienna, Nationalbibliothek, Cod. 2617.—See text p. 67 and 102.

47–51. *Master of King René*: 47. Cœur and Désir at the Magic Well. 48. Love takes Possession of Cœur's Heart. 49. Cœur meeting the Dwarf Jalousie. 50. Désir meeting Humble Requête. 51. The Knights at the Hermit's Cell. (See also text ill. XII.) Miniatures from the *Livre du cuer d'amours espris* of King René of Anjou. 11⅜ × 8½ in. Vienna, Nationalbibliothek, Cod. 2597.—See text p. 63.

52. See under plate 46.

53 and 54. *Master of the Annunciation of Aix:* 53. The Prophet Isaiah. 54. The Prophet Jeremiah. Inside paintings of the wings of the Altar of the Annunciation at Aix, Eglise Saint-Sauveur. Panels. Vierhouten (Holland), D. G. van Beuningen coll.; Brussels, Musées Royaux des Beaux-Arts.—See text p. 68 and 102.

55–57. *Paul of Limburg and Jean Colombe:* 55. November. 56. Procession of Supplicants against the Plague. 57. *Colombe:* Requiem. Miniatures from the *Très riches Heures* of the Duc Jean de Berry. Chantilly, Musée Condé.—See text p. 75.

58. *Colombe:* The Annunciation. Miniature from the *Prayerbook of Anne de Beaujeu.* (See also text ill. XV.) New York, Pierpont Morgan Library, MS 677.—See text p. 78.

59. *Colombe:* The Building of Troy. Single miniature from a *Recueil des histoires de Troye.* 20¼ × 13 in. Berlin, Staatliches Kupferstichkabinett, No. 4645.—See text p. 77.

60. *Colombe:* Masinissa receiving Scipio Africanus and Lelius. Miniature from the *Romuléon* of Roberto della Porta. Translated by Sébastien Mamerot. Paris, Bibliothèque Nationale, Ms. fr. 364.—See text p. 77 and 102.

61 and 62. *Colombe:* 61. St. Veronica. 62. Bathsheba. Miniatures from the *Prayerbook of Louis de Laval.* Paris, Bibliothèque Nationale, Ms. lat. 920.—See text p. 78 and 103.

63. *School of Fouquet:* Banker in his Office. Miniature from the *Livre intitulé de richesse.* Paris, Bibliothèque Nationale, Ms. fr. 9608, fol. 11 v.—See text p. 72.

64–66. *Bourdichon:* Altar of the Crucifixion. 64. Crucifixion. Centre panel. 65. Jesus carrying the Cross. Left wing. 66. Entombment. Right wing. Triptych. Panel. 56¼ × 111⅜ in. Loches, Eglise Saint-Antoine.—See text p. 82.

67 and 68. *Bourdichon:* 67. Margaret of Rohan. 68. Crucifixion. Miniatures from the *Prayerbook of Margaret of Rohan*, wife of Duc Jean d'Angoulême. Princeton, N. J., Princeton University.—See text p. 84.

69 and 70. *Bourdichon:* 69. David in Prayer. 70. Frère Jean Bourgeois. Miniatures from the *Prayerbook of Frère Jean Bourgeois.* 9¼ × 6¼ in. Innsbruck, Universitätsbibliothek, Cod. 281.—See text p. 84.

71. *Bourdichon:* Three Prophets. Miniatures from a *Livre d'Heures dit de Bourbon-Carency.* $4\frac{1}{2} \times 3\frac{3}{8}$ in. Paris, Bibliothèque de l'Arsenal, Ms. 417.—See text p. 81 and 103.

72. *Bourdichon:* Virgin and Child. Single Miniature. Private collection, England.—See text p. 85.

73. *Bourdichon:* Virgin and Child · Calvary. Centre panel of an altar-piece. Triptych. $45 \times 29\frac{1}{4}$ in. Naples, Museo Nazionale.—See text p. 85 and 103.

74. *Bourdichon:* The Adoration of the Magi. Miniature from the *Prayerbook of Duc Charles d'Angoulême.* Paris, Bibliothèque Nationale, Ms. lat. 1173.—See text p. 84.

75–78. *Bourdichon:* The four States of Society. Four single miniatures. Average size $6\frac{3}{4} \times 5\frac{1}{4}$ in. Paris, Ecole des Beaux-Arts (Jean Masson coll.).—See text p. 86.

INDEX OF NAMES

The titles of the works of the four main artists Jean Bourdichon, Jean Colombe, Jean Fouquet and the Master of King René are listed under their names.
All Books of Hours are listed as Prayerbooks.

Alberti, Leon Battista 26
Alexandre, Guillaume 34
Alphonso I, King of Aragon 56, 59
Alvarez di Toledo, Cardinal 81
André, Piètre 55
Angelico, Fra 19, 25, 26
Angoulême, Charles d' 84
Angoulême, Jean d' 84
Anjou, Duke Charles of 10, 56
Anjou, Duke Louis II of 75
Anjou, Marie d' cf. Marie, Queen of France
Anjou, Duke René of cf. René, King of Sicily
Anne de Beaujeu, Regent of France 35, 77–78, 81, 86
Antonello da Messina 85
Armagnac, Catherine of 82, 84
Armagnac, Jacques of, Duke of Nemours 34, 45, 76
Attavante 86

Baer, Leo 34
Bapteur, Jean 76
Barthélemy de Clerc (de Cler or d'Eilz) 67
Baude, Henri 22, 23
Beauvau, Louis de 56
Bedford, Duke John of 9, 12, 23
Bellechose 48
Beroaldo, Filippo 8
Berry, John Duke of 22, 34, 36, 45–46, 75
Bersuire, Pierre 35
Birmann, Peter 21
Blum, André 91
Boccaccio, cf. Fouquet, Jean: Miniatures, and Master of King René: Miniatures
Boll, Franz 75, 91
Bouchot, Henri 91
Bourbon, Cardinal Charles of 77

Bourbon, Duke John II of 82
Bourbon, Louis of 77
Bourbon, Duke Pierre of 22, 29, 33, 78, 86
Bourdichon, Jean
  Miniatures:
  Jean Marot: "Voyage de Gênes" 81
  Miniatures of the life of St. Gregory 79
  Miniatures of Notre Dame de Pitié 79
  "Papaliste" of Queen Charlotte 79
  Prayerbook of Cardinal Alvarez di Toledo 81
  Prayerbook of Charles d'Angoulême 81, 84, 85.—Ill. 74
  Prayerbook of Queen Anne of Brittany 81
  Prayerbook with the coat of arms of the Aragons 81
  Prayerbook of Frederick III of Aragon 86
  Prayerbook of Catherine of Armagnac 82, 84
  Prayerbook ordered by a member of the house of Bourbon 81.—Ill. 71
  Prayerbook of Frère Jean Bourgeois 84, 86.—Ill. 69 and 70
  Prayerbook of Charles VIII 86
  Prayerbook of Margaret of Rohan 84.—Ill. 67 and 68
  Prayerbook in the Rothschild collection 81
  Quatre états de la société 86, 87.—Ill. 75–78
  Virgin and Child, single miniature 85.—Ill. 72
  Panel-Paintings:
  Portraits of Charles VIII as a youth 80, 84
  Portraits of Queen Charlotte 79, 84
  Portraits of the monk Francis of Paola 78
  Portrait of Louis XI in profile 80.—Ill. XVI
  Portrait of Admiral Malet de Graville 80

III

Portrait of Mademoiselle de Tarentes 84
The Virgin on clouds 86
Two Pictures of the Virgin enthroned 86
The Virgin in Glory 86
Triptych of Loches 82, 84, 85.—Ill. 64–66
Triptych at Naples 85–86.—Ill. 73
Other works:
Ceiling in the Castle of Plessis 78
Designs for an equestrian Statue of St. Michael in the Castle of Plessis 78
Tabernacle in the Castle of Plessis 78
Twentyfour pictures on parchment for King Louis XI 78
View of the city of Caudebec on parchment 78
Bourgeois, Frère Jean 83
Bourrée, Jean 13
Bouts, Dirk 19, 21
Brentano, Georg 21
Briçonnet, Jean 30
Budé, Catherine 51
Burgundy, Duke John of, (Jean-sans-peur) 9
Burgundy, Duke Philip of, (Philip the Good) 23, 33, 60

Caillemesnil, Pierre cf. Colombe, Jean: Miniatures
Campin, Robert 24
Carpaccio 37
Champion, Pierre 91, 92
Champollion-Figeac, Jean-François 21, 92
Charenton, Enguerrand 53, 56, 68
Charles VI, King of France 9, 48
Charles VII, King of France 7, 9–12, 14, 19, 21, 23–24, 26–33, 37, 44, 51, 60, 64, 82–83, 88, 92–93.—Ill. VIII
Charles VIII, King of France 8, 35, 71, 78, 81, 84, 88, 93
Charlotte, Queen of France 76, 79, 84
Chartier, Alain 10, 15
Chastellain, Georges 14, 22

Chevalier, Etienne 13, 16–19, 25–30, 36–43, 45–52, 64, 77, 82, 84, 86.—Ill. III and V
Clément, Pierre 26, 92
Clève, Marie de 33, 55
Clouet, François 20
Clouet, Jean 20, 86
Cœur, Geoffroy 75
Cœur, Jacques 14, 25, 29–30, 75, 77–78, 92–93.—Ill. II
Colantonio del Fiore 68
Colin d'Amiens 30, 55
Colombe, Jean
Miniatures:
"Apocalypse" 76
Pierre Caillemesnil: "Livre des douze Perilz d'enfer" 76
Raoul Lefèvre: "Recueil des histoires de Troye" 77.—Ill. 59
The Life of Christ 77
Sébastien Mamerot: "Passages d'outre-mer" 77–78
Prayerbook of Anne de Beaujeu 77–78.—Ill. XV, 58
Prayerbook of Jacques Cœur 75, 78.—Ill. II
Prayerbook of Hélène de Comines 77
Prayerbook of Philippe de Comines 34
Prayerbook of Louis de Laval 77–78.—Ill. 61 and 62
Prayerbook of Duke René II of Lorraine 77
Prayerbook of Adelaide of Savoy 77
Roberto della Porta: "Romuléon" 77.–Ill. 60
"Très riches Heures" of the Duke of Berry 22, 36, 75–77, 91.—Ill. 55–57
"Vie de saint Louis" 77
Colombe, Michel 8, 33, 72, 78
Comines, Hélène de 77
Comines, Philippe de 33, 34
Corneille de Lyon 20
Cossa, Giovanni 56
Couart, Jean 72
Courcelles, Thomas de 25
Cousinot, Guillaume 13, 37

Cox, Trenchard 91
Crespy-le-Prince, Charles 21
Croy, Diane de 40

Delf, Coppin 55, 60, 67, 71
Deschamps, Eustache 15
Dimier, Louis 91
Dufresne de Beaucourt, Gaston 92
Dürer, Albrecht 24
Durrieu, Paul 22, 43, 91

Espingues, Evrard d' 34
Estampes, Jean d' 25
Eugene IV, Pope 24–25
Eyck, Jan van 19–24, 34, 36, 48, 53, 68
Eycken, Jan ten 34

Fabriano, Gentile da 25
Faure, Pierre 43
Ferdinand I, King of Naples 81
Fichet, Guillaume 8
Filarete, Antonio Averlino 22, 24, 52
Florio, Francesco 22, 30, 33
Folarton, Allart 72
Fouquet, Jean
  Miniatures:
  Boccaccio: "Des Cas des nobles hommes et femmes malheureux" 30, 40–43, 46–47, 67.—Ill. VI
  "Grandes Chroniques des Rois de France" 30, 40–44, 46–47, 52.—Ill. VII, 28–30
  "Histoire ancienne jusqu'à Jules César et des faits des Romains" 47.—Ill. 37
  Flavius Josephus: "Antiquités Judaïques" 22, 34, 40, 44–47, 76.—Ill. 32–35
  Livy: "Histoire Romaine" 35, 47.—Ill. 36
  Manuscript at Paris 40
  Prayerbook of A R 40
  Prayerbook of Pierre de Bourbon 33, 40
  Prayerbook of Etienne Chevalier 16, 25–26, 30, 36–43, 45–47, 52, 64, 77, 82, 84, 86.—Ill. I, III, IV, 1–27

  Prayerbook of Marie de Clève 33
  Prayerbook of Philippe de Comines 33, 34
  Prayerbook of Diane de Croy 40
  Prayerbook of Charles de Guyenne 33, 40
  Prayerbook at The Hague 40
  "Statutes of the Order of St. Michael" 33
  Panel-Paintings:
  Altar-piece of the Ascension of the Virgin at Candes 33
  Altar-piece of the Pietà of Nouans 19, 30, 52–53, 82, 84.—Ill. 41 and 42
  Diptych of Melun 19–21, 26–30, 37–38, 48–52.—Ill. V, 38
  Portrait in profile of Louis II of Anjou 51
  Portrait of Marie of Anjou 21
  Portrait of Charles VII 21, 26, 30, 51–52.—Ill. VIII
  Portrait of the Chancellor Guillaume Juvénal des Ursins 30.—Ill. 40
  Portrait of Pierre de Luxembourg 51
  Portrait of a Young Man 53.—Ill. 43
  Portrait of Pope Eugene IV 24
  Other works:
  Decorations and plans for the triumphal entry of the new king, Louis XI 30
  Designs for a painted canopy to be used at the triumphal entry of the King of Portugal 34
  Medallion representing Pentecost 52
  Self-portrait 16, 52.—Frontispiece
  Study for a portrait of Guillaume Juvénal des Ursins 51.—Ill. 39
Francesca, Piero della 19, 26, 48, 64
Francis I, King of France 8, 20, 72, 79, 84, 86, 89
Francis of Paola 78–80
François, Jacques 78
Frébois, Noël 44
Frederick III, Emperor, King of Naples 12, 81
Froissart, Jean 19
Froment, Nicolas 53, 68

Gaguin, Robert 8

Gaignières, Abbé 21
Ganz, Paul Leonhard 92
Gasparino da Bergamo 8
Gaucourt, Charles of 77
Gaufier, Guillaume 13
Gerson, Jean Charlier de 30
Ghiberti, Lorenzo 26
Gilbert, Jean 29
Godefroy, Denis 21, 43, 51–52
Godefroy de Batave 20
Goes, Hugo van der 19, 21
Gonzalves, Nuno 34, 55
Grandmaison, Charles de 92
Gréban, Arnould de 38, 39
Greene, Belle da Costa 92
Guillaume de Nangis 43
Guyenne, Charles Duke of 33
Guyot, Bénigne 23
Gyrard, Laurens 13, 43

Haincelin of Hagenau (Hans of Hagenau) 23
Hannes, Pierre de 30
Harcourt, Guillaume d' 35
Harrsen, Meta P. 92
Henri IV, King of France 20
Henry VI, King of England 12
Hermann, Julius Hermann 92

Jacques de Besançon 23
Jacques, Charles 91
Jean Bernard, Archbishop of Tours 30, 53
Jean-le-Sage 72
Joanna II, Queen of Naples 56
Josephus, Flavius cf. Fouquet, Jean: Miniatures
Juvénal des Ursins, Guillaume 30, 51.—Ill. 39 and 40
Juvénal des Ursins, Jean 10, 23, 25, 37

Labande, Léon Honoré 91, 92
Laborde, Count Louis de 8
Lamy, Perronnet 76

La Sale, Antoine de 15
Lauer, Philippe 91, 92
Launay, Jean de 72
Laurana, Francesco 56
Laval, Gui de 60
Laval, Jeanne de 60, 67
Laval, Louis de 77–78
Lecoy de la Marche, Albert 92
Lefèvre, Raoul cf. Colombe, Jean: Miniatures
Leidinger, Georg 92
Lemaire, Jean 22, 88
Lemoisne, Paul André 91
Le Nain, Louis 53, 89
Leo X, Pope 79
Leonardo da Vinci 39
Leroquais, Abbé Victor 81, 92
Lescuyer, Adenot 67
Limburg, Paul of 19, 22, 34, 45–46, 59, 75, 76.—Ill. 55 and 56
Lippi, Fra Filippo 25
Litemont, Jacques de 30, 72
Livy cf. Fouquet, Jean: Miniatures
Lochner, Stephan 19
Lorenzetti, Costanza 92
Lorraine, Duke René of 68, 77
Louis XI, King of France 7, 12, 23, 30–35, 37, 56, 68–80, 82, 88–91.—Ill. XVI
Louis XII, King of France 81
Lyna, Frédéric 92

MacGibbon, David 92
Mâle, Emile 38, 82, 92
Malet, Louis, seigneur de Graville 80
Malouel, Jean 48
Mamerot, Sébastien cf. Colombe, Jean: Miniatures
Marcello, Jacopo Antonio 56.—Ill. X
Marie, Queen of France 21
Marot, Jean 88 (cf. also Bourdichon, Jean: Miniatures)
Martin V, Pope 24, 25

Martin, Henry 91, 92
Masaccio 25, 53
Masolino 25
Master of 1456 55, 91.—Ill. IX, 44
Master of the Annunciation of Aix 68, 91.—
  Ill. 53 and 54
Master of the Duke of Bedford 23
Master of the Duke of Berry 22.—Ill. 31
Master François 8, 23, 39
Master of Moulins 86
Master of King René of Anjou
  Miniatures:
  Boccaccio: "Theseïde" 67.—Ill. XIII, 46, 52
  King René: "Book of tournaments" 21, 60.
    —Ill. 45
  King René: "Livre du cuer d'amours
    espris" 63–67, 91.—Ill. XII, 47–51
  Le mortifiement de la vaine plaisance 67.—
    Ill. XIV
Master of the Rohan prayerbook 19
Maximilian, Emperor 88
Medici, Cosimo de' 29
Memling, Hans 21
Mignard, Pierre 20
Miretto, Giovanni 76
Molinet, Jean 22, 88
Montaiglon, Anatole de 92
Montferrat, Blanche of 76
Montluçon, Jean 75
Moreau, Jacques 59
Müntz, Eugène 8, 25, 92

Nattier, Jean-Marc 20
Nicholas V, Pope 26

Olschki, Leonardo 92
Orléans, Charles of 10, 33, 40, 59–63

Paul II, Pope 25
Pératé, J. 25
Perls, Klaus G. 91
Petit Dutaillis, Charles 92

Petrarch 8, 29
Petrus Christus 24
Pico della Mirandola 8
Piero da Milano 56
Pisanello 19, 25, 39
Pognon, Edmond 93
Poitiers, Aliénor de 44
Poyet, Jean 72
Poyet, Mathelin 29, 55
Premierfait, Laurent de 40
Provence, Duke René of cf. René
Prutz, Hans 26, 93

Quatrebarbes, Count Théodore de 93

Raphael 26
Raulin, Jean 80
Raulin, Yves de 23
Réau, Louis 91
René, King of Sicily, Count of Provence,
  Duke of Anjou and Lorraine 10, 12, 53–68,
  75, 77–78, 92–93
Renouvier, Jules 93
Reuchlin, Johannes 8
Roberto della Porta cf. Colombe, Jean:
  Miniatures
Robertet, François 22, 44, 75
Robertet, Jacques 22
Robertet, Jean 22, 33, 63
Rochechouart, François 35
Rohan, Margaret of 84.—Ill. 67

Savoy, Adelaide of 77
Savoy, Duke Charles I of 10, 75, 76
Schiavone, Giorgio 64.—Ill. X
Sigismund, Emperor of Austria 44
Sluter, Claus 40
Smital, O. 91
Sorel, Agnes 11, 19–20, 29, 48, 75, 82
Standonck, Jan 80
Stein, H. 91
Sterling, Charles 52, 91

Strohmer, Erich v. 93
Summonte 63

Thouars, François 30

Uccello, Paolo 29

Vallet de Viriville, Auguste 93
Vasari, Giorgio 26

Villon, François 7, 15, 16, 22, 23
Vitry, Paul 93
Vossler, Karl 80, 89, 93

Wescher, Paul 93
Weyden, Rogier van der 19, 21, 22, 24, 53
Winkler, E. 91
Witz, Conrad 19, 53

Designed by:

Jan Tschichold

Colour photographs:

Steiner & Co., Basle (XII, XIII)

Four colour blocks:

Steiner & Co., Basle (XII, XIII).—A. Seemann & Co., Leipzig (V).—
F. Bruckmann, Munich (IX).—Pierre Tisné, Paris (I, VIII).

Half tone engravings:

F. Schwitter AG., Basle.—Steiner & Co., Basle.—F. Bruckmann, Munich
(XVI, 38, 40, 42−44, 53, 54).

Photographs:

Öffentliche Kunstsammlung, Basle (XI, 67, 68).—Universitätsbibliothek,
Innsbruck (69, 70).—Braun & Co. S.A., Mulhouse (1, 10, 11, 13, 16, 18,
21, 26, 27).—Bayrische Staatsbibliothek, Munich (II).—A. Schneider,
Munich (VI).—Peter A. Juley & Son, New York (22).—Wildenstein & Co.,
New-York (14).—Pierpont Morgan Library, New York (XV).—Archives
Photographiques, Paris (45).—Bouan, Paris (VII, 29, 30, 32−35).—A. Gi-
raudon, Paris (Frontispiece, III, IV, 2−9, 12, 15, 17, 19, 23−25, 37, 41,
55−57).—D. Anderson, Rome (71).—Nationalbibliothek, Vienna (47−50).